Religion in America

Advisory Editor

Edwin S. Gaustad

LIFE, TIMES, AND CHARACTER

OF THE

RIGHT REVEREND

BENEDICT JOSEPH FLAGET

Martin J. Spalding

ARNO PRESS & THE NEW YORK TIMES
New York 1969

Reprint edition 1969 by Arno Press, Inc.

*

Library of Congress Catalog Card No. 71-83441

*

Reprinted from a copy in
The State Historical Society of Wisconsin Library

*

Manufactured in the United States of America

SKETCHES

OF THE

LIFE, TIMES, AND CHARACTER

OF THE RT. REV.

BENEDICT JOSEPH FLAGET,

SKETCHES

OF THE

LIFE, TIMES, AND CHARACTER

OF THE RT. REV.

BENEDICT JOSEPH FLAGET,

FIRST BISHOP OF LOUISVILLE.

BY M. J. SPALDING, D. D.

BISHOP OF LOUISVILLE.

" *Quasi sol refulgens, sic ille refulsit in templo Dei.*—Eccl'cus, L. 7.
As the sun when it shineth, so did he shine in the temple of God.

LOUISVILLE, KY.

WEBB & LEVERING.

1852.

PRINTED BY J. F. BRENNAN, LOUISVILLE, KY.

To the

MOST REV. FRANCIS P. KENRICK, D. D.

ARCHBISHOP OF BALTIMORE,

AND TO THE OTHER

MOST REV. AND RIGHT REV. ARCHBISHOPS AND BISHOPS

OF

OUR HIERARCHY IN THE UNITED STATES;

These Sketches

OF THE LIFE, TIMES, AND CHARACTER OF ONE,

WHO WAS LONG AN ORNAMENT OF THEIR BODY,

AND A MODEL OF

EVERY SACERDOTAL AND EPISCOPAL VIRTUE,

ARE MOST RESPECTFULLY INSCRIBED,

BY THE AUTHOR.

PREFACE.

If our early missionaries labored much, they wrote but little. Their time was too much occupied in the discharge of severe ministerial duties, to allow them much leisure for recording their proceedings. Hence, our early religious history is involved in no little obscurity; and the inquirer, who wishes to trace the origin and progress of our various missions, has to contend with many difficulties. Among these, the principal is the paucity of well ascertained facts and dates. Materials there are, indeed, here and there in abundance; but they are scattered, unconnected, often vague in their accounts, and, still more frequently, merely local, personal, or otherwise unimportant in their details.

A heavy labor is thus imposed on the historian, who wishes to analyze and condense these documents, to reconcile their various statements, and reduce them to order; and, above all, to extract from them what is most useful and interesting. Sometimes, when he fancies that he is about to attain his end, by falling on a hidden treasure, his joy is suddenly changed to disappointment, on discovering that some important links are wanting in the narrative, which he has no clue for finding.

Yet the annals of our Church should be written some day or another; and the longer the work will be delayed, the more difficult will it become. Already all of our first Bishops, and all of our earliest missionary priests,—with a single exception,—have descended to the tomb. In this condition of things, the time seems opportune, for "gathering up the fragments, lest they be lost."

This is what has been attempted, to a certain extent, for our Western missions, in the following Sketches. Besides being a willing labor of filial piety, they are intended,—not, indeed, fully to meet a want which has been long felt,—but to make an essay in that direction. The life of Bishop Flaget is identified with the early history of the Catholic Church in the West and South, for a period of more than forty years. The first Bishop who came to the West, he labored here for several years alone; and he lived to see *eleven new* Dioceses—including an Apostolic Vicariate—springing up within the limits of the vast territory, either comprised in his original Diocese, or placed for some time under his episcopal supervision. Two of these became, before his death, archbishoprics; nor was he at all displeased, to behold the glory of the mother-see thus paling before that of her younger, but more favored daughters.

The principal sources, from which the facts contained in the following pages have been drawn, are the following:

1. The personal *Reminiscences* of the prelate himself. These regard chiefly the earlier portion of his life, up to the time of his consecration. During his latter years, he frequently in conversation recurred to this period, of which his recollections were distinct and vivid, in every thing except dates. Copious notes of these conversations were taken down at the time, without his knowledge, by his private Secretary, Rev. P. J. Lavialle; and the author has availed himself of the incidents and details contained therein.

2. His own manuscript *Journal*, commenced in 1812, and continued till 1834; with an additional separate account of his visit to Rome in 1836. This Journal, though it deals in general with local details and accounts of personal movements, contains many interesting incidents and important facts; but it is chiefly valuable, as fixing the dates of several occurrences, otherwise involved in doubt. It is written in French, in a pleasing and animated style; and it abounds in pious remarks and reflections, which, of course, were not intended for publication.

3. His extensive and voluminous *Correspondence;* containing chiefly the Letters written to him by different persons in Europe and America, with a few copies of important ones, written by himself to Rome, and to some distinguished personages. Nearly three thousand of these Letters have been examined. Every one acquainted with such researches, will understand how difficult and laborious is the process of gleaning a few

important facts from a huge mass of correspondence, running through more than forty years, most of which is taken up with details of merely transient interest. Yet, with the valuable assistance and patient labor of the Rev. C. J. Böeswald, the author has been enabled to gather from this correspondence several facts of sufficient interest to deserve preservation. To the same ecclesiastic he is also indebted for an able analysis of the Bishop's Journal, composed of thirty-four small manuscript volumes.

4. The *French Life* of the holy prelate, written by the Abbé Desgeorge, his traveling companion during his last visit to Europe. This work, though beautifully written, is necessarily meagre, and occasionally inexact in what regards some minor details of the Bishop's life and administration in America. The accomplished writer made the most, however, of the scanty materials he had at hand; and his work has been found valuable, chiefly as containing copious extracts from letters written by the prelate to members of his family, and to other persons in France. Appended to these Sketches will be found a translation from the Second Part of the French Life, devoted to a portraiture of the spirit and virtues of the Bishop;—those portions only having been selected for republication, which contained interesting incidents and anecdotes of his foreign travel, or a striking estimate of his character, founded on an intimate acquaintance with him for eighteen months.

5. The author has also to return his thanks to the Archbishops of Baltimore, St. Louis, Cincinnati, and New Orleans, and to the Bishop of Pittsburgh, for the communication of documents or valuable information on the early history of their respective Dioceses. The details regarding the early religious history of Vincennes were kindly furnished, from the ancient parish Registers, by the Rev. E. Audran, Pastor of the Cathedral of St. Francis Xavier; while for the facts connected with the early missions lying along the borders of the Mississippi, the author has derived valuable assistance from the researches of the Rev. Edmond Saulnier, Chancellor of the Archdiocese of St. Louis.

It is a task of some difficulty, and of no little delicacy, to treat properly of persons and events so near our own times; and it is quite possible, that the author of these imperfect Sketches has often said either too much or too little; and that, in such a multiplicity of details, he has fallen into some inaccuracies. The only merit he can claim, is to have bestowed some labor on supplying an acknowledged want; and if his attempt should have the effect of stimulating some one better qualified and gifted with more leisure, to devote himself more successfully to the work of rescuing our early religious history from obscurity, his humble efforts will not have been made wholly in vain.

LOUISVILLE, KY.
Easter Monday, 1852.

CONTENTS.

CHAPTER XV.

APPENDIX.

SKETCHES

OF THE

LIFE, TIMES AND CHARACTER

OF

BISHOP FLAGET.

CHAPTER I.

HIS CHILDHOOD, YOUTH, ORDINATION, AND FIRST YEARS OF PRIESTHOOD.

1763—1792.

His Birth—Parentage—Brothers and Aunt—Words of his dying Mother—Love for Orphans—Incident of Childhood—Presentiment—Vocation to the Ministry—Confirmation—Bishop De Bonald—He joins the Sulpicians—Solitude of Issy—He is at Nantes, and at Angers—French Revolution—His calmness amidst its Horrors—Retirement at Billom.

ONE of the most striking evidences going to prove the divine origin and character of the Catholic Church is founded on the fact, that, in every age of her eventful history, God has been pleased to raise up men, who were indued with the Spirit which animated the first Apostles, and who brought forth similar fruits of holiness. Looking over the pages of ecclesiastical history, we cannot fail to remark constant and palpable proofs of this ever watchful Providence, directing all things strongly, yet sweetly, to the great purpose for which Christ died on the cross,—the salvation of men. New confessors of the faith, new doctors, and new apostles spring up at the very periods, when their respective services are most required by the emergency;—whether for the strengthening of the faithful, the confutation of innovators and infidels, or the bringing of new sheep into the One Sheepfold of the One Shepherd.

Among the apostolic men whom God has raised up during these latter times, few have been more distinguished for virtue, long continued labors for the glory of God, and usefulness to the Church of Christ, than the subject of these Sketches. He shines forth conspicuous among the band of devoted missionaries, who have "spent and been spent," in laying the foundations of the Catholic Church in North America.

Bishop Flaget was born on the night of November 7, 1763, in the small town of Contournat, lying in the *commune* of St. Julien, not far from Billom, in Auvergne, France. His parents were honest cultivators of the soil, in humble circumstances, but of respectable family, and distinguished for their sincere and unaffected piety. His father died before his birth, and his bereaved mother was sustained in her heavy affliction by a strong faith in God's holy providence. At the birth of her son, some one present having exclaimed, that "he was a child of *benediction*," he was called BENEDICT,*—a name not uncommon in the family.

* "Monseigneur Flaget, eveque de Bardstown et Louisville;—sa Vie, son Esprit, et ses Vertus: par le pretre qui accompagnait le Prelat pendant les voyages qu'il fit en Europe pour l'oeuvre de la Propagation de la Foi. A Paris. 1851."—p. 4. The name which

His father had been twice married; two daughters had been born to him in the first, and three sons in the second marriage. Of the latter, our BENEDICT was the youngest. His two elder brothers lived, like himself, to a very advanced age. The oldest became a priest, was a confessor of the faith during the stormy times of the French revolution, and died parish priest of Billom,—which office he filled during the last twenty years of his life,—at the age of eighty-four, universally esteemed and beloved. The second became a notary public; and, after having amassed a considerable fortune, died in his eighty-eighth year. The youngest was destined to become an apostle in a far distant land.

When the little BENEDICT was but two years old,* his pious mother departed this life. While on her death bed, an aunt of her children stood by, bathed in tears; and, holding the youngest in her arms, she lamented that one so tender was so soon to be left a desolate orphan. The mother, raising her eyes to heaven, and pouring forth a fervent prayer, calmly exclaimed: "Be not solicitous; God will take care of the child!"† She

---

the child bore in the *Patois* of the country was *Benuet*—a corruption of the French *Benoit*.

In quoting this work hereafter, we shall simply refer to it as the "French Life."

* Reminiscences of his own Life, by Bishop Flaget; written down, as he narrated the facts, by his secretary, Rev. P. J. Lavialle. The author of the French Life says, that he was in his fourth year at his mother's death. We follow the account of the sainted Bishop himself, whose recollections of the earlier period of his life were distinct and vivid. Unless where another source is indicated, most of the incidents in his youth are taken from these "Reminiscences."

† Reminiscences, &c.

soon afterwards tranquilly breathed her last; and God heard her prayer!

The faithful aunt now became the mother of the young orphans; and she devoted the remainder of her life to rearing them up in the love and fear of God. In this she was assisted by a brother of the deceased father, the Abbe Benedict Flaget, canon of the collegiate church of Billom.* He received the aunt and her adopted children into his house, and lent efficient aid in raising and educating them;—with what success, their subsequent lives clearly proved.

Having thus become an orphan himself at so early a period of his life, the subject of these Sketches ever afterwards cherished sentiments of the most lively sympathy for those left by Providence in a similar condition. It was the object dearest to his heart to provide for their temporal and spiritual comfort. He often spoke most feelingly on the subject, in the latter years of his life; and nothing was more grateful to his feelings, than to see assembled around him those little ones, for whom he had been able to provide a shelter in establishments erected under his auspices.

He never forgot the good aunt, who had taken the place of his mother. In a letter to one of his brothers, written nine years after his arrival in America, he speaks of her in the following terms:

"My heart bounds at the very remembrance of my aunt. If she be yet living,—and I hope that God has preserved her life till now,—I cast myself on her neck, I water it with my tears; words fail me to express to her my gratitude. * * * The idea that she is with

* French Life—p. 4.

you and your virtuous wife, assures me as to her well-being. * * * * Now that the Americans have free intercourse with the French, please see some banker at Clermont, who has business transactions with a merchant at Bordeaux or Havre, in order that I may be able to contribute something to the comfort of this good aunt. I would despoil myself to clothe her, I would deprive myself of nourishment to feed her; and I would thus be doing only what she has done a thousand times for me. I think I do not flatter myself on this point; my heart is not ungrateful; it seeks but the occasion to manifest its gratitude."*

From the reminiscences of the Prelate in his old age, it would appear that this aunt had not spoiled him by over indulgence. She often corrected the waywardness of his childhood; and she was very strict, and sometimes even rigid in her discipline. She was always kind; but, at the same time, she exacted the most punctual obedience to her commands.

On one occasion, when he had left the house without her permission, and had thereby caused her much solicitude for his safety, she sent him supperless to bed, and in a dark room. The afflicted child, while sobbing in his little apartment, fancied that he beheld an apparition of his deceased mother, who, with a calm, but sorrowful countenance, bade him be of good cheer. The aunt, alarmed by his outcry, soon came to his relief; and on hearing his account of the apparition, she relented, took him kindly in her arms, and remitted his punishment. He remembered, also, that she took

* Letter, May 18, 1801. French Life—pp. 8, 9.

care to have the holy sacrifice offered up for the repose of his mother's soul.

At a very early age, the young BENEDICT was sent to the college of Billom. At the age of seven, he was already so far advanced as to be placed in the grammar class. In this college he continued his studies until he had completed his classical course.

During his childhood, he seems to have had some presentiment of the life to which God afterwards called him; for he was often heard to say, that "he would go far, very far from home, and that they would see him no more."*

Having conceived, from his most tender years, an ardent wish to devote himself to the service of God in the holy ministry, and having taken all the precautions, dictated by Christian prudence, to be enabled to decide wisely in a matter of so much importance, he at length determined to embrace the ecclesiastical state. In order to enjoy greater facilities for pursuing the course of studies required for this sublime vocation, at the age of about seventeen he was sent to the episcopal city of Clermont. Here he made his course of philosophy, and attended the class of theology for two years, in the university; boarding, in the meantime, with two young men of wealth, towards whom he discharged the office of private tutor, in consideration of their defraying his expenses.

It was here, also, that he had the happiness of receiving the sacrament of confirmation from the hands of Monseigneur De Bonald, Bishop of Clermont, whose age and infirmities had not permitted him to visit

* French Life—p. 5.

Billom. He was, at the time, in his eighteenth year. Having long cherished a tender devotion towards St. Joseph, the special patron of youth, and especially of orphans, he took his name in confirmation. He received the sacrament with sentiments of the most lively faith, and with those emotions of tender piety for which he was always distinguished. He was thereby greatly strengthened in his purpose of devoting his whole life to the service of God and the salvation of his neighbor.

The Sulpicians, so celebrated for their ability in training up youth for the ecclesiastical state, were then conducting in Clermont a seminary for the higher clerical studies. The young candidate for the ministry was forcibly struck by the learning, piety, and strict observance of this body of priests; and he determined to place himself under their direction. He accordingly entered their seminary, having obtained a free scholarship established by Bishop De Bonald.*

---

* He subsequently returned thanks for this favor, in a graceful letter written to the famous philosopher De Bonald, Peer of France, the Bishop's relative, who had presented him with a copy of his works: "Through the aid of the burses established at the Seminary of Clermont by Monseigneur De Bonald, one of which I obtained after the requisite examination, I made my seminary course under the eyes of that illustrious prelate. It was he who initiated me into the sanctuary; from him I received sub-deaconship; and by his permission I entered the Society of the Sulpicians. Finally, in 1792, the time at which Monsieur Emery charged me with the mission to the United States, I had the unspeakable pleasure of receiving at Paris the blessing of that holy and wise prelate; who folding me in his arms, conjured me, in presence of heaven, to go as an apostle to the country to which I had been called; in order to establish therein that faith, which was tottering, or rather seemed lost, in France. These words sank deeply into my heart; and I have never forgotten them."—*Letter, May* 19, 1829.

Under the enlightened guidance of this venerable prelate, he pursued his ecclesiastical studies with great confidence; and without his advice he took no important step.

He was so much pleased by the manner of life followed by his new instructors, that, with the permission of Bishop De Bonald, he resolved to apply for admission into their congregation. They likewise had conceived a high opinion of his piety and other good qualities; and his application was favorably received. He became a member of their congregation on the 1st of November, 1783;* when he had almost completed his twentieth year. He now continued his studies with renewed ardor, and daily advanced in the path of perfection. Obedience, to which he had been trained from his infancy, had become a settled habit with him; and it now cost him comparatively but little, no matter how painful to nature the object of the command.

At the canonical age, he received the holy order of sub-deaconship; and thereby bound himself irrevocably to the service of the Church at her holy altars.

Having remained for nearly two years under the instruction of the Sulpicians at Clermont, and completed the course taught in that seminary, and not having as yet reached the age required for the priesthood, he was sent to the solitude of Issy, near Paris, to prepare himself for ordination. Here he remained about three years; continuing his studies, and grounding himself more and more in the sublime principles and difficult practices of the spiritual life.

These were, perhaps, the happiest years of his life.

* Sulpician Register. For a copy of this valuable document, we are indebted to the present Archbishop of Baltimore.

He always viewed religious solitude as "a paradise upon earth"; and he never tired of being near the holy altar, and paying his homage to Jesus, reposing thereon in the sacrament of His love. The office of Sacristan, with which he was charged, afforded him the opportunity he so much coveted; and it was here that he grew up, under the shadow of the altar, in that tender and abiding devotion to the Blessed Sacrament, which, through all the vicissitudes of his long life, he always so warmly cherished and so constantly practised.

The Rev. Gabriel Richard, afterwards for so many years an American missionary, stationed chiefly at Detroit, was then Superior of the Seminary at Issy; and here both these distinguished ecclesiastics imbibed in solitude that spirit of prayer and fortitude, which fitted them to become apostles in the new world.

After his promotion to the priesthood when at Issy, Monsieur Flaget was sent by his Superiors to the Seminary of Nantes; where he was for two years professor of dogmatic theology. He here also fulfilled, for a time, the office of procurator, during the illness of the incumbent.

The professor of moral theology in the Seminary of Nantes having been appointed Superior of that of Angers, asked that Monsieur Flaget, for whom he had conceived a special friendship, might be permitted to accompany him to the latter city, as professor of dogma. The request was granted. In a few months, however, the storm of the French revolution broke out with fury in that portion of France; and the Seminary of Angers was closed. The professors sought shelter in private families, or wherever they were most safe against the rage of the infuriated Jacobins, who thirsted for the blood of every priest of God.

In this sad emergency, Monsieur Flaget applied for counsel to Monsieur Emery, the superior general of the society, and under his advice, he retired for a time to the bosom of his family at Billom. This occurred in the year 1791, when he was in the twenty-eighth year of his age.

While all was confusion and bloodshed around him, strong in faith and in hope, he possessed his soul in peace. His heart was indeed torn with anguish by the news of desecrated temples, of violated altars, of priests massacred while faithfully ministering to God, and of holy virgins immolated in the cloister; but his confidence that God would protect His Church never for a moment faltered. He infused much of his own serenity amidst the storm into the minds of others. Better days were coming.

CHAPTER II.

THE YEARS OF HIS PRIESTHOOD IN AMERICA.

AT VINCENNES.

1792—1795.

French revolution—Exiled French clergy in England and America—Monsieur Flaget sails for America—Sent to Vincennes—Delay in Pittsburgh—General Wayne—Incidents—Journey to Louisville and Vincennes—State of Religion there—His labors—Small-pox—Improvements in agriculture and manufactures—Early religious history of Vincennes—He is recalled to Baltimore—Goes by New Orleans—Arrival in Baltimore.

The storm which spreads devastation in its course, is controlled by Providence for purposes of good. It scatters far and wide the seed, and thus causes to spring up goodly plants, yielding abundant fruit in distant lands; which, but for its wild agency, would have remained deprived of this resource for beauty and usefulness. So was it with the tempest of the French revolution. It scattered the good seed of the Gospel into remote regions, where it took root and fructified "for the healing of the nations." The zealous and exemplary clergy of France, persecuted and hunted down at home by the enemies of all social order, and of its only solid basis—Religion,—followed the evangelical counsel, and fled abroad into distant countries; where, though many privations awaited them, they might at least hope to labor in peace for the salvation of men.

Thus the loss of France became the gain of other lands less favored with Religion. England and the United States, in particular, felt the beneficial effects of this partial dispersion of the French clergy. The exemplary piety, the patient endurance, the high-toned politeness, and the unalterable meekness of the French priests who sought shelter in England, could not fail to excite the admiration, and win the esteem even of the prejudiced and proud British Protestants. There is little room to doubt, that the religious change which has since taken place in the English Protestant mind, had its commencement in the favorable impression made by the exemplary lives of the exiled French clergy; whose prayers also, no doubt, drew down a blessing on their kind entertainers.

In the United States we are still more largely in debt to the zeal of those devoted men. Examples proving this are numerous and familiar; one of the most illustrious is the subject of the present Sketches.

In his retirement at Billom, Monsieur Flaget earnestly implored the divine light for his guidance under the difficult circumstances in which he found himself placed. The horrors of the revolution continued with unabating fury, and he saw no prospect of his being soon able to devote himself usefully to the holy ministry in his native land. In this difficulty, the inward voice which he had thought he heard in his early childhood, warning him that he was to go far away from home, again echoed through his heart; and he decided to offer himself for the missions of the United States. There the harvest was indeed great, and the laborers few. Bishop Carroll had lately been consecrated; and while his jurisdiction extended over all the States, the number of his priests was lamentably small, and entirely inadequate to the wants of so vast a mission.

That he might not, however, act with precipitation in a matter of so much importance, he went to Paris to consult his Superior, Monsieur Emery. Under his direction, he made a spiritual retreat, and to him he laid open the inmost recesses of his heart in a general confession. The result was, that Monsieur Emery advised him to carry out the intention he had conceived; and accordingly, he lost no time in preparing for his departure to his distant mission.*

For this purpose, he repaired to Bordeaux; from which port he sailed for Philadelphia in January, 1792. His traveling companions were, the Rev. MM. Chicoisneau,† David, and Badin; the first named, lately Superior of the Sulpician Seminary of Orleans; the second, a Sulpician priest, like himself, and his intimate friend; the third, a secular sub-deacon, of the diocese of Orleans. The two last become subsequently for many years his missionary associates in Kentucky.

The missionaries reached Philadelphia on the 26th, and Baltimore on the 29th‡ of March.§ Here they were delighted to find that a colony of French Sulpi-

* It would appear also, from hints thrown out in the subsequent correspondence of the Bishop, that Monsieur Emery advised his going to America with a special view to his taking the mission of Vincennes.

† Sulpician Register.

‡ Idem. The French Life states that they arrived on the 28th.

§ Sulpician Register.

cians had arrived six months before, and that many of them were old friends.

On the day after their arrival, they went in a body to pay their respects to Bishop Carroll; but they met this venerable prelate already on his way to render them the first visit. Apologizing for their tardiness, they were placed completely at their ease by the graceful reply of the Bishop: "Gentlemen, you have traveled fifteen hundred leagues to see me; and surely it was as little as I could do to walk a few squares to see you!"

M. Flaget remained in Baltimore but two months. Having unreservedly offered his services to Bishop Carroll, he cheerfully accepted from the latter the distant mission of Vincennes; where there was a considerable number of French settlers, who had been long deprived of the services of a clergyman.

He accordingly set out on his journey in the month of May, in a wagon destined for Pittsburgh. He traveled alone,* with the conductor of the wagon; whose good will and friendship he won, though as yet he knew but a few words of English. In Pittsburgh he was detained for nearly six months, in consequence of the low stage of water in the Ohio. He carried with him letters of introduction from Bishop Carroll to Gen.

---

* The French Life of Bishop Flaget, as well as the Sulpician Register, states that he was accompanied in his journey by M. Levadoux. This is incompatible with his own Reminiscences, which are explicit and detailed on this point. He met MM. Levadoux and Richard only on his arrival at Louisville. They probably left Baltimore somewhat later; at least they did not travel in his company, else he would have mentioned the circumstance in one of his numerous conversations on the subject of this journey.

Wayne, who was stationed at that point, preparing for his great expedition against the Indians of the North West. The General received him with kindness, and offered him every attention and aid in his power.

During his detention in Pittsburgh, M. Flaget was not idle. He boarded in the family of a French Huguenot married to an American Protestant lady, by whom he was kindly and hospitably entertained. He said Mass every morning in their house; and during the day he devoted himself to the instruction of the few French inhabitants and Catholic soldiers.

The small-pox having broken out in the place, he was indefatigable in his attentions to those stricken with the loathsome disease. Forgetful of his own imminent danger, he generously devoted himself for their bodily and spiritual comfort. His zeal brought with it a blessing, and his heart was much consoled by these first fruits of his ministry in America.

An incident occurred while he was in Pittsburgh, which presented an occasion for the exercise of his charity and zeal. General Wayne, though a humane man, was a rigid disciplinarian. Four soldiers had deserted; and on being apprehended, they were promptly condemned to death by a court martial. Two of them were Irish or American Catholics, one was a Protestant, and the fourth a French infidel. M. Flaget visited them in prison; and though but little acquainted with English, he had the happiness to receive the Protestant into the Church, and to administer the sacraments to the two Catholics. They were in the most happy dispositions; and he mingled his tears of joy with theirs of repentance. The Frenchman proved obdurate; and the zealous priest could make no impression on his heart.

He accompanied the convicts to the place of execution; but his tender heart would not permit him to hear the fatal shot, by which they would be launched into eternity. So much was he moved, that on his hasty departure from the spot, he fell into a swoon; and on recovering, he found himself lying in a ravine by the way-side. Several hours had already elapsed since the execution; and the whole appeared to him like a dream. The Frenchman was pardoned by General Wayne, the moment before the order to fire, out of regard for the feelings of Monsieur Flaget; who had exhibited the most poignant grief that his unhappy countryman was so totally unprepared to die.

In November, he left Pittsburgh in a flat-boat bound for Louisville, which place he reached towards the end of the month. Cincinnati was then a mere fort; and there were but three or four cabins in Louisville. Here he had the happiness to meet with his old friends, Rev. MM. Levadoux and Richard, on their way respectively to Kaskaskias and Prairie du Rocher. At the foot of a tree with wide spreading branches, he made his confession to Monsieur Levadoux; his heart was filled with lively emotion; for he knew not how long it might be before he would have another opportunity to receive the grace of the holy sacrament of penance.

In Louisville, he stopped at the cabin of a French settler, who owned a hundred acres of land at the mouth of Beargrass creek, embracing the central portion of the present city. His host, who had no heirs, pressed him to take up his abode permanently at his house, promising to convey to him all his property, in case of compliance. But the disinterested missionary told him at once that he was a child of obedience, and that he must repair promptly to the station to which he had been sent by his superiors. This property is now worth probably more than a million of dollars!

General Wayne had commended him to the kind attention of Colonel George Rogers Clark, who then commanded a garrison on Corn Island, near the Falls of the Ohio. Colonel Clark armed a bateau, and accompanied him to Vincennes, showing him every attention on the way, and causing him at night to sleep under his own tent. So great was the friendship he then conceived for the humble missionary, that he ever afterwards spoke of him in terms of the highest praise, and exhibited every readiness to serve him.

M. Flaget arrived at Vincennes a few days before Christmas, 1792.* He found the church in a sadly dilapidated state. It was a very poor log building, open to the weather, neglected, and almost tottering. The altar was a temporary structure, of boards badly put together. He immediately set to work, to repair the church, and especially to refit and decorate, to the best of his power, the wretched altar, for the coming festival.

The congregation was, if possible, in a still more miserable condition than the church. Out of nearly seven hundred souls of whom it was composed, the missionary was able, with all his zealous efforts, to in-

* The precise day of his arrival, as appears from the Church Registers of Vincennes, was December 21st.

duce only twelve to approach the holy communion during the Christmas festivities! His heart was filled with anguish at the spiritual desolation which brooded over the place.

Yet he reposed his trust in God, and yielded not, for a moment, to discouragement. He determined to enter at once upon the work of reformation, in the same way that St. Francis Xavier had adopted among the degenerate Portugese at Goa;—by seeking to reach the hearts of the parents through those of the children. He accordingly opened a school for the latter, in which they were taught, along with the rudiments of learning, the principles of the catechism and the prayers of the Church. He also formed a class of singing, and those of the children who had the best voices were exercised in chanting French canticles.

His success was complete. The children became warmly devoted to their new teacher; they entered with relish into all his plans; they were seen hanging round him, as a father whom they loved. They sang the canticles, not only in the school and in the church, but also while laboring in the fields. Some of the more pious and promising among them were also instructed to serve Mass; and the service of the altar was rendered imposing by a number of these pious youths, arrayed in white within the Sanctuary. The hearts of the parents were moved at the spectacle. The most obdurate among them determined not to be outdone by their own children. They came to confession in great numbers; and the congregation soon wore a new appearance.

The pious pastor was consoled by the reflection, that

if but twelve adults could be found at Vincennes who were willing to approach the holy communion on his first arrival, he could say with truth,—as St. Gregory Thaumaturgus had said under similar circumstances of his episcopal city of Neo-Cæsarea,—that at his departure, there was probably not more than that number of persons who were not pious communicants!

The inhabitants of Vincennes had lived so long among the Indians, with whom many of them had intermarried, that they had contracted many of their savage habits. Like them, they were erratic and improvident, living chiefly by the chase, and purchasing their clothing and other necessaries with peltries at the different trading stations.

M. Flaget employed every effort to improve their social condition, and to teach them the useful industrial arts. He encouraged agriculture and domestic manufactures. He had looms made, and purchased a house with lands adjoining, with a view therein to train up youth to the different trades. His success might have been complete, had he not been recalled to Baltimore, before he had time fully to carry out his plans.

As it was, he succeeded in awakening the attention of the inhabitants to these important improvements. He was at the same time pastor, father, judge, and counsellor of these poor people. They applied to him in every difficulty and distress. He received nothing from them for his services. On the contrary, he exhausted his own slender resources, and even distributed the greater portion of his linen, in order to provide for the comfort of the poor and the sick.

Having, with all his occupations, considerable leisure time on his hands, he employed it in revising his theological studies. He was never idle, but was always engaged either in prayer, study, or missionary duties. Prayer and spiritual reading were his chief resources for comfort and strength, in the lonely situation in which Providence had placed him.

During his stay at Vincennes, the small-pox appeared in a malignant form among the inhabitants and the neighboring Indian tribes; and it raged at intervals for a year. He waited upon the afflicted with his usual tender devotedness, and forgetfulness of self. He visited the Miamis and other Indians of the vicinity, among whom the disease was most fatal. He had the happiness to baptize many on their death-bed; eight or nine among the Miamis alone.

So much was his heart moved by the forlorn condition of these savages, that he wrote to Bishop Carroll, offering his services as a missionary among them; adding, however, as a condition, that he should have an associate in the mission, of whom he might take counsel, and to whom he could go to confession;—for he could not bear the thought of being alone in the wilderness without the consolations of the sacrament of penance.

In this respect he had already suffered much. The nearest priest was stationed at Kaskaskias, or Prairie du Rocher; and the intervening wilderness swarmed with savages, some of whom were hostile. Whenever he went to confession, which was but once, or at most twice a year, he was compelled to cross this wilderness with an armed escort. Even with this necessary precaution, the journey was fraught with danger, as will appear from the following incident.

Two Indians were arraigned before the court at Kaskaskias for the murder of a white man. They pleaded, in evidence of their innocence, that they and their tribe might easily have slain the "Blackgown" with his young men, but that they had spared his life, and let him pass unhurt through their territory.

On being subsequently interrogated by a friend, as to the chief sources of his consolation and strength, while alone in Vincennes, he smilingly answered, with characteristic simplicity: "Two things sustained me at that time: first, the visits of the Blessed Sacrament, which every day consoled me and recruited my strength; and second, the memory of M. Emery; for I thought often within myself,—what would M. Emery think if I should do any thing foolish?"* His reverence for his superior rendered what might seem at first sight a human motive of conduct, really a divine one in his eyes.

Before following farther the missionary career of M. Flaget, it may be well to pause, and glance rapidly at the early history of Vincennes, up to the time of his arrival there in 1792. As this subject must be interesting to the Catholic reader, and as it is not inappropriate to the object of these Sketches, we may be permitted to enter into some details, derived from the Registers of the ancient parish of Vincennes; one of the oldest in the West.†

---

* French Life—p. 13.

† We are indebted to the Rev. E. AUDRAN, the present pastor of St. Xavier's Cathedral, Vincennes, for a condensed summary of

At what precise date Catholic missionaries first visited Indiana, is involved in some uncertainty; as is also the time when the French Post of Vincennes was first established. The late Bishop Brutè was of opinion, that the famous discussion which took place, some time before the year 1712, between the Jesuit missionary Mermet and the Indian medicine-man, occurred at, or near the present site of Vincennes.* Father Mermet

---

facts extracted by him principally from those venerable records, many of which are now defaced by time, and scarcely legible. We shall make a free use of this valuable communication.

* We subjoin the entire passage from the *Lettres Edifiantes*, Vol. 6—p. 333, &c:—

"The French had established a fort on the river *Ouabache;* they asked for a missionary, and the Father Mermet was sent to them. This Father thought he should also labor for the conversion of the *Mascoutens*, who had formed a settlement on the banks of the same river; a tribe of Indians who understood the Illinois language, but whose extreme attachment to the superstitions of their medicine-men rendered them exceedingly indisposed to listen to the instructions of the missionary.

"The course which Father Mermet took, was to confound in their presence one of their medicine-men, who worshiped the buffalo as his grand *Manitou*. After having insensibly led him to confess that it was not by any means the buffalo which he worshiped, but a *Manitou* of the buffalo, which is under the earth, which animates all the buffaloes, and which gives life to all their sick; he asked him whether the other beasts, as the bears, for example, which his comrades worshiped, were not equally animated by a *Manitou*, which is under the earth? 'Certainly,' replied the medicine-man. 'But if this be so,' said the missionary, 'then men aught also to have a *Manitou* which animates them.' 'Nothing can be more certain,' said the medicine-man. 'That is sufficient for me,' replied the missionary, 'to convict you of having but little reason on your side; for if man who is on the earth be the master of all the ani-

accompanied the *Sieur Tuchereau*, a Canadian officer, who wished to establish a military post at or near the mouth of the Ohio or Wabash; or, as the name of the latter is written in the Letters of the early Jesuit missionaries, the *Ouabache*.* The supposed founder of Post Vincennes, from whom at least the place took its name, was *Francis Morgan de Vinsennes*, supposed by Bishop Hailandiere to have been of Irish extraction. Some descendants of his family are believed to be living to the present day at St. Malo in Brittany, France. He was commandant of a small French fort on the Wabash, and was killed in 1736, in an expedition against the Chickasaw Indians, which he had undertaken in company with M. D'Artaguiette, of the French settlements in the Illinois country.

A Jesuit missionary, F. Senat, accompanied this unfortunate expedition. When those who survived the murderous engagement with the savages fled with precipitation, this devoted priest remained behind, to solace and assist the wounded. He was taken prisoner by the Chickasaws, and burned to death at the stake,

---

mals—if he kills them, if he eats them, then it is necessary that the *Manitou* which animates the men should also be the master of all the other *Manitous*. Where is then your wisdom, that you do not invoke him that is the master of all the others?' This reasoning disconcerted the medicine-man, but this was the only effect which it produced; for they were not less attached than before to their ridiculous superstitions."—*Letter of F. Marest, dated Caskaskias, November* 19, 1712.

* From the old French maps, some of which are still preserved in the library of the Cathedral at Vincennes, it appears that the Ohio was called the Wabash: the former river had not probably been fully explored at that time.

with all the atrocities of savage vengeance, praying for his executioners to the last breath. The retreat of the French was conducted with extraordinary skill and bravery by M. Voisin, a young officer only sixteen years of age.*

The church records of Vincennes open April 21, 1749. They begin simply and absolutely, without title page or introduction, with a certificate of marriage between Julien Trattier, of Montreal, Canada, and Josette Marie, the daughter of a Frenchman and an Indian woman. This record is written on a detached sheet, afterwards appended to the Register by the resident clergyman, with the proper certificate of its genuineness. The only baptisms recorded during this year are those of two Indian adults.

The residing priest, a Jesuit, was then F. Sebastian Louis Meurin; who, the Register states, performed also the functions of the civil court.† There was, even at that early period, a rude church or chapel; and the young woman, whose marriage is the first recorded in the Register, was buried in the cemetery adjoining, in December, 1750:—her grave is under the present cathedral.

From the appearance of the Registers, it would seem that all the marriages, baptisms, and burials, were not recorded; but it is evident that the population of the place was then very small. All the certificates, except those of deaths, are signed by M. de St. Ange, Lieutenant of marine, commandant for the King

---

* Charlevoix. Vol.—p. iv 297. Edit. 12.

† *Faisant les fonctions curiales.*

at Post Vincennes. The last official act of F. Meurin was the burial of the wife of a corporal in the garrison, March 17, 1753.

He was succeeded by another Jesuit, F. Louis Vivier, whose first act is a marriage recorded May 20, 1753. On the 24th of November following, he buried Pierre Leonardy, lieutenant of the garrison. His last record is dated August 28th, 1756. The number of baptisms and marriages is still very small, but steadily increasing. Half of these is of *red*, or *Indian slaves*, belonging to the commandant, to discharged soldiers, and to the handful of inhabitants, most of whom were Canadians.

The next priest was the Jesuit F. Julien Devernay, who remained at the Post till 1763. His last official act is dated October 24th, of that year. About this time the Jesuit society was driven from France; and he was the last missionary of the order stationed on the Wabash.

From a record preserved at Vincennes, it appears that there was, at the time of which we are speaking, another Jesuit post and French missionary station higher up the Wabash, called *Fort Ouiatenon*, near the site of the present city of Lafayette. The missionary resident here was F. Dujaunay; and the name of the commandant, Marchand de Ligneris, Knight,* Captain of infantry, &c. There was also a Jesuit mission still farther north, on the St. Joseph's river, near the present site of Southbend; and a Jesuit Father was interred there.

Several years elapsed after the departure of the

---

* *Ecuyer.*

Jesuits, before another priest visited Vincennes. Private baptism was given meantime by a layman, Etienne Philibert, notary public, who duly registered the names.

In February, 1770, M. Gibault, Vicar General of the Bishop of Quebec for Illinois and the adjoining countries, made a visit to Vincennes. He renewed many marriages contracted before witnesses in the absence of a priest, and supplied the baptismal ceremonies over the children who had already received lay baptism. He remained until March 19th, when he returned to Kaskaskias, his usual place of residence. He continued for several years to pay occasional visits to this Post, where he remained generally for some weeks or a month. But the duties of this indefatigable missionary were too numerous and laborious for any one man; he was, for a long time, the only priest in Illinois and Indiana. His zeal and energy were admirable, and his labors almost surpassing belief.

He also did much to conciliate the minds of the French settlers on the Mississippi and the Wabash towards the American government, then struggling for independence. Thus we find that, in July, 1778, he spent two weeks at Vincennes, and exerted himself successfully in inducing the French inhabitants to declare in favor of the United States against Great Britain. The oath of allegiance to the American government was administered by him in the church with the utmost solemnity. The inhabitants entered with zeal into his plans, which proved of great service to the American cause.*

His course was the more deserving of our commen-

---

* See on this subject Dillon's History of Indiana. Vol. i.

dation, from the fact that, being from Canada, he was a subject of England, and risked much in adopting so decided a position. The Indian tribes he also contributed greatly to conciliate and render friendly to the Americans. There is no doubt, that the efforts of this good priest saved the effusion of much blood, and facilitated our conquests in the North-west.

Vincennes was already looked upon as an important post, and the town was thriving. Peace and mutual confidence prevailed between the inhabitants and the numerous Indian tribes in the vicinity. It is a remarkable fact, highly creditable to the French settlers, and indicative of the humanizing influence of the Catholic Religion, that during the period of which we are speaking, there is not found, among the numerous deaths recorded, a single instance of a murder committed by an Indian; nor is there in the Registers any intimation of hostile feelings entertained by even one of the tribes against the whites.

What happened in that vicinity a few years after the conquest of the place by the Americans, presents, unfortunately, a picture strongly contrasting with the above;—violence and murders became but too common occurrences on both sides.

It does not appear, that any great number of the Indians residing along the Wabash embraced the Christian faith. The Jesuit missionaries were withdrawn, ere they were able to make a very deep or general impression; and from their Letters it would seem that these Indians were not so well disposed towards Christianity as the Illinois, and other tribes bordering on the Mississippi. Still, many of them became Christians, especially when sick.

Not long after M. Gibault had administered the oath of allegiance to the American government at Vincennes, Governor Hamilton, with a small party of troops from Detroit, took possession of the town, in the name of the King of England. Colonel George Rogers Clark, in the ensuing February, 1779, marched a small body of troops from Kaskaskias, and retook the place, February 27th. Several French inhabitants of Kaskaskias volunteered and joined this expedition; and on the day before their departure from the town, M. Gibault had harangued and blessed the heroic little band.

In July, 1779, M. Gibault again visited Vincennes, and remained there three weeks, discharging the usual missionary duties. Five years now elapsed without a visit from a priest; when at length M. Gibault reappears in 1784, accompanied by another priest, Rev. M. Payet. Both these missionaries set zealously to work as usual, supplying baptismal ceremonies over infants privately baptized by the notary Philibert, revalidating marriages, and administering the sacraments.

In May, 1785, M. Gibault came again to Vincennes, to continue there as resident pastor. From this date several English names appear on the Registers, and the Catholic population increased rapidly. In 1781, there had been 40 baptisms, by Philibert; in 1788, there were 53 baptisms by M. Gibault. In July, 1786, for the first time, a man was buried who had been killed by the Indians. Indian or *red* slaves are still occasionally mentioned in the Registers.

On the 11th day of October, 1789, the good M. Gibault finally left Vincennes, having been probably recalled to Canada by the Bishop of Quebec. A layman, Pierre Mallet, appointed for this purpose by M. Gibault, now acted as "guardian of the church"; until the arrival of M. Flaget, in 1792. The people assembled on Sundays in the church, and the "guardian" read the Mass prayers, after which the gospel of the day was read or chanted, and the bans of matrimony were published. Those who wished to contract marriage did so in church, in presence of witnesses, of whom Mallet was always one. The records mention during this period a casual visit to the town by a priest from New Madrid.

From the above details, which if somewhat tedious, are still well worth preserving, we may infer how difficult was the charge imposed on M. Flaget, when he was sent to Vincennes, and how much need there was of a priest in that place. His labors were so exhausting in serving those sick with the small-pox and in other ministerial duties, that he himself fell very ill in October, 1793; but his vigorous constitution soon brought him safely through. In that year there were no less than seventy-six deaths among his parishioners.

M. Flaget remained nearly two years and a half at Vincennes, when he was suddenly recalled to Baltimore by his superiors, much to the regret of Bishop Carroll.* The people of Vincennes were devotedly attached to him; and to spare their feelings, he took his departure as though he were going on one of his usual visits to Kaskaskias. It was only on the re-

* "*Me admodum invito,*"—says Bishop Carroll in a Letter to the Cardinal Prefect of Propaganda, dated June 17, 1807.

turn of his escort, that the people learned his final departure. He left Vincennes towards the end of April, 1795.*

At Kaskaskias, he embarked on the Mississippi, and descended to New Orleans. Here he was hospitably received by the superior of the Capuchin convent, where he lodged during his stay. He took the first vessel bound for the North, and reached Baltimore in the fall of 1795.†

Here he met his old friends and associates, and rejoiced to be again in the bosom of civilization, surrounded by all the aids and consolations of Religion.

---

* His last official act in Vincennes was a baptism, recorded April 23d, as appears from the Registers of the parish. In his old age, he was under the impression that he remained in this place about three years. He probably confounded the date of his return to Baltimore with that of his departure from Vincennes.

† The French Life says he was recalled to Baltimore in 1794, (p. 15): but this is inaccurate by one year, as will appear from the facts stated in the text. Both the Sulpician Register and Bishop Flaget's Reminiscences agree in the statement, that he was absent about three years at Vincennes, where he arrived towards the end of 1792.

CHAPTER III.

THE YEARS OF HIS PRIESTHOOD IN AMERICA.

AT GEORGETOWN—IN HAVANA—AT BALTIMORE.

1796—1808.

College at Georgetown—College Life—George Washington—M. Flaget is sent to Havana—Difficulties—Yellow Fever—A Foster Mother—M. Calvo—Obstacles removed—Great rejoicing—Remains in Havana—Louis Philippe—Contemplates a Foreign Tour—Returns to Baltimore—College duties—Attends convicts—Distress about friends—The higher ways of perfection—Wishes to become a Trappist.

SHORTLY after his arrival in Baltimore, M. Flaget was sent to the college of Georgetown, of which his friend M. Dubourg was then President. The college was under the immediate jurisdiction of Bishop Carroll, who intended to deliver it up to the society of the Jesuits, so soon as they might be able to assume the charge. The principal professors were already Jesuits, who, during the period of the suppression of their Society, observed their rules privately, so far as circumstances allowed, without a regular organization.

M. Flaget remained about three years in Georgetown college, discharging the difficult office of chief disciplinarian, and teaching Geography and French. He blended firmness with his characteristic sweetness, while controlling the waywardness of the youth under his charge. They both loved and feared him. On one occasion he was compelled to punish with severity one of the students; who meeting him many years afterwards, threw himself into his arms, and with tears implored pardon for the fault committed, and thanked him for the correction administered.

The students were much attached to him; and his chief desire was to form their minds to Christian knowledge, and their hearts to the love and practice of virtue. He attended them in their vacations, and participated in their innocent amusements. Among his pupils there was one to whom he was most tenderly attached, on account of the talents and application, combined with openness and solid piety, which he remarked in him; this was BENEDICT I. FENWICK, afterwards Bishop of Boston.

While living at Georgetown college, he had twice the pleasure of seeing, and shaking by the hand, GEORGE WASHINGTON, then President of the United States. The first occasion was, when he accompanied the faculty of the college to pay a visit of compliment to the Father of his country; the second, when Washington himself returned the visit at the college. On both occasions he shared, to the full, in the general admiration awakened in all by the dignity and benignity of the first President; and this favorable impression remained lively on his mind to the close of his mortal career. Nearly fifty years after the death of that truly great man, he continued to speak of him with praise.

The Jesuits having become sufficiently strong to

take the entire administration of the college in Georgetown, the Sulpicians were withdrawn; and M. Flaget was sent by his superiors to Havana. The Rev. M. Babade, a Sulpician, having previously visited the Island, had produced so favorable an impression, that a number of the principal inhabitants sent to Baltimore an earnest petition for a colony of the Society, to found there a college. M. Dubourg was, in consequence, sent on to examine the ground; and he was soon followed by M. Flaget, who left Baltimore in November, 1798.* The captain of the vessel on which he sailed was so much pleased with him, that he gave him a free passage.

But when the three Sulpicians were preparing to open their college in Havana, under apparently favorable auspices, unforeseen difficulties were suddenly interposed, which frustrated their purpose. The Archbishop was old and blind, and the administration was entirely in the hands of two Vicars General, who were brothers. These unfortunately yielded to a feeling of national jealousy, and informed the Sulpicians, that, as they were foreigners, they could not be permitted even to say Mass in Havana! The result was, that MM. Dubourg and Babade determined to return without delay to Baltimore. M. Flaget was unable to join them; for he was unexpectedly stricken down with

* The Sulpician Register says that he sailed from Baltimore for Havana, in November, 1797. But this date does not seem to tally with the time of his stay at Georgetown college, nor with that of his residence on the Island. He remained here about three years, and returned to Baltimore late in 1801. This appears from his own Reminiscences, and especially from his Correspondence with his family in France. See French Life—p. 18.

the yellow fever, and was soon lying at the point of death.

In this emergency, he was not forgotten nor neglected. His sufferings, and the hardships endured by himself and associates, awakened a lively sympathy in Havana. An aged lady of high rank undertook to be his nurse, providing him abundantly with new linen and every thing that was necessary for his comfort. She went farther; she adopted him as her son, and discharged towards him all the tender offices of a mother.

On his recovery, a wealthy and generous Spaniard,—Don NICHOLAS CALVO,—took him to his house, and begged him to live in his family, and take charge of the education of an only son. M. Flaget's heart was moved by all this kindness; but he replied, that he could do nothing without the permission of his superiors, to whom he would write on the subject.

Upon one condition, however, he strongly insisted, as a necessary preliminary to his stay in the Island:—that if within three months he could not receive permission to celebrate the holy sacrifice, his position would become wholly unbearable, and he should be compelled to take his departure for Baltimore. The answer from his superiors was favorable; and meantime, M. Calvo was using every possible effort to obtain the requisite permission. All his exertions were fruitless; the two Vicars were inflexible in their refusal. He began to lose hope; when, a few days before the expiration of the three months, the aged Archishop died, and the administration fell into the hands of the Chapter, composed of the canons of the Cathedral.

Don Nicholas Calvo now lost no time in waiting on the Dean of the Chapter, accompanied by his Reverend friend. No sooner had M. Flaget made known his application, than the Dean replied: "Yes, Senor Abbate! I grant you those faculties; and I rejoice that the first act of my administration is one of *justice!*" The two former Vicars General were sitting, at the time, by the side of the Dean; and as Bishop Flaget long afterwards playfully remarked: "It was a lesson for them!" *

The rumor of his restoration soon spread through the city, and it diffused universal joy. His foster mother, assisted by other ladies, had an altar in the church of the Capuchins magnificently adorned for his use on the morrow; and a large concourse, as on a festival, assisted devoutly at his first Mass in Havana. Previously, he had heard Mass every morning in this church, receiving frequently the holy communion. The superior of the convent attached to it, was the same person who had entertained him so hospitably in New Orleans, while he was on his way from Vincennes to Baltimore.

All obstacles to his remaining on the Island having been thus removed, he devoted himself with zeal to the education of M. Calvo's son. Many others applied to engage his services for their children also; but he firmly declined, alleging that, though M. Calvo might consent to the arrangement, the mission which obe-

---

* These details are derived from the Reminiscences of the Bishop himself.

dience had assigned him was confined to the instruction of his (M. Calvo's) son, whose studies might suffer, should a portion of his time be devoted to other pupils.

He had commenced the study of the Spanish language on his voyage to Havana; he now soon became so proficient in it, as to be able to converse fluently with the natives. He remained, however, in his beloved retirement, and visited no one, except occasionally the family of the good lady who had adopted him, and who had been so kind to him in his illness.

During his sojourn in Havana, he became acquainted with Louis Philippe and his two brothers, then in exile from France. When they were about to leave the Island for the United States,* the inhabitants, sympathizing with their misfortunes, made up a large sum of money,† and appointed M. Flaget to present it in their name to the illustrious exiles. This office was most grateful to his feelings, and he discharged it with his usual tact and grace. This act was remembered long afterwards, when Louis Philippe was King of the French, and he Bishop of Bardstown.

His pupil, meantime, made rapid progress; and the parents became daily more and more attached to the preceptor. They offered him a splendid plantation, if he would remain with them permanently on the Island;

* The departure of the exiles from Havana was owing, Bishop Flaget afterwards thought, to certain diplomatic representations made by Napoleon to the Spanish Court.

† The sum, as stated by him in his Reminiscences, was about $14,000:—possibly it was that number of francs, or something over $2,700.

but he declined, saying that he did not belong to himself. They then proposed to settle on him an annuity of one thousand dollars; and desired him to accompany their son in a tour through Europe. He was at first much pleased with this proposal; for he had always cherished a wish to visit the different capitals of Christendom. On the other hand, he feared the distraction of spirit usually attendant on traveling, and bethought himself of the maxim laid down by Thomas A Kempis: "Those who travel much are rarely sanctified,—as often as I have been among men, I have returned less a man." He wisely resolved to leave all to the decision of his superiors.

The question was, however, soon solved by a calamity, which suddenly deprived him of his dear friend. M. Calvo died in May, 1801; and his afflicted widow could not think of parting with her only son, in her desolate condition. The European tour was consequently abandoned; and M. Flaget thought seriously of returning to Baltimore. While awaiting an answer to a letter he had written to his superiors on the subject, he labored to console the widow, and to advance still more the studies of the son. The death of M. Calvo greatly afflicted his sensitive heart. He thus speaks of it in a Letter to France:

"Providence, the designs of which I cannot too much admire, has again interposed to fill my days with bitterness. The death of my own father could not have caused me greater grief; I have shed a torrent of tears; I have fallen into a state of extreme languor, so far as to cause apprehensions for my health. * * * He lived but forty-two years; but, in my opinion, these were worth an age." *

Having received letters from Baltimore advising his speedy return, he at once set about his preparations for departure. He persuaded the mother that her son would advance more rapidly in the college of Baltimore, than by studying alone, and she willingly permitted him to accompany his beloved preceptor to that city. Twenty-two other youths were also entrusted to his care, to be placed in that college.

Towards the close of the year 1801,† he rejoined his old friends in the seminary of Baltimore. He handed to his superior the large sum of money, which he had been compelled to accept, as some compensation for his services; retaining nothing for himself.

His heart was filled with joy at beholding himself once more in a religious community; where he could breathe freely the pure air of solitude, and where every exercise and duty had its allotted time and place. He felt like a weary mariner returning to port.

His time was divided between prayer, study, his duties in college, and the exercise of the holy ministry. He was ready for every call, and he sought to sanctify all his actions by referring them to God. Thus he tranquilly passed the eight years of his life, intervening between his return from Havana in 1801, and his journey to France in 1809.

---

* Letter, May 28, 1801. French Life—p. 18.

† The Sulpician Register has 1800—the dates of his Letters written from Havana prove that it should be 1801. He remained on the Island about six months after the death of M. Calvo, which took place in May, 1801. His departure was therefore some time in the November following.

During this period he was called upon, more than once, to visit and prepare those who were condemned to death. Though the office was a very painful one to his feelings, yet he discharged it with cheerfulness, whenever directed to do so by his superiors. Having been often, during the previous years of his ministry, placed under the necessity of preparing convicts for their last end, it was believed that his experience fitted him for this duty; * while his mildness, unction, and tenderness of heart, were well calculated to make a deep impression on the most obdurate.

His own heart was feeling and exquisitively sensitive; and though his mind was firmly anchored in obedience, and he willingly engaged in the discharge of the duties assigned him by Providence, yet he occasionally suffered greatly from melancholy. Europe was then passing through the startling vicissitudes of Napoleon's administration, and communication with his friends in France was very precarious. At one time, solicitude for his distant brothers and friends, from whom he had received no intelligence for many months, caused him to fall into a slow nervous fever, from which he suffered for eight weeks. On receiving favorable intelligence from them, a little later, his sadness gave place to joy, and his fever disappeared. In his answer, he said:

"You see that my dark melancholy has disappeared, to give place to my natural gaiety; but if I am gay at the distance of fifteen hundred leagues, what would I be, were I by your side? In truth, I might be in

* He assigns these reasons himself in a Letter to his brother in France, December 1, 1808. French Life—p. 22.

danger of falling into dissipation, and becoming to you a subject of scandal. Let us, then, remain as we are, until the designs of Providence will be more fully explained on the subject. I shall never interpose any obstacle to my re-union with a family which I love as I do myself; but I would never dare take upon myself to ask it, for fear I might be doing my own will, rather than that of God." *

Three years later, he wrote to his brother, the curate, on the same subject—his return to France, strongly urged on him by some of his friends:

"It is very difficult to uproot a tree which has been for seventeen years in a good soil. Let this be said, *en passant*, my dear brother, in order that we may both accustom ourselves to the thought of never more seeing each other in this lower world. My heart is very heavy in making you such an adieu; but it is as well to make it to-day as to-morrow. The sorrow would be always the same; and the sacrifice once made, we would labor seriously, both of us, to be re-united, as soon as possible, in the bosom of God." †

These thoughts of his relatives in France did not, however, interfere with his progress in the interior life. He became daily more and more disengaged from flesh and blood. That beloved solitude, which he had tasted at Issy, had lost none of its charms for him. He even panted after a higher perfection than that which seemed attainable in his present manner of life. When the Trappists arrived in Baltimore, in August, 1804, he thought it a stroke of Providence in his behalf. After

* Letter, September 3, 1805. French Life—p. 24.

† Letter, December 1, 1808. Idem—p. 25.

some reflection, he applied to their superior, Rev. Father Urban Guillet, for admission into that most rigorous order. His petition was favorably received, and he was happy in the thought of burying himself in silence and solitude.

But unforeseen obstacles arose, and his entrance into the order was postponed. God had other views on His servant.

CHAPTER IV.

HE IS APPOINTED BISHOP OF BARDSTOWN.

1808—1811.

Increase of Catholics—Bishop Carroll—New Sees—Four new Bishops appointed—M. Flaget named Bishop of Bardstown—He refuses—Interview with Bishop Carroll—Correspondence—Goes to France—M. Emery—Obliged to accept—Singular present—Embarks for America—Incident on voyage—Consecrated—Apostolical poverty—Sets out for his Diocese—Journey from Louisville to Bardstown—Ceremonial of his Inauguration at St. Stephen's—Early Missions of Kentucky recapitulated.

THE population and resources of the United States were rapidly increasing every year. Europe was pouring her tide of emigration into this promising portion of the new world, which, under the influence of free institutions, bade fair to advance continually in prosperity. The Catholic population, through immigration and other causes, was also constantly augmenting.

Meantime, the awful burden of the episcopacy, which he had borne alone for seventeen years, weighed heavily on the shoulders of the venerable Bishop Carroll, whose advanced age and increasing infirmities required solace and assistance. His Diocese embraced the whole territory of the United States.* The num-

* It was bounded by Louisiana and the Mississippi river on the South and West. The Archbishop of Havana, at the time of Bishop

ber of his clergy was also lamentably small, and totally insufficient for the growing wants of so vast a mission.

Under these circumstances, Bishop Carroll thought seriously of applying to the Holy See for the erection of new bishoprics, which would relieve him of a portion of the charge, become much too weighty for one man. He accordingly determined to recommend the erection of four new episcopal sees, to be located at Boston, New York, Philadelphia and Bardstown.

While he was revolving these thoughts in his mind, and thinking of the most suitable subjects to be presented for each of the contemplated sees, M. Badin, who had been already laboring with indefatigable zeal for fifteen years in Kentucky, arrived in Baltimore, in the spring of 1807. He had undertaken this journey, chiefly to lay before Bishop Carroll a statement concerning the condition and prospects of his extensive mission. He confirmed the Bishop's purpose of proposing the erection of a new bishopric in the West, and recommended M. Flaget, as the one best suited for the new see of Bardstown. The latter had already been a missionary in the West; and his piety, zeal, and robust constitution,—to say nothing of his other qualities,—eminently qualified him for the place.

Bishop Carroll received favorably the suggestion of M. Badin. On the 17th of June, 1807, he accordingly wrote to the Cardinal Prefect of Propaganda, recommending M. Flaget in the following terms:

"For several years he was stationed at a place called *Post Vincennes*, lying between the waters of the Ohio

Carroll's appointment, held jurisdiction over Upper and Lower Louisiana, as ordinary, until the erection of the See of New Orleans, in 1793.

and the Lakes of Canada; where, with the greatest industry and the most hearty good will of all, he labored in promoting piety, until, to my great regret, he was recalled to fill some office in this seminary. He is at least forty years of age; of a tender piety towards God; of most bland manners; and if not profoundly, at least sufficiently imbued with theological knowledge."*

The recommendation of Bishop Carroll was adopted by the Holy See. While Baltimore was made an archbishopric; the four new sees were erected; and M. Flaget was appointed first Bishop of Bardstown. His jurisdiction extended over all the vast territory of the West and North-west; lying between the Lakes on the North, and the 35th degree of north latitude on the South; and stretching from the Atlantic States on the East to the Mississippi river on the West.†

* "Per plures annos stationem habuit in loco, *Post Vincennes*, inter fluvios Ohio et lacus Canadenses interjecto, ubi summa industria, et propensissima omnium benevolentia sese in fovenda pietate exercuit, donec, me admodum invito, ad munus quoddam in hocce seminario perficiendum revocatus fuerit. Ætatem habet ad minus 40 annorum; tenera in Deum pietate; blandissimis moribus; et si non profunde, saltem sufficienter doctrina theologica imbutus."

We are indebted for this extract to the present Archbishop of Baltimore.

† We have not been able to find the Bulls of Bishop Flaget. From certain passages in his reports to the Holy See, drawn up in 1816 and in 1836, we would infer that the see of Bardstown, strictly speaking, comprised only the two States of Kentucky and Tennessee; and that the new Bishop held jurisdiction over the remaining territory, as administrator or vicar apostolic, only until the establishment of other sees therein. Whenever, therefore, in the sequel, we speak of his vast Diocese, the term is to be understood with this qualification.

The Bulls of Bishop Flaget were dated April 8, 1808; and they reached Baltimore in September of the same year; having been transmitted, owing to the troubled state of Europe, through the papal Nuncio at Lisbon. The newly elected prelate was at Emmittsburgh, when the documents arrived. On receiving information of the event, he was so much surprised, that he could scarcely credit the intelligence. Rumor had fixed the appointment on his intimate friend, M. David. He hastened to Baltimore, in order to have his solicitude relieved. But the first person he met, on the steps of the seminary, was M. David; who, embracing him, confirmed the news, congratulated him on the appointment, and, with tears, offered his services for the new mission. "They told me," said the good man, "that I was to be the Bishop of Bardstown. I did not believe it; but I determined that, should this happen, I would invite you to accompany me:—now, the case being happily reversed, I tender to you my services without reserve." Bishop Flaget was much affected; he warmly thanked his friend, and accepted his services, in the event that it should please God not "to suffer this chalice to pass away from him."

Entering into his own heart, and sincerely believing that he possessed not the good qualities for which his friends gave him credit, he became persuaded that it was his duty to use every possible effort to shake off a responsibility, which he felt to be entirely above his strength. He pleaded, chiefly, that in consequence of his constant employment in colleges and on the missions, he had not enjoyed leisure to become sufficiently grounded in theological knowledge. His reluctance to accept the episcopacy did not spring from the mere *nolo episcopare;* but from the dictates of a timid conscience, and of a deeply rooted humility.

He implored his brother Sulpicians to come to his assistance, in this emergency. They took some days to consider; and after having made a novena, to recommend the important affair to God, they united in advising him not to accept. A delegation from the college with the superior, M. Nagot, at their head, accordingly called on Archbishop Carroll, to lay before him, in the strongest possible light, the reasons upon which their advice was based.

The firm prelate was not, however, shaken, either by the unwillingness of the Bishop elect, or by the advice of his brethren. "What, gentlemen," said he, "you have prayed! Think you, then, that before proposing your brother I did not pray, and that the Cardinals who surrounded the Holy Father, and the Sovereign Pontiff himself, did not pray? Well, I tell you plainly, that M. Flaget must accept."*

This decided stand taken by the new Archbishop did not, however, overcome his reluctance to accept. In a letter to his brother, the curate, written some months after, he simply says: "It is a Sulpician who has been appointed Bishop of Bardstown;—but he has refused."†
Even in August, of the ensuing year, he had not only not accepted, but he had persuaded himself that he had been, or would soon be entirely relieved of the burden.

Having referred the whole matter to his superior, M.

---

* See French Life—pp. 28, 29.

† Letter to brother, December 1, 1808.—*Ibid.*

Emery,—proposing only as a necessary condition for his acceptance, under any event, that three or four Sulpician priests should be given him as associates,—and having received no answer to this letter, he concluded that M. Emery, not being able to comply with the condition, had declined to interfere in a matter of such delicacy. The news of his appointment had made him ill; but now that he regarded himself as relieved from the heavy burden, he breathed freely,—"the first time for a year."*

"Who would have ever been able to guess," he adds, "forty years ago, that my name would one day resound in the ears of the cardinals in consistory, and that his Holiness would have given himself the trouble to send me Bulls? In truth, all this appears to me so marvelous, that whilst I write it, I almost think I am dreaming."†

His first thought had been to go immediately to France to cast himself in the arms of M. Emery, and to implore him to avert the storm; but the opposition of the President of the college, M. Dubourg, who feared to lose him entirely, had frustrated this purpose.‡ Now, however, not having heard from M. Emery, and new apprehensions arising, he could bear the suspense no longer; and, with the consent of his brethren, he departed for France, late in the year 1809.

But what was his surprise and sorrow, when on seeing M. Emery, the first words he heard from the lips of the stern superior were: "My Lord, you should

* Letter to brother, December 1, 1808. French Life—pp. 28, 29.

† *Ibid.*

‡ *Ibid.*

have been already in your Diocese! The Pope has given you an express order to accept; I can, if you wish, show you his commands."

No resource being now left him, he resolved at once to accept; and henceforward, to the end of his life, he considered himself as belonging wholly to the Diocese of Bardstown. Having received from M. Emery the assurance, that his acceptance would not break the long cherished bonds which connected him with the Sulpician congregation, and that the usual three Masses would be said by all its members for his repose after death, he now fully resigned himself to the holy will of God, and placed himself unreservedly in His hands.

After a brief visit to his family and friends at Billom, he went to Saint Flour, with a view to procure laborers for the new vineyard committed to his care. The superior of the seminary in that city was M. Levadoux, his old friend and associate in the missions of the West, well acquainted with the wants of his new Diocese. His application was successful. With the aid of M. Levadoux, he obtained a band of zealous missionary recruits; and he hastened his preparations to depart with them for America.

Many of his friends strongly urged him to be consecrated in France, that they might have the happiness to witness the ceremony:—"No, no," said the prelate; "Archbishop Carroll has taken the responsibility of procuring my appointment, and he alone shall finish the work which he has begun."

On visiting M. Emery to take his leave, he received from the hands of the latter a singular parting present,—a box of needles, and a French book on cookery! With admirable *sang froid*, the superior observed, on handing him the articles: "These needles, my Lord, may be of great service to you in the midst of your savages; and as I greatly mistrust their manner of cooking, take also this book."*

On the 10th of April, 1810, he embarked from Bordeaux, accompanied by the Rev. M. Brutè, M. Chabrat, sub-deacon, and MM. Deydier, Derigaud, Romeuf, and another young man, a deacon, who afterwards joined the Jesuits at Georgetown. The vessel on which they sailed was twice overhauled and detained by English frigates. and was even in danger of being carried into an British port; but Providence averted this calamity. Napoleon having promulgated his continental system, the English government claimed the right of visiting every vessel trading with France. After a long and tedious voyage of nearly three months, he arrived safely in Baltimore, some time early in the July† following.

As an immediate preparation for his consecration, he made, in the vicinity of Baltimore, a retreat of *forty days*, in imitation of Christ's Retreat in the wilderness; during which precious period of grace, he imbibed much of that apostolic spirit, which he manifested so conspicuously throughout the FORTY years of his episcopacy. On the 4th of November, the feast of St. Charles Borromeo, to whom he had always cherished a particular devotion, he was consecrated by Archbishop

* French Life—p. 34.

† This date of his arrival in Baltimore is given by M. David in a letter to a friend in France, dated November 20, 1817.

Carroll in the Cathedral of Baltimore. The assistant prelates were the lately consecrated first Bishops of Boston and Philadelphia, Doctors Cheverus and Egan.* The Bishop of Boston preached an affecting and eloquent sermon. The venerable Archbishop of Baltimore could not restrain his tears at the touching spectacle presented to his view on this solemn occasion.

Ten days after his consecration, the Archbishop convened the three new Bishops, and held with them several conferences, in which many important points of discipline were agreed on and settled by mutual consent. It was not, however, deemed advisable to hold a Provincial Council, until the Bishops would become better acquainted with the condition and wants of their respective Dioceses. We will here give the Preamble, or first of the resolutions thus provisorially adopted;—the most important of the acts themselves have been published in our collection of the Provincial Synods, made by authority of the Bishops.

"It appears to the Archbishop and Bishops now assembled, that the holding of a Provincial Council will be more advantageous at a future period, when the situation and wants of the different Dioceses will be more exactly known. This Provincial Council will be held, at farthest, within two years from the first of November, 1810; and in the meantime, the Archbishop and Bishops will now consider together such matters as appear to them most urgent; and they recommend an uniform practice in regard to their

---

* Dr. Connolly, a Dominican, had been consecrated in Europe first Bishop of New York; but he died at Naples, on the eve of his intended departure to take possession of his see.

decisions, until the holding of the said Provincial Council."*

The new Bishop now ardently desired to repair immediately to the theatre of his future labors; but insuperable difficulties arose, which delayed his departure till the following spring. The principal obstacle was his truly apostolic poverty; he had not wherewith to defray the necessary expenses of his journey.

He corresponded on the subject with M. Badin, now his Vicar General in Kentucky; and the latter opened a subscription, with a view to raise the requisite sum. But the poverty of the Catholics, most of whom were new settlers, subsequently induced him to suspend the collection. The Bishop approved of this proceeding; for he was aware of the destitution of his new flock, and he wished to do nothing to alienate their affections.

He wrote to M. Badin: "May the will of God be done! I would prefer a thousand times to walk, than create the slightest murmur." And again: "Be pleased to take notice, that we are seven or eight persons, and have but one horse among us. I intend to let M. David, as being the slowest of foot, have the use of this horse; I and my other companions will perform the journey on foot, with the greatest pleasure, and without the slightest reluctance. This manner of pilgrimage will be more to my taste; and unless I am greatly deceived, it will not derogate from my dignity. I, however, leave everything to your prudence."†

---

* From an old copy of the Acts, in an English translation; dated November 15, 1810; found among the papers of Bishop Flaget.

† Taken from M. Badin's "Statement of the Missions of Ken-

While he was placed in these difficulties, a number of generous friends in Baltimore came to his relief, by contributing the necessary amount. We will here let him speak for himself; laying before our readers an extract from a Letter to the directors of the Association for the Propagation of the Faith, in France:

"To give you a clear idea of the bishoprics of the United States, I propose to lay before you a brief statement of the condition in which I found myself, after the Holy See, on the representation of Bishop Carroll, had nominated me to the bishopric of Bardstown. I was compelled to accept the appointment, whether I would or not; I had not a cent at my disposal; the Pope and the Cardinals, who were dispersed by the revolution, were not able to make me the slightest present; and Archbishop Carroll, though he had been Bishop for more than sixteen (*twenty*) years, was still poorer than myself; for he had debts, and I owed nothing. Nevertheless, my consecration took place on the 4th of November, 1810; but for want of money to defray the expenses of the journey, I could not undertake it. It was only six months afterwards, that, through a subscription made by my friends in Baltimore, I was enabled to reach Bardstown, my episcopal see."*

At length, on the 11th of May, 1811, the Bishop and his suite left Baltimore for the West. They traveled over the mountains to Pittsburgh; whence they

---

tucky," published in Paris in 1822—p. 37, seq. An English translation of this correspondence was published in the U. S. Catholic Miscellany; December 1, 1824.

* Annales de la Propagation, &c. Vol. iii—p. 189.

embarked on the 22d in a flat-boat, chartered specially for the purpose.* They were thirteen days in descending the Ohio river to Louisville, where they arrived on the 4th of June.

A Canadian priest—M. Savine—had joined them; and on the boat, all the exercises were conducted as in a regularly organized seminary. Though "M. David's health was in as bad a condition as the Bishop's funds,"†—it having been greatly shattered on the missions of Maryland,—yet he presided over all the spiritual exercises, the order of which had been previously fixed by the Bishop.

"The boat on which we descended the Ohio became the cradle of our seminary, and of the church of Kentucky. Our cabin was, at the same time, chapel, dormitory, study room and refectory. An altar was erected on the boxes, and ornamented so far as circumstances would allow. The Bishop prescribed a regulation which fixed all the exercises, and in which each had its proper time. On Sunday, after prayer, every

* At Pittsburgh, the Bishop met with Father Edward Fenwick, of the order of St. Dominic, who was returning from Maryland with his nephew, N. D. Young, and some others of the order. Father Fenwick had already considerable experience in traveling, and he was well acquainted with the West. He offered his services to accompany the Bishop in the boat; while his young companions conducted the horses of the prelate and his suite by land through Ohio. In the descent of the river, Father Fenwick acted as purveyor and general superintendent. This information is derived from the Rev. N. D. Young, O. S. D.

† Letter of M. David to a friend in France, dated November 20, 1817, and published in the "Journal de Marseilles," &c., October 17, 1818.

one went to confession; then the priests said Mass, and the others went to communion. After an agreeable navigation of thirteen days, we arrived at Louisville, next at Bardstown, and finally at the residence of the Vicar General."*

At Louisville, the Bishop met the good M. Nerinckx, who had come to welcome him in the name of the clergy, and to escort him to Bardstown and St. Stephen's.

We cannot better relate his journey to Bardstown, or describe his sentiments in taking possession of his see, than in his own words, contained in a Letter,—half playful and half serious,—written to his brother in France, a few days afterwards:

"While we were there, (in Louisville,) the faithful of my episcopal city put themselves in motion to receive me in a manner conformable to my dignity. They despatched for my use a fine equipage drawn by two horses; and a son of one among the principal inhabitants considered himself honored in being the driver. Horses were furnished to all those who accompanied me, and four wagons transported our baggage.

"It was then, for the first time, that I saw the bright side of the episcopacy, and that I began to feel its dangers. Nevertheless, God be thanked, if some movements of vanity glided into my heart, they had not a long time to fix their abode therein. The roads were so detestable, that, in spite of my beautiful chargers and my excellent driver, I was obliged to

* Letter of M. David to a friend in France, dated November 20, 1817."—*sup. cit.*

perform part of the journey on foot; and I should have so traveled the entire way, had not one of my young seminarians dismounted and presented me his horse. * * *

"The next day, the sun was not yet risen when we were already on our journey. The roads were much better; I entered the carriage with two of my suite. I was not the more exalted (*fier*) for all this; the idea that I was henceforward to speak, to write, and to act as Bishop, cast me into a profound sadness. How many sighs did I not breathe forth while traversing the four or five remaining leagues of our journey!

"At the distance of a half league (a mile and a half) from town, an ecclesiastic of my Diocese, accompanied by the principal inhabitants, came out to meet me. So soon as they had perceived us, they dismounted to receive my benediction. I gave it to them, but with how trembling a hand, and with what heaviness of heart! Mutual compliments were now exchanged, and then we all together proceeded towards the town. This *cortege*, though simple and modest in itself, is something very new and extraordinary in this country. It was the first time a Bishop was ever seen in these parts (*deserts*); and it was I, the very last of the last tribe, who was to have this honor!

"In entering the town, I devoted myself to all the guardian angels who reside therein, and I prayed to God, with all my heart, to make me die a thousand times, should I not become an instrument of His glory in this new Diocese. O, my dear brother, have compassion on me, overloaded with so heavy a burden, and pray fervently to God that He would vouchsafe to lighten it."*

The Bishop entered Bardstown,—where there was as yet no church,—on the 9th of June; and he reached St. Stephen's, the residence of M. Badin, on the 11th. Here he was met by the clergy of his Diocese, and was greeted by a large concourse of his people, anxious to see their Bishop. The ceremony of his installation is thus described by M. Badin:

"The Bishop there found the faithful kneeling on the grass, and singing canticles in English: the country women were nearly all dressed in white, and many of them were still fasting, though it was then four o'clock in the evening; they having entertained a hope to be able on that day to assist at his Mass, and to receive the holy communion from his hands. An altar had been prepared at the entrance of the first court, under a bower composed of four small trees which overshadowed it with their foliage. Here the Bishop put on his pontifical robes. After the aspersion of the holy water, he was conducted to the chapel in procession, with the singing of the Litany of the Blessed Virgin; and the whole function closed with the prayers and ceremonies prescribed for the occasion in the Roman Pontifical."†

Under circumstances so simple, yet so touching, did the first Bishop of the West enter into formal possession of his see.

We will close this chapter with a summary sketch of

---

* Letter, July 2, 1811. French Life—p. 41, seq.

† "Statement of M. Badin"—*sup. cit.*

the early Catholic missions of Kentucky, up to the period of the Bishop's arrival.

The first missionary who came to Kentucky was the Rev. Father WHELAN, an Irish Franciscan, who had served as chaplain in the French navy sent out to our assistance during the war of the revolution. After the close of the struggle, he remained in America, and was employed in different missions. It is believed that he was sent out to Western Pennsylvania, and stationed for some time at Sugar creek.* When he was selected for the distant mission of Kentucky, he was living with the Jesuits at New Town, Maryland.

Father Whelan was appointed missionary to our State by the Very Rev. Dr. Carroll, then Vicar General of the London Vicar Apostolic, in the spring of 1787. He traveled to Kentucky with a colony of Catholics from Maryland. Before his departure, it was reported to Dr. Carroll that there were already in Kentucky about fifty Catholic families, who had been for several years deprived of all pastoral aid and consolation. The tide of emigration was then setting rapidly towards this new territory, in what was then the far West; and the number of Catholics was yearly increasing. The latter were almost entirely from Maryland.

While watching over the infant missions of Kentucky, Father Whelan had to contend against many difficulties. He found that many abuses had crept in among the Catholics, in consequence of their long continued spiritual destitution amidst the waving forests. With zeal and energy he sought to extirpate these

* This fact was furnished by the Bishop of Pittsburgh.

scandals, and to bring his flock to the knowledge and practice of their Religion. He was only partially successful in his efforts. He remained not quite three years on this mission, enduring many privations. He had not the satisfaction to be able to erect a single church or chapel. Having encountered much opposition from the Protestants, and having unhappily met with difficulties on the part of a portion of his own flock, he returned to Maryland in the spring of 1790. He was afterwards engaged on the missions of Maryland, chiefly on the Eastern Shore; and he seems to have died there about the year 1805 or 1806.

The next priest who came to our State was the Rev. WILLIAM DE ROHAN, born in France, of Irish parentage, and a reputed doctor of the *Sorbonne*. He arrived in Kentucky in the summer of 1790; and he was of considerable assistance to the Catholics, until the arrival of Father Badin in 1793. He passed the last years of his life at St. Thomas' seminary, and died piously there, about the year 1832.

The Rev. Father BADIN, as we have seen, had come to America in the same ship which bore to our shores the Rev. MM. Flaget and David. He reached Baltimore in the spring of 1792. Being only a sub-deacon, he entered the seminary, and continued his studies with zeal and success. He was ordained by Bishop Carroll, in the old cathedral of St. Peter's, on the 25th of May, 1793. *He was the first priest ever ordained in the United States;* and he was destined to be the real founder of our missions in Kentucky.

Appointed, soon after his ordination, to this difficult and remote missionary district, he accepted the post tendered him by Bishop Carroll, with fear and trembling indeed, but still with courage and cheerful confidence in God. He was accompanied to the West by the Rev. M. BARRIERES, an older clergyman, likewise from France, who had been named Vicar General by Bishop Carroll.

"The two missionaries left Baltimore on the 6th of September, 1793, and traveled, like the Apostles, on foot to Pittsburgh, over bad roads, and a rugged wilderness country. On the 3d of November, they embarked on a flat-boat, which was descending the Ohio in company with six others. These boats were all well armed, for fear of an attack from the Indians. About that time, however, General Wayne was preparing his great expedition against them; and they had enough to do to defend their own wigwams, without prowling about near the frontier settlements.

"The boats were seven days in going down to Gallipolis; and between this place and Pittsburgh, the travelers saw but two small towns—Wheeling and Marietta. The two priests remained for three days at Gallipolis, the inhabitants of which place were French Catholics, who had been long without a pastor. They heartily welcomed the missionaries, who, during their brief stay, sang High Mass in the garrison, and baptized forty children. The good French colonists were delighted; and shed tears on their departure. They were but a remnant of a large French colony of about 7,000, who had emigrated to America four or five years previously. A French land company had purchased for them a large territory on the Scioto river; but the title to these lands proved defective: the colonists were defrauded, and many of them returned in disgust to France, bitterly inveighing against Yankee shrewdness in bargaining.

"The two missionaries landed at Limestone, or Maysville, where there were at that time about twenty families. They proceeded on foot to Lexington, a distance of about sixty-five miles. They passed the first night in an open mill, six miles from Limestone, lodging on the mill-bags, without any covering, during a cold night, late in November. On the next day, they passed the battle-ground of the Blue Licks, where M. Barrieres picked up the skull of one of those who had fallen there eleven years before. He carried it with him, and retained it as a relic of the disastrous battle, and as a *memento* of death. On the first Sunday of Advent, M. Badin said Mass, for the first time in Kentucky, at Lexington, in the house of Dennis M'Carthy, an Irish Catholic, who acted as clerk in the commercial house of Colonel Moyland, brother of the then Bishop of Cork.

"The missionaries had with them but one chalice; and after having offered up the Holy Sacrifice, M. Badin traveled sixteen miles to the Catholic settlement in Scott county, where M. Barrieres said Mass on the same day. Preparations were then in progress to erect in this place a frame church. M. Badin remained in Scott county for about eighteen months, occasionally visiting the other Catholic settlements in Kentucky; M. Barrieres proceeded immediately to take charge of the Catholic families in the vicinity of Bardstown.

"The difficulties of the times, and the rude state of society in the infant colonies, soon determined M. Barrieres to leave the country. His habits had been already formed, and he thought that he could not adapt himself to the new state of things in the wilderness. Accordingly, about four months after his arrival in Kentucky, he left the State. In April, 1794, he departed from Louisville, in a pirogue for New Orleans, which, with all Louisiana and Missouri, was then in possession of the Spaniards.

"The Spanish government was at that time apprehending an attack on Louisiana from the French Republic; and M. Barrieres, being a Frenchman, was arrested and detained for some time at New Madrid. He immediately wrote to Baron Carondolet, the Spanish Governor of Louisiana, representing the objects of his visit: and the Baron soon liberated him, and permitted him to proceed, without farther molestation, to New Orleans. Shortly after his arrival in this city, he went to Attakapas, where he labored zealously in the missions for nearly twenty years. In 1814, he sailed for Bordeaux, where he died eight days after his arrival. About twenty-three years before, he had escaped from a prison of this city, and from the death which probably awaited him at the hands of the French Jacobins; and he had sailed from this port for America: and now he returned to the same place, but to breathe his last.

"M. Badin was now left alone in the heart of the wilderness. Keenly as he felt the desolation of heart which this state of isolation brought with it, he yet reposed his whole trust in God, who abundantly consoled him in all his tribulations. He remained alone for nearly three years, and was at one time twenty-one months without an opportunity of going to confession. He had to form the new congregations, to erect churches at suitable places, and to attend to the spiritual wants of the Catholic settlements scattered over Kentucky; and he had to do all this alone, and without any advice or assistance. Well might he exclaim: 'Oh! how much anguish of heart, how many sighs, and how many tears, grow out of a condition so desolate!' Still he was not cast down, notwithstanding all his perplexities.

"His mind was also soothed by the cheering voice of friendship. The nearest Catholic priest was M. Rivet, who was stationed at Post Vincennes in 1795, shortly after the departure from that station of the illustrious missionary pioneer, the Rev. M. Flaget. In France, he had been professor of rhetoric in the college of Limoges: and he still continued to write Latin poetry with ease and elegance. He occasionally sent his Latin poems to M. Badin, who also excelled in this species of composition. When the French revolution burst over Europe, M. Rivet took refuge in Spain, where the Archbishop of Cordova made him his Vicar General, for the benefit of the numerous French refugees who had taken shelter beyond the Pirrenees.

"He and M. Badin mutually consoled each other, by carrying on as brisk a correspondence as the difficulties of the times would permit. There were then, however, no post offices in the West; and the frowning wilderness which interposed between these two friends rendered the exchange of letters extremely difficult; and wholly precluded the possibility of their visiting each other; even if this had been permitted by the onerous duties with which each was charged. M. Rivet had discovered at Vincennes a precious document of the old Jesuit missions among the Indians of the North-west. It consisted of two large folio volumes in manuscript, containing the Mass, with musical notes, and explanations of it, together with catechetical instructions, in the Indian language. This document has probably since disappeared.

"When M. Badin first came to Kentucky, he estimated the number of Catholic families in the State at three hundred. These were much scattered; and the number was constantly on the increase, especially after Wayne's victory in 1794, and the treaty of Greenville in the following year. There was then but one Catholic in Bardstown—Mr. A. Sanders, to whose liberality and generous hospitality the clergy of the early church in Kentucky were so much indebted.

"He found the Catholics suffering greatly from previous neglect, and in a wretched state of discipline. Left alone with this extensive charge, he had to exert himself to the utmost, and, as it were, to multiply himself, in order to be able to meet every spiritual want of his numerous flock. As the Catholics were then almost wholly without churches or chapels, he was under the necessity of establishing stations at suitable points, in private houses. These stations extended from Madison to Hardin county—a distance of more than a hundred and twenty miles; and to visit them all with regularity, he was compelled almost to live on horseback. He estimates that, during his sojourn in Kentucky, he must have rode on horseback at least 100,000 miles. Often was he exhausted with his labors, and weighed down with the 'solicitude of all the churches.'

"His chief stations during this time were those at Lexington, in Scott county, in Madison county, in Mercer county—where there were then about ten families—at Holy Cross, at Bardstown, on Cartwright's creek—two miles from the present church of St. Rose—on Hardin's creek, on the Rolling Fork, in Hardin county, and at Poplar Neck, on the Beech Fork.

"In all these places, except Madison and Mercer counties, there are now fine brick churches; but at the period of which we are speaking, there was not one of any kind, except a miserable log chapel, on the site of the present church of Holy Cross; and this had been erected at the instance of M. De Rohan, before the arrival of M. Badin in Kentucky. This temporary hut was covered with clapboards, and was unprovided with glass in the windows. A slab of wood, roughly hewed, served for an altar. Such was the first Catholic church in Kentucky! As it was situated near the centre of the Catholic settlements, M. Badin soon took up his residence near it; and it then became the central point of his mission, and the *alma mater* of Catholic churches in the State. He subsequently erected a temporary chapel at his own residence, three miles from Holy Cross: this he called St. Stephen's, after his patron Saint.

"M. Badin was indefatigable in his efforts to awaken piety, and to restore a proper discipline among his flock. He insisted particularly on having servants and children taught the catechism. At every station he had regular catechists, whose duty it was to teach them the elements of the faith. He displayed on all occasions particular zeal in the instruction of poor servants of color. Whenever he visited a Catholic family, it was his invariable custom to have public prayers, followed by catechetical instructions. He every where inculcated by word and example the pious practice of having morning and evening prayer in families. He was in the habit of repeating to children, in his usual emphatic and pointed manner, the following maxims: 'My children, mind this—no morning prayer, no breakfast; no evening prayer, no supper:' and, 'my children, be good, and you will never be sorry for it.'"*

Father Badin was at length consoled by the arrival of other missionaries. The Rev. M. Fournier reached Kentucky in 1797. "He was a native of the Diocese of Blois, in France; and, when driven from his native country by the French revolution, he took refuge in England. In London he taught the French language for about four years, in order to obtain a subsistence. Weary of this manner of life, and panting for a field of action more congenial to his zeal for the salvation of souls, he sailed for America, which he reached towards the close of the year 1796. He at once offered his services to Bishop Carroll; who gratefully accepted them, and immediately sent him to Kentucky to the assistance of M. Badin, of whose melancholy condition he had been already well apprised.

"M. Fournier, after a long and painful journey, in the dead of winter, reached Kentucky in February,

* Sketches of the Early Catholic Missions of Kentucky—p. 61, seqq.

1797. M. Badin received him with open arms, and extended to him for several months the hospitality of his own log cabin of St. Stephen's. M. Fournier soon purchased one hundred acres of ground, on the Rolling Fork—the site of the present Holy Mary's—and, after having erected a temporary hut, removed thither in 1798. He then took charge of a portion of M. Badin's stations. He attended the congregation situated on the Rolling Fork, on Hardin's creek, on Cartwright's creek, on Rough creek in Hardin county; with those at Danville, and in Madison county. When we reflect that a distance of least one hundred and twenty miles intervened between the two extreme points of this circuit, we will probably come to the conclusion, that, like his fellow-laborer in the same field, he was certainly in no lack of employment.

"He was an excellent priest; pious, zealous, laborious, and punctual to all his appointments. He was of the ordinary size, and had a thin visage, furrowed with care, but still beaming with habitual cheerfulness. His manners were extremely popular; he soon caught the spirit, and adapted himself to the manners of the country; and he had not one personal enemy. He spoke English remarkably well, and preached sermons which had the triple merit of being solid, short, and intelligible to the meanest capacity.

"When not engaged in his missions, he was almost constantly laboring on the little farm adjoining his residence. His death was caused by the rupture of a blood-vessel, through over exertion in raising large beams of wood, to be sawed into plank. It was so sudden, that his friend, M. Badin, arrived only in time to assist at his funeral. His body was interred at the church of Holy Cross. He had not yet reached his fiftieth year.

"Another French priest, M. Salmon, reached Kentucky in February, 1799. He was from the same Diocese (of Blois), and was an old and long tried friend of M. Fournier; with whom he had been a fellow student in the diocesan seminary of Blois, as well as his associate in exile from his country. The two friends had met and passed some years together in London. After the arrival of M. Fournier in Kentucky, he wrote to his friend in London, who followed him as soon as he could make the necessary arrangements. He was about forty-two years of age, of a delicate frame; and, like M. Fournier, was well versed in the English language.

"M. Badin, who was Vicar General, assigned him the stations at Hardin's creek, Poplar Neck, Mr. Gardiner's, and Bardstown. He was zealous and indefatigable in the discharge of all his missionary duties. Especially did he labor without intermission for the instruction of children and servants in their catechism. In whatever Catholic house he visited, he made it an invariable rule to examine the children on their knowledge of their Christian duties.

"His zeal was rewarded with abudant fruits; though it pleased God, in the unsearchable ways of His Providence, speedily to put an end to his labors and sufferings on this mission. He had been in Kentucky but nine months, when his career was suddenly cut short by death. He was the first priest who died on this laborious mission,—and he fell a martyr to his zeal.

"In the discharge of his duties, he had caught a violent cold, which confined him to his bed for six weeks, in the house of M. Badin. When convalescent, he determined to visit the station at Mr. Gwynn's, where he had an appointment to meet a Protestant lady whom he was instructing and preparing for baptism. He was a bad horseman, and was still very feeble from his previous sickness. It was the 9th day of November, 1799; and the snow covered the ground, concealing a road which was rugged and difficult. M. Badin endeavored to dissuade him from undertaking the journey, in his debilitated condition; but he was firm in his resolution, and departed at an early hour in the morning.

"About a mile from Bardstown, on the road to Mr. Gwynn's, he was thrown violently from his horse, and was dashed against a tree. He was stunned and mortally wounded, in the breast and head. In his struggles, he succeeded in dragging himself to a tree, against which he leaned his head and shoulders, and thus sat upright, near the road side. From 12 o'clock until night he remained in this dreadful situation, surrounded by the snow, benumbed with the cold, and in the very agonies of death.

"The good Mr. Gwynn, on hearing of his perilous situation, was deeply affected. He flew to the spot, where he discovered that his worst anticipations were more than realized. M. Salmon seemed on the very point of death. He was immediately placed on horseback, and conveyed, with as much tenderness as possible, to the residence of Mr. Gwynn, about a mile distant. Messengers were speedily despatched for physicians, and for the V. Rev. M. Badin. The latter arrived at 2 o'clock the same night, having rode about sixteen miles in little more than two hours. He found M. Salmon insensible, reciting occasionally prayers in Latin, and acting as though he fancied himself at the holy altar. M. Badin administered to him the last sacraments, and remained with him till his death, which took place on the following night, the 10th of November. His remains were conveyed to the church of Holy Cross, where they were interred with all the ceremonies of the Roman Ritual.

"The worthy partriarch of the American Church, Bishop Carroll, seemed to take a special interest in the missions of Kentucky. In the same year of M. Salmon's death, he sent out another zealous missionary to labor in this distant field. The Rev. Mr. Thayer arrived in Kentucky in the year 1799. He was the first native of America who exercised the holy ministry in our State. He had been a Presbyterian or Congregationalist minister at Boston; and had been reared with all that bitter hostility to the holy Catholic Church so common to his sect.

"He left Kentucky in 1803; and subsequently went to Ireland. He exercised the holy ministry for many years in Limerick, where he contributed greatly towards the revival of piety. The year of his death we have not been able to ascertain with precision; but it certainly occurred some time before the year 1822. When M. Badin was in Paris during this year, he received, from a respectable Irish gentleman of Limerick, a glowing account of his zealous labors and edifying death. Among other particulars, the gentleman alluded to mentioned the fact, that Mr. Thayer had induced about two hundred of his penitents to make their meditation daily."*

For two years—from 1803 to 1805—Very Rev. M. Badin was again left alone in the vast missions of Kentucky. After the death of his intimate friend, Rev. M. Rivet, at Vincennes, his situation became still more isolated and painful. There was no priest nearer to him than those stationed at the missions on the banks of the Mississippi, and at Detroit. Alone in the immense forests, he labored with earnest zeal for the spiritual profit of his large and scattered flock; and God crowned his efforts with abundant fruits. Abuses were every where rebuked or extirpated: piety was seen to revive; children and servants were instructed; and it became a matter of wonder and edification, that one zealous priest could accomplish so much good.

In the summer of 1805, he was consoled by the arrival of another valiant missionary; who was to labor in this portion of the vineyard for nearly twenty years, with so much devotedness and success, as to be fairly entitled to the name of the second founder of our Western missions. This holy priest, whose name is still held in benediction, and whose "fruits yet remain," was the Rev. CHARLES NERINCKX. "He was born on the 2d of October, 1761, at Herffelingen, in Haynault.† His parents were distinguished for their virtues and their strong attachment to Religion. His father was a physician of some eminence in the profession; and his mother seems to have been a woman of great piety.

* Sketches of the Early Catholic Missions of Kentucky—p. 73, seqq.

† In Belgium.

His studies completed, he was ordained priest in 1785: and in the following year was appointed *curè*, or pastor of Malines, the archiepiscopal city. He filled this important post for eight years, and gathered there the abundant first-fruits of his ministry. The good people of Malines yet remember his piety and laborious zeal, the effects of which they still feel. The rectory of Everbery Meerbeke, half way between Malines and Brussels, having become vacant by the death of the aged incumbent, M. Nerinckx was appointed to fill it by the general suffrage of a board of examiners; who, after the searching examination, or *concursus*, recommended by the Holy Council of Trent for such cases, unanimously awarded him the palm over all other candidates. Though loath to leave Malines, where the people were much attached to him, yet he hesitated not to enter upon the new field of labor thus opened to him by Providence.

"It was natural that a man of so much zeal, and one who had done so much good, should be viewed with an evil eye by the infidel leaders of the French revolutionary movement, who had recently taken possession of Belgium. An order for his apprehension was accordingly issued; and M. Nerinckx was compelled to fly from his dear parish, which he left a prey to the devouring wolves. In 1797 he secreted himself in the hospital at Terremonde, which was under the charge of twelve or fifteen Hospitalier nuns, of whom his aunt was superioress. Here he remained for seven years, during all of which time he carried his life in his hands. He acted as chaplain to the hospital, the former incumbent having been banished to the Isle of Rhe.

He bore his persecutions with entire resignation to the holy will of God, and edified all by the practice of every virtue. He encouraged the good nuns to persevere in their heavenly calling of mercy. He said Mass for them every morning at 2 o'clock, and then retired to his hiding place before the dawn.

"Beset with dangers, and uncertain as to the duration of the dreadful storm which was then sweeping over Europe, M. Nerinckx at length determined to bid adieu to his unhappy country, and to emigrate to the United States. Here 'the harvest was great, and the laborers few;' and no impediment was placed in the way of a free exercise of Religion, according to each one's conscientious convictions. He accordingly made his escape, in a vessel which sailed from Amsterdam to the United States, on the 14th of August, 1804.

"He had a long and dangerous passage of ninety days. The old and rickety vessel was often in imminent danger of foundering at sea; and to add to the distress, a contagious disorder carried off many of the passengers and crew. Still they were not chastened under the rod of affliction; the heart of M. Nerinckx often bled over their wickedness, which he was wholly unable to check; and he afterwards was in the habit of styling this ill-fated ship, 'a floating hell.' The captain, in particular, was a very profane and wicked man. M. Nerinckx was wont to ascribe his preservation from shipwreck, to a special interposition of Divine Providence.

"He reached Baltimore about the middle of November; and immediately offered his services to the patriarch of the American Church—Bishop Carroll—for whatever mission in the United States he might think proper to assign him. The Bishop received the good exile with open arms, and immediately sent him to Georgetown to prepare himself for the American mission by learning English, with which, as yet, he was wholly unacquainted. M. Nerinckx was then in his forty-fifth year; and yet he applied himself with so much ardor to the study of our language, as to be able in a few months to speak and write it with considerable facility.

"Bishop Carroll was well aware of the forlorn condition of M. Badin, who was alone in Kentucky; and he determined to send the new missionary to his assistance. And had he sent us no other, Kentucky would still have ample reason to be forever grateful to him for the invaluable treasure he gave in M. Nerinckx.

"The good missionary hesitated not a moment to comply with the wish of his new superior. He left Baltimore in the spring of 1805; and, after a long and painful journey, reached Kentucky on the 5th of July following. He immediately applied himself zealously to the labors of the mission, which he cheerfully shared with M. Badin, the Vicar General. For the first seven years he resided with M. Badin, at St. Stephen's; afterwards, he took up his residence chiefly near the church of St. Charles, which he had erected on Hardin's creek, and named after his patron Saint. But he was seldom at home: he lived on his scattered missions, and passed much of his time on horseback.

"His labors in the arduous field upon which he had now entered were as great as their fruit was abundant. With his whole soul, he devoted himself to the work of the ministry. He even seemed to court labors and sufferings for their own sake. Of a powerful frame, and of herculean constitution, he never spared himself. His rest was brief, and his food was generally of the coarsest kind. He usually arose several hours before day, which hours he devoted to prayer and study. In fact, he seemed to be always engaged in mental prayer, no matter how numerous or distracting were his employments.

"He appeared to live solely for God, and for his neighbor. Performing his duty was his daily bread. And though old age was fast creeping over him, yet he relaxed in nothing his exhausting labors. His soul was still fresh and vigorous; and God so preserved his health, that, even at the age of sixty, he seemed gifted with all the strength and vigor of youth.

"He seldom missed offering up the Holy Sacrifice daily, no matter what had been his previous fatigues or indisposition. Often was he known to ride twenty-five or thirty miles fasting, in order to be able to say Mass. His missionary labors would be almost incredible, were they not still so well remembered by almost all the older Catholics of Kentucky.

"His courage was unequalled: he feared no difficulties, and was appalled by no dangers. Through rain and storms; through snows and ice; over roads rendered almost impassable by the mud; over streams swollen by the rains, or frozen by the cold; by day and by night, in winter and in summer; he might be seen traversing all parts of Kentucky in the discharge of his laborious duties. Far from shunning, he seemed even to seek after hardships and dangers.

"He crossed wilderness districts, swam rivers, slept

in the woods among the wild beasts; and while undergoing all this, he was in the habit of fasting, and of voluntarily mortifying himself in many other ways. His courage and vigor seemed to increase with the labors and privations he had to endure. As his courage, so neither did his cheerfulness, ever abandon him. He seldom laughed, or even smiled; but there was withal an air of contentment and cheerfulness about him, which greatly qualified the natural austerity of his countenance and manners. He could, like the great Apostle, make himself 'all to all, to gain all to Christ.' He appeared even more at home in the cabin of the humblest citizen, or in the hut of the poor negro, than in the more pretending mansions of the wealthy.

"He was averse to giving trouble to others, especially to the poor. Often, when he arrived at a house in the night, he attended to his own horse, and took a brief repose in the stable, or in some out-house; and when the inmates of the house arose next morning, they frequently perceived him already up, and saying his office, or making meditation. He made it an invariable rule never to miss an appointment, whenever it was at all possible to keep it. He often arrived at a distant station early in the morning, after having rode during all of the previous night. On these occasions, he heard confessions, taught catechism, gave instructions, and said Mass for the people generally after noon; and he seldom broke his fast until three or four o'clock in the evening.

"In swimming rivers, he was often exposed to great danger. Once, in going to visit a sick person, he came to a stream which his companion knew to be impassable. M. Nerinckx took the saddle of his friend—who refused to venture—placed it on his own, and then remounting the horse, placed himself on his knees on the top of the two saddles, and thus crossed the flood which flowed over his horse's back. On another occasion he made a still more narrow escape. He was swept from his horse, which lost its footing and was carried away by the current; and the rider barely saved himself, and reached the other shore, by clinging firmly to the horse's tail!

"On one of his missionary tours, he narrowly escaped being devoured by the wolves, which then greatly infested those portions of Kentucky which were not densely settled.

"M. Nerinckx often manifested his great bodily strength in the course of his laborious life. He erected no less than ten churches in Kentucky; two of which—those of Holy Cross and of Lebanon—were of brick; and the rest of hewed logs. He was not content with directing the labors of others: he was seen intermixing with the workmen, aiding them in cutting timber, in clearing out the undergrowth, and in every other species of hard labor. He generally worked bareheaded under the broiling sun: and, in removing heavy timber, or as it is commonly called, *rolling logs*, he usually lifted against two or three men of ordinary strength! He built his own house, chiefly with his own hands; and was wont to say cheerfully, 'that his palace had cost him just $6,50 in money!'

"He had charge of six large congregations, besides a much greater number of stations, scattered over the whole extent of Kentucky. Wherever he could learn that there were a few Catholic settlers, there he established a station, or erected a church. The labor which he thus voluntarily took on himself, is almost incredible. To visit all his churches and stations, generally required the space of at least six weeks.

"He never took any rest or recreation. He seemed always most happy, when most busily engaged. He seldom talked, except on business; or on God, on virtue, or on his missionary duties. On reaching a church or station, his confessional was thronged with penitents, from the early dawn until mid-day. Before beginning to hear confessions, he usually said some prayers with the people, and then gave them a solid and familiar instruction on the manner of approaching the holy tribunal. If he seemed austere out of the confessional, he was in it a most kind, patient, and tender father. He spared no time nor pains to instruct his penitents; all of whom, without one exception, were deeply attached to him. To his instructions, chiefly in the confessional, are we to ascribe the piety and regularity of many among the living Catholics in Kentucky.

"But it was on the children and servants that he lavished his labor with the greatest relish. Thoroughly to instruct them, and prepare them for their first communion, was his darling enjoyment. He thought no time nor labor, that was devoted to this favorite object, too long or ill-spent. For this purpose, he usually remained a week at each of the churches and stations. During this time, he had the children and servants daily assembled, and devoted his whole time to them.

"God blessed his labors with fruits so abundant and permanent, as to console him for all his toils and privations. He witnessed a flourishing church growing up around him, in what had recently been a wilderness, inhabited only by fierce wild beasts and untameable savages. He saw, in the virtues of his scattered flock, a revival of those which had rendered so illustrious the Christians of the first ages of the church. M. Badin had laid the foundation; and, like a skillful architect, he reared the superstructure, in that portion of the flock entrusted to his charge. The results of his labors prove how much one good man, with the blessing of God, can achieve by his single efforts, prompted by the lofty motive of the Divine glory, and directed by simplicity of heart to one noble end."*

The next missionaries who came to Kentucky were members of the Order of St. Dominic. They belonged to an English province of the Order, who, persecuted in their own country, fled to Belgium, and there established a flourishing college at Bornheim; of which Father Thomas Wilson was president, and Father Edward Fenwick, procurator. In the spring of 1805, this institution was forcibly seized on by the French troops. Father Wilson and the other English members escaped to England; Father Fenwick was cast into prison, from which he was, however, soon released, in consideration, that being a native of Maryland, he was

---

* Sketches of the Early Catholic Missions of Kentucky—p. 131, seq.

an American citizen, whom the French did not dare retain in captivity.

Having joined his brethren in England, Father Fenwick petitioned that they should be permitted to emigrate to America. This was granted, and Father Fenwick was named provincial.

"The members of the Order who accompanied F. Fenwick to the United States were three in number: FF. Thomas Wilson, William Raymond Tuite, and R. Anger; all natives of England. They presented themselves to Bishop Carroll, who welcomed them warmly to his extensive Diocese, which then embraced the whole territory of the United States. When F. Fenwick applied for advice as to the most suitable location for the new Dominican province, Bishop Carroll recommended the distant and destitute missions of Kentucky. To his tender solicitude for the prosperity of our infant missions, we had, early in the same year, been indebted for the invaluable services of M. Nerinckx; and now we were to be in debt to the same goodness, for a whole band of zealous and efficient missionaries.

"In the fall of the year, 1805, F. Fenwick paid a visit to Kentucky, to examine the country, and to decide on the most fitting situation for the new establishment. Having satisfied his mind on the subject, he returned to Maryland, late in the same, or early in the following year. In the spring of 1806, he and his brethren removed to Kentucky, where they established themselves in the present Washington county, on a farm which had been purchased with the rich patrimony of F. Fenwick. The new establishment was called St. Rose, after the Virgin of Lima—the proto-saint of the Dominican Order in America. Thus F. Fenwick was the founder of the Dominican Order in the United States; and he was afterwards destined to be the father and founder of the missions of Ohio, and its first Bishop.

"Having thus founded St. Rose's, F. Fenwick determind to commit the destinies of the new establishment to another, whom, in his humility, he sincerely believed better qualified than himself to conduct it with success. He accordingly obtained from the General of the Order permission to resign his office of superior, in favor of F. Thomas Wilson, who, by an extraordinary privilege, was named provincial for an indefinite period.* F. Fenwick then became a private member of the Order; preferring rather to live under obedience than to incur the responsibility of commanding."†

He now devoted himself almost entirely to the missions. He felt a great relish for the holy work of seeking out and saving sinners. With a peculiar tact, he turned the conversation to Religion; and while those into whose company he was thrown were placed completely at their ease in his presence, he seldom failed to produce a very favorable impression on their minds. He reclaimed many sinners, and converted many Protestants. He and his religious associates were among our most efficient early missionaries.

As we shall see a little later, they laid the foundations of Catholicity in Ohio.

---

* *Usque ad revocationem.*

† Sketches of the Early Catholic Missions of Kentucky—p. 152,

CHAPTER V.

FIRST THREE YEARS OF HIS EPISCOPACY—JOURNEY TO BALTIMORE.

1811—1814.

Extent of his Diocese—Fewness of priests—First priest ordained in the West—Statistics—His *episcopal palace*—Retreats and clerical conferences—Subjects of uneasiness—Resources for comfort and strength—His seminary—Father David—Zeal of seminarians—Thomas Howard—Prospects of the seminary—Severe missionary labors—Visitations and privations—Journey to Baltimore—Visits the Northern portion of his Diocese—And passes through Ohio—Incidents of travel—His impression of Baltimore—Returns.

In entering upon his episcopal career in the West, Bishop Flaget had much need of strong faith and unwavering reliance in Providence. Human resources were but few and slender. With a Diocese extending over so vast a territory, and having Catholic settlements scattered over it at points the most remote from one another, he had need of a large and intrepid missionary band to supply even the most necessary spiritual wants of his flock.

Yet, on his arrival in Kentucky, he found only three secular priests, besides four Dominican fathers established in their convent of St. Rose. The Rev. MM. Nerinckx and O'Flynn were the only missionary associates of M. Badin, among the secular clergy. The Canadian priest—M. Savine—who accompanied him from Baltimore, remained but a few months in Kentucky before he was sent to attend the congregations of Cahokias and St. Louis; and including M. David, the total number of his clergy, both secular and regular, amounted to but eight.

On the Christmas day after his arrival, he had the happiness to add another to this number, by the ordination of Rev. M. Chabrat, which took place at St. Rose's. He was the first priest ordained in the West, as M. Badin had been the first in the East.

We shall have occasion, a little later, to refer to the religious statistics of that portion of his Diocese which lay outside of Kentucky. In the State itself there were about a thousand Catholic families, with an aggregate population not exceeding six thousand souls. There were thirty congregations, ten churches or chapels already built, and six in progress of erection. Besides the Dominican convent of St. Rose, established in the spring of 1806, there were a few poorly furnished pastoral residences, and six plantations,—most of them of little value,—belonging to the Church.

Such was the condition of that part of his Diocese which was more immediately under his eye, when he entered upon the administration. The resources, real and personal, were certainly not very abundant; nor were the prospects, according to any merely human standard of judging, very promising. He had almost every thing to create. But the less he possessed of human means, the more firmly did he rely on the assistance of that God, who created all things out of nothing.

He resided during the first year at St. Stephen's—the present Loretto;—with MM. Badin and Nerinckx, M. David and the seminarians. His accommodations were of the apostolic order, and his *palace* would have done honor to the primitive Bishops of the Church.

"M. Badin had for his own lodging but one poor log house; and in consequence of the expenses he had lately incurred in building a house for a monastery, which was burnt down ere it had been completed, it was with great difficulty that he was enabled to build and prepare, for the residence of his illustrious friend and the ecclesiastics who accompanied him, two miserable log cabins, sixteen feet square. One of the missionaries was compelled to sleep on a matress in the garret of this strange episcopal palace, which was whitewashed with lime, and contained no other furniture than a bed, six chairs, two tables, and a few planks for a library. Here the Bishop resided for a year, esteeming himself happy to live thus in the midst of apostolical poverty."*

Among the subjects which engaged his early pastoral solicitude, the sanctification of his clergy, and the ordering of an uniform discipline, were not the least prominent. The more effectually to secure these ends, he frequently convened the missionaries in spiritual retreats, followed by synods, or rather conferences, on various points connected with pastoral duties and the administration of the sacraments.

---

* M. Badin's Statement—*sup. cit.*

The first of these conferences took place at St. Stephen's, on the 20th of February, 1812.* Eight priests attended; and various points were discussed; some of which were settled, and others adjourned to a subsequent meeting, held at the same place on the 21st of the ensuing May. Among the points under consideration at these conferences, a principal one was the distribution of the Diocese into missionary districts, with defined limits;—a matter of no little difficulty, when the small number of missionaries and the vast extent of territory were taken into account. To give some idea of these districts, it may be observed that the one assigned to M. Nerinckx embraced nearly half the State, extending from Washington to Union county;—a territory in which there are, at present, more than thirty organized congregations!

Many other subjects awakened his solicitude during this early period of his administration.

1. The proposed departure of M. Nerinckx for Europe, on business connected with the missions and the founding of the Loretto Society, gave him no little uneasiness. He could not hope to supply the place of this courageous missionary, and he accordingly induced him to defer his departure for three years.

2. He had no Cathedral, nor even a church or residence of any kind in Bardstown, his see; and he had no means for erecting one. He had thoughts of engaging, as architect, a Mr. Weiss, of Baltimore; but as the prospect of obtaining the funds requisite for even

---

* Bishop's Journal, February 20, 1812. This is the first entry on the Journal, to which so frequent reference will be made in the sequel.

a respectable commencement were very gloomy, he deferred the project to more favorable times, committing it to the hands of Providence.

3. Difficulties arose as to the settlement of various legal questions connected with the church property in Kentucky, which it required several years to adjust in a satisfactory manner.

4. The solicitude of all the churches weighed heavily on his mind and troubled his delicate conscience: the vastness of the work to be done, and the fewness of the laborers, formed the principal elements of the difficulty.*

In the midst of all these perplexities, his resources for consolation and strength were frequent visits to the Blessed Sacrament, and constant prayer. He often retired from the agitation of public life into the depths of his cherished solitude; where he without interruption communed with God in holy retreat. Thus we find him making a spiritual retreat, February 12, 1812; and again, April 18—20, of the same year.

He derived much consolation from this last; and he records the sentiment: "God is very good,—I desire to love Him and to make others love Him."† Towards St. Joseph he cherished a tender devotion; he confidently committed himself and all his spiritual children and friends to his patronage; frequently breathing the prayer: "St. Joseph, my Patron, pray for all the friends who have thought of me."‡

In the sad dearth of missionaries, he naturally turned

---

* Condensed from different entries in his Journal.

† Journal, *in loco*, 1812.

‡ *Ibid*, March 19, 1812.

his eyes to his infant seminary, the future hope of the Diocese. In a long conversation with his intimate friend, M. David, on this subject, he was much cheered by the prospect of soon being able to see, reared up under his own eye, zealous priests who might worthily minister at the holy altar, and break the bread of life to his people.

Father David had been already appointed by M. Emery superior of the seminary; and a better choice could not have been made. Solidly grounded in theological knowledge, and in the practice of those higher virtues which make up the interior and spiritual life, he was regular and systematic in every thing he said and did, as well as industrious and indefatigable in his exertions. He devoted himself with untiring zeal to his office. It mattered not whether he had twenty seminarians under his charge, or only two or three; his interest and labors for their advancement were all the same. He began with only three seminarians; in five years, the number had swelled to fifteen, of whom five were students of theology. We will let him speak on the subject, in his own simple language:*

"There (at St. Stephen's) our seminary continued its exercises for five months. The Bishop lived in a log cabin which had but one room, and was called the *episcopal palace*. The seminarians lodged in another cabin, all together, and myself in a small addition to the principal house. A good Catholic (Mr. THOMAS HOWARD,) who had labored for sixteen years to make an establishment for the Church, then bequeathed to

* In his Letter to a friend in France, November 20, 1817—*sup. cit.*

the Bishop a fine plantation:* and in November, 1811, the seminary was removed thither. After five years we finally succeeded in building a brick church, sixty-five feet long by thirty wide. The interior is not yet sufficiently ornamented, for want of means; it is, however, in a condition sufficiently decent for the celebration of the divine offices. The Bishop officiates in it on the great festivals; and in it three ordinations have already taken place."

The young seminarians seem to have entered fully into the spirit which animated their superior, whom they greatly esteemed and loved; and they labored with a zeal worthy those primitive times of our missions, when every thing was to be founded:

"They made bricks, cut wood, &c., to build the church of St. Thomas, the seminary, and the convent of Nazareth. The poverty of our infant establishments compelled them to spend their recreations in labor. Each day they devoted three hours to work in the garden, in the fields, or in the woods. Nothing could be more frugal than their table, which was also that of the Bishops,† and in which water is their ordinary drink; nothing, at the same time, could be more simple than their dress."‡

Such devotedness could not fail of being blessed by God: "We have at length succeeded," writes Father David, "thanks to God, in building a seminary thirty

* The farm of St. Thomas,—named after the Patron Saint of the donor.

† Bishop Dubourg was at St. Thomas' at the time to which this account refers.

‡ M. Badin's "Statement"—*sup. cit.*

feet square. The second story, which is a garret, serves as a dormitory, and may contain twenty-five persons; it is habitable in winter."*

Though some of these details belong to a later period, yet they are given here, in order that what concerns the early history of the seminary might be presented in the same connection.

The missionary labors undertaken by Bishop Flaget, during the first year of his administration, are scarcely credible. He was almost incessantly engaged in the confessional, in administering the sacraments, and in visiting the sick. He was always the leading missionary, and he had to supply the place of his priests, whenever they were indisposed, or absent on distant missions. Scarcely a day passed without a sick call, which, in most cases, he was compelled to attend himself. It was common with him to ride thirty, forty, and even fifty miles, to visit the dying.

One instance, which we find recorded in his Journal, will give some idea of his labors at this period. During the first four months of the year 1812, he rode eight hundred miles on horseback, on missionary duty. He was heard to observe in his old age, that in those early years, he did not remember to have often passed four days continuously under the same roof! † He lived the greater portion of his time on horseback. Yet he was seldom known to miss saying Mass; having, more than once, rode from twenty to thirty miles fasting, in order to have the consolation of ministering on that day at the holy altar. It required an herculean consti-

---

* Letter—*sup. cit.*

† Slightly modified from the account in the French Life—p. 53.

tution to undergo so much fatigue; and God, who sweetly proportions the means to the end, had accordingly blessed him with a strong frame, and with almost uniterrupted good health.

At this time, when nearly every thing in Western social life is so much changed for the better, we can scarcely imagine the privations to which the Bishop and his missionary priests were exposed at the period in question. Whithersoever he went, he was, indeed, cheerfully accommodated with the best food and lodging which his hospitable entertainers could provide. But these were, in general, necessarily such as to tax heavily even *his* confirmed habit of mortification. The food, as well as the manner of preparing it, was not what he had ever been accustomed to; while the room in which he lodged was frequently open to the weather. We do not read in his Journal, that he ever once put in requisition the French cookery book, so kindly presented to him by the considerate M. Emery, on his departure from France!

His episcopal visitations were but a continuation of his arduous missionary labors. Before the year 1815, he had twice visited all the congregations lying in Kentucky.* In his Report, presented to the Sovereign Pontiff while he was in Rome in 1836, he refers to the manner in which he performed these early visitations of his Diocese:

"In order properly to fulfill the task imposed on me, I was compelled to traverse a territory six or seven times more extensive than Italy; and it was, in many respects, after the manner of the apostles that I had to

---

* Journal—*Ibid.*

undertake all these journeys: for I had absolutely nothing, except the blessings with which the venerable Archbishop of Baltimore had crowned me; to which he added a portable Pontifical, the chief riches of my episcopal chapel. Yet I must say, that, in the midst of this poverty, I was rich in hopes.

"In the long journeys upon which I entered in order to know my flock and to be known by them, I was sometimes alone; and at others, accompanied by a priest who imparted to me the information which he had acquired. Every Sunday, I found myself in a parish church, to fulfill therein all the offices of a missionary. * * In the course of the week, I visited the neighboring stations, devoting to each one or two days, to say Mass, hear confessions, and teach catechism."

We will close this chapter with a summary account of the Bishop's journey to Baltimore, in the fall of 1812, extracted from his Journal.

On the 10th of June, 1812, he had received a letter from M. Bruté, written in the name of Archbishop Carroll, stating that it was in contemplation to convene a Provincial Council in the following November, and requesting his attendance.* He had other motives likewise for making this journey. He desired to take the advice of the Archbishop in reference to the question of church property in Kentucky, concerning which there was some difference of opinion between himself and his Vicar General. He wished also to obtain

* As we have already seen, the Bishops in their meeting at Baltimore, in November, 1810, had resolved to hold a Provincial Council, at a time not later than November 1, 1812.

additional seminarians, and to procure a copy of the rules established by St. Vincent of Paul for the government of the sisters of charity;—a branch of which admirable society he contemplated establishing in his own Diocese.

He moved his effects to St. Thomas' on the 10th of August, and immediately set about making the necessary preparations for his journey. He convened his clergy, and held with them a conference,—the third in this year,—on matters connected with the missions. He ordered public prayers on occasion of the war just commencing with Great Britain. On the 8th of September, he visited St. Charles, to take leave of the sisters of Loretto, lately established there by M. Nerinckx; and on the same evening he returned to the seminary of St. Thomas.

On the next day, he started on horseback, accompanied by the Rev. M. Chabrat. Determining to visit a portion of the Diocese, *en route*, the travelers passed through Shelby county; where, at the house of a Mr. Howell, they performed the usual missionary duties. M. Chabrat preached twice, "with great fire and unction," to a large audience, composed mostly of Protestants. The subjects of his sermons were: the use of time; and the necessity of baptism. Thence they proceeded to Flat creek, where, not having been expected, they found but few in attendance. The next congregation visited was that in Scott county. Here M. Chabrat left the Bishop to return to his missionary station; and he was replaced by Father Badin, with whom the Bishop continued his journey. At Lexington, they were hospitably entertained by Mr. Tibbatts.

There were about thirty families in this congregation at that time; but Religion was found to be in a languishing condition. Only seventeen approached the sacraments; and even this number was considered by M. Badin as extraordinary, and in consequence of the impulse given by the Bishop's visit.

They left Lexington on the 29th of September, and proceeded on horseback, by the way of Paris and the Blue Licks, to Washington, in Mason county, where they were kindly received by Mr. O'Neill. They said Mass at his house, and the Bishop preached on the holy sacrifice, without,—he thought,—producing any very deep impression on the hearts of his hearers. Father Badin accepted an invitation from the people of the town to preach in the court house. His subject was baptism, and his audience large and attentive, consisting almost entirely of Protestants. When he had concluded, a Catholic, who had never before avowed his Religion, came forward and presented his five children for baptism. A Dr. Watts also, who had married a Protestant lady, took courage to confess his faith, and promised to have his children baptized on the Bishop's return.

At Limestone,—now Maysville,—they found but one Catholic, a Mr. Gallagher. The Bishop remarks with pain, that Religion was almost entirely disappearing from this quarter of his Diocese, to which few Catholics had ever emigrated; that the black population was sunk in the most deplorable ignorance; and that the whites were involved in a sad religious indifference. A zealous priest, he adds, might form a respectable congregation at Lexington, with numerous stations between that town and the Ohio river.*

On the 7th of October, the missionaries crossed the Ohio river, and entered the young, but thriving State of Ohio. The first Catholic they met in this State was William Cassel, a German,† whose children they baptized. The road from the river to Chillicothe was "covered with Methodist preachers," whose mistaken zeal struck forcibly the mind of the Bishop; and he thought that, in this respect, their example might well serve to arouse the energy of the lawfully appointed heralds of truth. At Chillicothe they found a few Catholics, who were, however, ashamed to confess their faith, and who even attended the Protestant meeting houses. But between Chillicothe and Lancaster, they were hospitably entertained by a Catholic family, who had remained firm and unshaken in their attachment to the Church.

On the 10th of October they reached Lancaster; where they found three or four Catholic families of high standing in society, and baptized five children. The Bishop cherished hopes that in time a good congregation would be formed here; but he remarked with regret that "the devotion to the Holy Virgin seemed unknown," in these parts.‡

After leaving Lancaster, on the way to Somerset, the missionaries stopped at a log cabin on the road side, to

---

* Journal, *in locis.*

† He induced this man and his wife to remove to Kentucky. They were very piously disposed, and lived for many years in one of the religious establishments.

‡ Journal—*Ibid.*

procure some refreshments. The people there considered them land speculators, and asked whence they came? When they heard that the travelers had come from Kentucky, the landlord exclaimed: "From Kentucky? I have been for a long time thinking of Kentucky, with my wife! They say there are churches and priests there. Wife! we must go thither; it is thirteen years since we saw either a church or a priest; and my poor children!"——

Here Bishop Flaget, deeply moved, interrupted him: "No, my children, stay where you are; I am your Bishop; I will endeavor to send you a priest, at least once a year, to console you:—are there any more Catholics in this neighborhood?" We may imagine the joy imparted by this intelligence. He was informed by the head of the family, whose name was FINK, that there were two other Catholic families at a distance of three miles; like himself, of German origin. Their name was DITTOE. The Bishop did not delay to pay them a visit; and he offered up the holy sacrifice at one of their houses, on the 11th of October.

This was the first time that a Bishop had ever said Mass in Ohio; and the second time that the clean oblation was offered up within the limits of the State:—the first occasion having been when M. Badin, stopping at Gallipolis in 1793, on his way to Kentucky, said Mass there for the French inhabitants.* The above date may then be considered, in some respects, as the birth-day of Catholicity in Ohio.

The Dittoes, with the assistance of their neighbors,

---

* Ohio was then only a territory.

had purchased 320 acres of land for the church, a portion of which was already cleared. The Bishop visited this land, and advised them to erect thereon a house, which might serve as a residence for a priest, and also as a temporary chapel. They promised to comply with his advice, and he was cheered with the hope that, at no distant day, Catholic worship would be performed there with great splendor;—the Germans having a great taste for music.*

Continuing their journey, the travelers proceeded to Baltimore by the way of Wheeling and Emmittsburgh, at which latter place they arrived on the last day of October. Wherever they stopped for repose or refreshment, they made inquiries for Catholics; of whom they found but few on their route. M. Badin created quite a sensation, by publishing every where on the road, "to the right and to the left," that they were not speculators, but genuine Catholic priests and missionaries!†

The Provincial Council, to attend which had been one of the principal objects of the Bishop's visit to Baltimore, was not held, for some reason not indicated by the Bishop in his Journal.‡

---

* Journal, *in loco.*

† This characteristic incident is duly recorded by the Bishop in his Journal.

‡ We gather from some hints thrown out in the Bishop's correspondence, that perhaps the principal reason was the difficulty, or rather impossibility, of communicating with the Sovereign Pontiff, then in prison. Archbishop Carroll felt a delicacy in holding a Provincial Council without the previous sanction of the Pope; and he therefore deemed it advisable to defer it till better times would dawn on the Church and its visible head. In a letter written from

He, however, exerted himself to accomplish the remaining purposes of his journey; in which he was but partially successful. The times were so hard, that it was not deemed advisable to take up a collection in Baltimore; M. Badin, however, not so easily deterred, was busily engaged in soliciting subscriptions among the Catholics in Washington city.

Meantime, winter set in with great severity; and the Bishop, much to his regret, was detained in Baltimore till the ensuing spring. He expresses his reluctance in being thus kept away from his beloved Diocese, in the following rather singular comparison: "An olive tree transplanted to Lapland, would not be more out of place than I am at Baltimore, where I am detained by snow and bad roads."*

He took apartments in the seminary, where he was warmly welcomed by his Sulpician brethren. His numerous old friends in Baltimore paid him every possible attention. "My sojourn at Baltimore," he says, "very agreeable to nature under every point of view, becomes painful on account of the *dissipation* into which it draws me, in spite of myself. From morning till evening, my room is filled with persons who come to see me: some to hear me speak on the condition of Religion in the place of my new abode; and others,—these forming the greater number,—to ask information

---

Baltimore, September 16, 1812, M. Tessier, in the name of the Archbishop, had informed Bishop Flaget that the Council had been postponed indefinitely; but the prelate had already started for Baltimore before the letter reached him. The Bishop wrote from Baltimore to Father David, that hopes were entertained of the Council being convened during the Lent of 1813.

* Journal—*Ibid.*

concerning Father David. The most painful thing for me is my being almost compelled to take my meals out of the seminary; and this unfortunately happens but too frequently."*

On the 22d of April, 1813, he set out on his return to Kentucky, and passed some days very pleasantly at Emmittsburgh. Here he was joined by Father Badin. Accompanied by him and his brother, Vincent Badin, and by some others, he continued his journey westward.

They stopped for four days with a Mr. Arnold, ten miles from Cumberland; where, at the request of Archbishop Carroll, he administered confirmation,—sixty persons approaching the holy communion. He gave confirmation also at Brownsville. This seems to have been the first episcopal visit ever made to these two places.

At Brownsville, the party embarked, with their horses, in "a family boat," and they arrived safely at Limestone; whence they continued their journey, by the way of Lexington and Frankfort, to St. Thomas'.

The remainder of the year 1813, and the first months of 1814, were passed by the Bishop in the visitation of his Diocese, and in the performance of arduous missionary duties. In the midst of his multiplied journeys and labors, the holy prelate sought daily to keep himself more and more closely united with God in prayer. He often exclaimed with the Psalmist: "Turn away my eyes, that they may not see vanity."†

* Journal, November 18, 1812.

† Journal, April 29, 1814.

"We should constantly purify our intentions, and occupy our minds with holy things: visits are always dangerous for an ecclesiastic."*

He experienced no little difficulty, in inducing the congregations which he visited to acquiesce in any fixed plan for securing a regular support to their pastors. At St. Charles and St. Rose, for instance, there were a few who opposed the assessment, which he had established. Vested in his episcopal *insignia*, he addressed the refractory in the strongest terms, from the altar; threatening that, in case they persisted in their refusal, he would no longer consider them as belonging to the Church. Exhibiting habitually a mildness and sweetness of character, which won all hearts, he could still be severe, whenever a sense of duty compelled him to act with vigor.

He ardently desired to rear up missionaries suited to the times, and filled with the apostolic spirit. "O, what a happiness for me," he exclaimed, "if I could form a generation of holy missionaries! But in this, O my God, may Thy holy will be done, and not mine!"†

Returning from his missions, his heart overflowed with holy joy, when he found himself in the midst of his dear seminarians at St. Thomas'. We find the following entry on the subject in his Journal:‡ "Recreation with the seminarians;—I love to be in the midst of them. I reproach myself with not being sufficiently grave in their company."

---

* Journal, January, 1814.

† Journal, April 9, 1814.

‡ May 13, 1814.

CHAPTER VI.

JOURNEY TO VINCENNES AND ST. LOUIS—MISSIONARY DUTIES.

1814—1816.

Petition from Catholics of Vincennes—Governor Harrison—Spiritual destitution—Religious history of Vincennes from 1795 to 1814—M. Rivet—Indian missions—The *praying chief*—M. Olivier—Early history of Kaskaskias and other French settlements—Succession of priests therein—Bishop Flaget visits Vincennes—Cahokias—St. Louis—Florissant—St. Charles—Kaskaskias—St. Genevieve—And Prairie du Rocher—Sets out on his return—Again in Vincennes—Painful rumor and ludicrous incident—Returns to Kentucky—Severe missionary labors—M. Nerinckx departs for Europe—An inward voice—Discussion with preacher Tapscott—Two tributes to Archbishop CARROLL.

BISHOP FLAGET, having now visited the greater portion of the Catholic congregations of Kentucky, had leisure to turn his attention to more distant missions placed under his jurisdiction. Already, in 1812, the Catholics of Vincennes had sent him an earnest petition to have a resident pastor. In this document, they freely admitted that they had been heretofore very remiss in their duties as Catholics, but promised amendment in the future. General Harrison, then Governor of the North Western Territory, and residing at Vincennes, had united also in the petition, promising every aid in his power to promote the interests of the mission.

The Bishop was much moved by this exposition of their wants by his old parishioners; who appear to have had no resident priest since the death of his own immediate successor in the pastorship, M. Rivet, which had occurred in February, 1804. But, in his sad paucity of missionaries, he was not able immediately to provide for the necessities of this congregation; which continued, for some time longer, to be only occasionally visited by the French clergyman stationed in Illinois.

To understand more clearly the state of spiritual destitution to which the old parish of Vincennes was now reduced, it will be necessary to go back a little, and trace its religious history in some detail, from the time M. Flaget left it in 1795, to that of his return on his visitation as Bishop in 1814;—two years after the reception of the petition just mentioned.* As on this occasion, he continued his journey through Illinois and Upper Louisiana (Missouri), and visited all the Catholic settlements lying on both sides of the Mississippi, it may not be inappropriate to glance also at the early history of these Catholic colonies, before we proceed to describe the first episcopal visitation with which they were ever favored.

The impression which M. Flaget had made on the minds and hearts of the Catholics at Vincennes, while there as a simple missionary, was deep and lasting. "He had stripped himself of all the linen he had brought with him to Vincennes, in favor of the sick and indigent. The tender care with which he visited

* We have already spoken of the history of Vincennes before 1792.

the sick will never be forgotten; and the impression it made upon the population will last as long as there shall be an old man left, to relate to his children's children the history of old times."*

His immediate successor in the mission was M. Rivet, a most zealous and laborious missionary, who left behind him at Vincennes memories scarcely less favorable than M. Flaget himself. This good man devoted his time, in a special manner, to the instruction and conversion of the various Indian tribes roaming over the plains watered by the Wabash. This he, in fact, viewed as the chief object of his mission to Indiana. In the Registers, he styles himself, "Missionary appointed for the savages, exercising the ministry, *for the moment*, in the parish of St. Francis Xavier." God rewarded his zeal with abundant fruits. The Registers show the baptism and marriage of many Indians of different tribes, during his residence in Vincennes. The greatest number was of Potowattamies; but there were also many from the tribes of Miamis, Shawnees, Charaguis, Piamkeshaws, Weas or *Ouias*, Sioux, and Kaskaskias. The first marriage he records was that of a Potowattamie to a Shawnee.

Some of these Indian converts were most exemplary. He mentions with special praise an old chief, called Louis in baptism, but better known as "the old praying man, or chief."† He died on White river, during

* From a letter of Rev. E. AUDRAN, of St. Francis Xavier's Cathedral, Vincennes. We are indebted to this worthy ecclesiastic for the details which follow, derived by him chiefly from the Registers of the church.

† "Le vieux priant."

the winter encampment with his tribe. His death was most edifying. It occurred but a few days after his return from Vincennes; whither he had gone, as was his custom, to receive the sacraments of penance and the holy Eucharist at Christmas.

Before M. Rivet's time, though some of the Indians had been converted to the faith, no general impression seems to have been made on their hearts. The Jesuit missionaries were withdrawn, ere they had been able to effect much general good among savages, who, from their accounts, seemed but little disposed to embrace the Gospel. M. Gibault had too much to do to devote any considerable time to their conversion; and the same may be said of M. Flaget, whose stay in Vincennes was besides too brief to permit his laboring with much general success among these poor children of the wilderness. Yet, as we have already seen, the latter baptized many, especially during the prevalence of the small-pox.

The state of continual agitation in which the country around that military post was involved, during the war of our revolution, was little favorable to the conversion of the Indian tribes, who were themselves engaged in the contest. We are sorry also to add, that after the occupation of Vincennes by the Americans, the state of mutual amity which had hitherto happily existed between the inhabitants and the neighboring tribes, was often interrupted. Murders became not unfrequent, and they were followed by swift revenge, which but increased the feud. The final result was, as we all know, that the Indians were driven from the graves of their ancestors, into the remote recesses of the Western wilderness.

In 1798—December 18—M. Rivet, for the first time, signs himself Vicar General of Bishop Carroll. There were about that time many Irish Catholic soldiers at Fort Knox, situated on the Wabash, three miles above Vincennes. M. Rivet baptized their children; and a mortality breaking out in the garrison, he buried several of the soldiers,—bearing honorable testimony in the Registers to their faith and piety. On the records, we find the name of Hon. William Clark, a good Catholic, one of the judges of the supreme court in the territory of Indiana.

M. Rivet had long been dying by inches of the consumption. Yet he remitted not his arduous labors. He remained at his post, faithful to the last. His last official act was the record of a baptism, January 31, 1804. Knowing that his time was short, he wrote to the Rev. Donatian Olivier, then residing at Prairie du Rocher among the French Catholics on the Mississippi, begging him to come and give him the last sacraments. But he died three days before the arrival of this good clergyman. He was not, however, unprepared. Finding that his death was near at hand, he wrote out his confession, sealed it, and directed it to be given to M. Olivier on his arrival. Thus died, in odor of sanctity, the good, modest, zealous M. Rivet.

After his death, the Catholics of Vincennes were visited from time to time by M. Olivier; and once or twice by missionaries from Kentucky. In the beginning of November, 1804, M. Olivier came and spent a month in the place, diligently attending to ministerial duties. In the following year—1805—he remained there during the two first weeks of July. On the 14th of April, 1806, MM. Badin and Nerinckx, from Kentucky, visited Vincennes, and remained until the 27th; baptizing many children, and assisting at several marriages, besides administering the other sacraments, as usual. In the same year, M. Olivier came again, November 13, and remained till the 1st of December.

Nearly eighteen months now elapsed before the next visit of M. Olivier, which occurred on the 1st of May, 1808;—he remained three weeks. On the 26th of September, of the same year, Father Urban Guillet, a Trappist, passed through the place, stopping there but one day.

During this interval, a layman—Zepherin Chesnet—gave private baptism, assisted at burials, &c. November 25, 1809, M. Olivier visited the town again, and remained a month. On leaving, he forbade Chesnet to do any thing of a sacred character in the congregation; having learned that his conduct had not been exemplary.

No records of baptisms or burials are therefore to be found, till the return of the missionary, November 20, 1810; when he was accompanied by M. Badin, Vicar General in Kentucky. They were both busily engaged in ministerial duties, and in revalidating marriages, which had been contracted before the civil magistrate. M. Olivier, on one day, renovated eight of such marriages in the church; having first caused the parties to prepare themselves for two weeks, during which time the bans were published.*

M. Olivier's next visit was in September and October, 1811. Two years now elapsed before he was able

* It seems that the decree of the Council of Trent on marriage was always considered as having been published at Vincennes.

again to come to the place;—in October and November 1813. His last visit to the parish was in May and June, 1814; when he went thither to meet Bishop Flaget, and conduct him to the Mississippi.

Considering the circumstances which surrounded the Catholics of Vincennes, and the small opportunities they had enjoyed for many years to be grounded in the knowledge and practice of their holy Religion, it is not at all wonderful that piety should have declined, and ignorance of religious duties prevailed, to a great extent. It is only remarkable, that, amidst so many disadvantages, faith was generally preserved, and religious fervor among even a few.

We are now enabled to see how heavy a responsibility rested on Bishop Flaget, when, after the lapse of nearly twenty years, he revisited, as Bishop, his old parishioners of Vincennes; whom he found in a condition scarcely less deplorable than that which caused him so much concern on his first visit, as a simple missionary, in 1792.

Post Vincennes, as we have seen, was founded by the French, as a military station, about or before the year 1710;* the French settlements on the Mississippi river were considerably older. Our information in regard to the religious history of these colonies is very

* From what has been said in a previous chapter, (Chapter ii.) it is certain that there was already a French post established on the Wabash in the the year 1712; for Father Mermet was sent thither as a missionary before that year, perhaps during the year previous. Father Marest's Letter, written November 9, 1712, says simply, that a post *had been* established, and Father Mermet *had been* sent, &c. In the same Letter we read that Father Mermet was back again in Illinois in 1711.

limited; the zealous missionaries who labored in founding them, and in administering to their spiritual wants, having been much more intent on unremitted efforts to extend the boundaries of Christian civilization, than solicitous to make out and leave behind them written records of their proceedings. The following facts, believed to be in the main accurate, are all that we have been able to glean from the scanty materials to which we could have access.

The first missionary station established among the Indians of Illinois was that of *St. Louis*, on the Illinois river, at or near the site of the present Peoria. This mission was founded by F. John Deguerre, a Jesuit from Lake Superior. From this point the zealous missionary visited several of the Indian tribes in the interior of the present State of Illinois; and while there exercising his apostolic functions, he was killed by the savages. Several others of the early missionaries likewise fell martyrs to their zeal: Father Gabriel de la Ribourde, a Franciscan, in 1680; F. Maximus Leberck, of the same order, in 1687; F. John D. Tetu, in 1728; and another Franciscan, F. Vercailler, was drowned in crossing the river in 1750.*

Father Marquette, having discovered the Mississippi in 1673, was filled with a burning zeal to evangelize the tribes living along its borders. He was returning from the North for this purpose, about two years later; but he died on his way. The mission was then entrusted to Father Daloes; who shortly afterwards was called to labor elsewhere. He was succeeded by Father

* Shepherd of the Valley, January 17, 1852. We have omitted some dates of very doubtful accuracy.

James Gravier, who may be considered as the founder of the missions among the Illinois Indians.*

Kaskaskias was founded about the year 1683. Father James Gravier, a Jesuit, was the principal instrument of Providence for the establishment of a French colony at this point. He was the first missionary to the Kaskaskias tribe of Indians, then numbering about two thousand warriors, He experienced, at first, much opposition from the "medicine-men," to whose jugglery the Indians clung with great tenacity.

Father Gravier having been compelled to return to Michilimakinac, the mission was entrusted to FF. Bineteau and Pinet, with whom F. Gabriel Marest was afterwards associated. On the death of the first and the departure of the second of these Fathers, the last named remained in sole charge of the mission; until the arrival of F. Mermet, in 1711.

F. Marest had before been stationed at the mission of St. Louis, in the great village of the *Peourias* Indians, on the Illinois river; where the French then had a military post.† Father Gravier returning to this station from Michilimakinac, received there from the savages a mortal wound, from which he soon died. The mission was in consequence for a time suspended. On the repentance of the *Peourias*, the missionary station among them was re-established; and Father De Ville was sent thither, about the year 1712.

The missionaries were in the habit of accompanying the Indians on their two annual hunts; the long one in the winter, and the short one in the summer season.

* Letter of Father Gabriel Marest, November 9, 1712.

† The same mentioned above.

Father Bineteau died of a fever he had contracted in following the summer hunt. He expired tranquilly in the arms of F. Marest.

Twenty-five leagues from Kaskaskias was the great village of the *Tamarouas;* among whom labored Father Bergier, a priest of the congregation of the foreign missions. This devoted missionary died here alone, joyfully embracing the crucifix,—sometime in 1712. Father Marest hastened to his assistance during his illness; but arrived only in time to assist at his interment.

There was also a mission called St. Joseph's, among the Potowattamies, on the St. Joseph's river. In 1711, it was attended by F. Chardon. In that year, F. Marest went thither, where he met his brother, then superior of the North-western missions.*

An old log house first served as a chapel in Kaskaskias. It was replaced by a stone church in 1714. In 1722, the population of French and mixed blood already numbered five hundred and eighteen.

A large portion of the tribe was converted to the faith. The new converts became most exemplary in their conduct; and their tender piety consoled the missionaries for all their previous labors and privations. They were divided into three classes: the first of which settled about two miles from Kaskaskias; the second at Cahokias; the third at Prairie du Rocher.

In 1750, the state of the missions in Illinois, both French and Indian, is given as follows by Father Vivier.† In the whole of Illinois and Upper Louisi-

* All these details are taken from the interesting Letter of F. Gabriel Marest—*sup. cit.*

† Letter dated "At Illinois, November 17, 1750."

ana (Missouri), there were then five French villages, containing one hundred and forty families; and three Indian villages (Christian), able to muster about three hundred warriors. These were divided into three stations, attended by Jesuit missionaries. The first was composed of about six hundred Illinois, all of them baptized with the exception of five or six; and it was attended by FF. De Guienne and Vivier; the second, composed of four hundred French and two hundred and fifty negroes, was served by F. Vatrin; the third, seventy leagues off, and much smaller, was attended by F. Meurin.*

The entire Indian missions of the North and West had been, some years previously, entrusted by the Bishop of Quebec to the French priests of the foreign missions. "There are three of these priests here, who have charge of the two French congregations; nothing can be more lovely than their character, or more edifying than their conduct. We live with them as if we were members of the same community."†

In 1832, the remnant of the Kaskaskias tribe removed to the Indian territory in the far West; where they had the inexpressible consolation of again finding their old fathers in God, the Jesuit missionaries.

The succession of priests attending to the missionary stations along the Mississippi, seems never to have been interrupted for any considerable time; from the date of their first establishment down to the present day. The French settlers and the Indian converts had always the happiness of kneeling at the altar, on

---

* This was located probably in the Wabash country.

† Letter dated "At Illinois, November 17, 1750."

which the holy sacrifice was offered up. The clergy generally resided at Prairie du Rocher; but occasionally at Kaskaskias, or Cahokias. The following list will exhibit the succession down to the year 18[illegible]7—so far as we have been able to ascertain it:

1683—1710—FF. James Gravier, Julian Bineteau and Henry Pinet; the last named founded the mission of Cahokias.

1710—FF. Gabriel Marest, Mermet, and De Ville.

1719—F. John Charles Guimeneau, superior of the mission, and Vicar General of the Bishop of Quebec, and Rev. Dominic A. Thaumur de la Source.

1724—Father A. F. X. De Guienne, superior and Vicar General, with FF. De Beaubois, Dumas, Tabarin, and others not known.

1735—F. Boularger, &c.

1739—Rev. MM. Mercier and Laurent.

1741—F. Truteau, &c.

1743—Rev. Joseph Gagnon, pastor of St. Ann's—died here in 1755.

1746—F. Tartarin, &c.

1750—FF. Aloysius Vivier, Gagnon, and Tourre.

1754—Rev. J. F. Forget.

1759—F. Watrin and two Franciscan Recollects, Hypolyte and Luke Collet, sent by the Bishop of Quebec; the latter remained till 1765.

1764—F. Aubert, &c.

1768—F. S. L. Meurin, the last Jesuit missionary in the West.

1770—1789 *—Rev. M. Gibault, Vicar General of the Bishop of Quebec for Illinois and the neighboring countries; with him were associated during a portion of this time, the Rev. MM. Bernard (1784), Payet (1785), and De St. Pierre, pastor of St. Genevieve.

1789—M. De la Valiniere, Vicar General, &c.; with whom were associated MM. Ledru, Gibault, and De St. Pierre.

1793—Rev. M. Levadoux, Vicar General; he remained but a short time.

---

* From Registers of Vincennes—*sup. cit.*

1793-8—Rev. Gabriel Richard and Rev. John Janin.
1799—1827—Very Rev. Donatian Olivier, Vicar General of Bishop Carroll.*

Between Kaskaskias and Cahokias there were formerly three different parishes: St. Philip's, St. Ann's, and St. Joseph's. The last named only now remains, it being that of Prairie du Rocher; the other churches seem to have been abandoned about the year 1788, in consequence of the encroachments of the Mississippi on the lowlands where they were established. The Registers of these parishes were kept at the old Fort Chartres: but they were subsequently removed to Prairie du Rocher or Kaskaskias.

As a specimen of the details recorded in these old Registers, we subjoin an extract from that of Prairie du Rocher:

"On the 24th of July, in the year 1768, I, the undersigned priest of the Society of Jesus, Vicar General of the Bishop of Quebec, having foreseen the approaching ruin of the church of St. Ann, near Fort Chartres, by reason of the encroachment of the Mississippi, gave orders to have the remains of the Rev. JOSEPH GAGNON, formerly pastor of Fort Chartres and the environs, taken from said church and transferred to that of St. Joseph, at Prairie du Rocher. The remains of Joseph Gagnon were buried near the sanctuary on the Gospel side; and those of Father Collet near the sanctuary on

* This list has been carefully compiled from various sources: the Letters of the Jesuit missionaries often quoted above; the records of the church of Vincennes; and lists published in the "Shepherd of the Valley," (January and February, 1852,) purporting to be taken from the Registers of Kaskaskias, Prairie du Rocher, and Cahokias.

the Epistle side. The ceremonies of the Church were previously performed, at which the inhabitants assisted, with feelings of reverence and grateful recollection of these good and zealous missionaries.

"In testimony whereof, I have subscribed this writing, with MM. BARBEAU and LECOMPTE.

"S. L. MEURIN, *Vic. Gen.*"*

The Rev. DONATIAN OLIVIER, the last named on the above list, was one among the most pious, zealous and efficient priests who ever labored in the missions of the Mississippi valley. He was universally esteemed and beloved; by the French Catholics, he was reverenced as a saint. His name is still held in benediction among them. He was for many years Vicar General of the Bishop of Baltimore, for all the missions extending over the present States of Indiana and Illinois. He usually resided, it appears, at Prairie du Rocher; but he visited Kaskaskias, Cahokias, Vincennes, and the other Catholic settlements. He was admirable for his child-like simplicity and unaffected piety, which traits he continued to exhibit, in the midst of his apostolic labors, till old age compelled him to abandon the field, and seek solace and prepare for death in retirement. He died on the 29th of January, 1841, at the seminary of the Barrens, in Missouri, at the advanced age of ninety-five years.†

Father Meurin was the last Jesuit missionary who attended the Catholic settlements on the borders of the

* Shepherd of the Valley, February 21, 1852. These learned articles were written by M. E. Saulnier, an old and zealous missionary, now residing at the cathedral of St. Louis.

† See his obituary in the "Catholic Advocate," vol. 6, p. 23.

Mississippi. About the year 1768, the Fathers of the society were withdrawn from the Western missions; and on the suspension of the order a few years later,—in 1773,—these splendid missionary establishments, which they had founded in the North and North-west among the various Indian tribes, began sensibly to languish. This was partly in consequence of the occurrence just mentioned, and partly because the British government, into whose hands the dominion of the Canadas had passed, viewed all Catholic missionaries with distrust. As the Jesuits successively withdrew from the different missionary stations, their places were supplied by other clergymen sent by the Bishop of Quebec; until the consecration of Bishop Carroll, in 1790. Then the latter was compelled, so far as he was able, to supply with priests those missions which lay within the limits of the United States.

With this rather long historical introduction, we will now proceed to give a summary account of the visit which Bishop Flaget paid to Vincennes, St. Louis, and the missions above mentioned, in the year 1814. Though his jurisdiction did not extend beyond the Mississippi river, yet at the request of Dr. Dubourg, administrator of the Diocese of New Orleans, he willingly assumed for a time the charge of all the missions lying in what was then called Upper Louisiana,—at present, the State of Missouri.

He was accompanied as far as Louisville by the Rev. MM. Badin and Chabrat; of whom he took leave on the 25th of May, to perform alone on horseback the journey to Vincennes. On the first night, he was obliged "to sleep with an American borderer." On the second, he sought repose on "a quilt, extended over a plank which was very uneven and knotty; he, however, slept soundly."

On the third day, the 28th, he reached Vincennes; and great was the joy of his old flock on seeing again their beloved pastor, who had been away from them for nearly twenty years. A large company came out to meet him on horseback, headed by the Rev. M. Olivier; and he was conducted into the town with great pomp. The good prelate was much moved; he remarked that "faith still existed in their hearts; a zealous priest would make saints of them."*

On the 30th of May, the Bishop visited the cemetery, attended by a great concourse of people who crowded around to enjoy the satisfaction of looking on the face of their first pastor. The *Libera* was sung over the grave of Rev. M. Rivet. On the same day he solemnly blessed a company of Rangers, who were setting out for the seat of war. They dismounted, and all together bent one knee to the earth, while, with uplifted hand, he invoked the blessing of God on them; exhorting them not to forget the God of battles, while fighting bravely under the banner of their country.

He remained for two weeks at Vincennes, which time he employed in the instruction of the children, in the duties of the confessional, and in the arrangement of temporal business, connected with the estate of M. Rivet, and with the general administration of church affairs. He found the congregation in a state of great spiritual destitution; in many, faith was

* Journal, May 28, 1814.

almost extinct; general ignorance of their Religion prevailed to an alarming degree, both among children and parents. Yet he yielded not to discouragement.

Assisted by M. Olivier, he devoted several days to the preparation of the candidates for confirmation, whose proficiency even surpassed his expectations. On June 5th, he administered this sacrament to eighty-six persons. He preached in English, as well as in French; to the great satisfaction of the Americans. He had the gratification "to hear the confessions of some sinners who had grown old in their iniquities."*

In his sermons, he inveighed strongly against existing abuses; particularly marriages out of the Church, and balls with dancing, which, it seems, were there carried to great excess. His discourses seem to have made a great impression on the people. He visited many of the French families: "I know," he writes, "that these poor people are very solicitous for such visits; but I know not whether they derive much profit from them."†

On the 14th of June, accompanied by M. Olivier, he started for the Mississippi. They were escorted by the company of French Rangers, to whom he was very grateful for their kind attentions. They soon entered on the vast prairies of Illinois, in which the Rangers amused themselves in hunting deer and wild turkeys; but without success. "These vast plains," the Bishop writes, "seem destined by the Creator for the rearing of millions of sheep."‡

---

* Journal, June 5, 1814.

† *Ibid,* June 6.

‡ *Ibid.*

On the 18th, they arrived at Cahokias, where they found the priest—M. Savine—"holding the handle of a skillet to make an omelette."* Bishop Flaget had not taken off his boots for four days! This congregation was free from debt, with a surplus fund of $200; every thing was in good order; and he heard many confessions, some of them of very old sinners. On the 26th, he confirmed one hundred and eighteen persons.

The good people of Cahokias conducted him in procession to the banks of the Mississippi, which he crossed in a canoe, with no companion but the oarsman. He entered St. Louis on the 30th, but without any public reception;—a circumstance remarked on as very unusual among those French settlements. He visited this city and the Catholic missions West of the Mississippi river, as was said above, at the special request of M. Dubourg; who held jurisdiction over Upper Louisiana, and had written to him on the subject.

Religion seems to have been in a worse condition at St. Louis than it was even at Vincennes. The 4th of July; which the Bishop spent here, was a day of great sadness for him; on account of the general religious apathy which prevailed. The rich, the fathers, the mothers, and the children over fifteen years, stayed away from the confessional; and he could make no impression whatever on their callous hearts.† He administered confirmation,—he does not state to how many;—and was attended in the ceremonies of the visitation by the Rev. M. Savine, and "the Father

---

* Journal, June 18, 1814.

† *Ibid.* Almost his own words.

Prior,"*—the latter a Trappist, who remained in America after his brethren had returned to Europe.

The ladies of St. Louis presented to him a fine cross and mitre. Greatly annoyed at the constant distractions occasioned by continual visits, he exclaimed: "My God! how happy were the ancient solitaries!"† Here he learned the intelligence of the downfall of Napoleon; and so great was his joy on the occasion, that he resolved to have a solemn *Te Deum* sung on his return to Kentucky, in case the news should be confirmed.

On the 8th of July, he departed for Florissant. The entire population of this village turned out with joy to welcome him. Two banners were borne by groups of boys and girls; and the procession, headed by chanters, conducted him solemnly into the church. This ceremony over, the people crowded around him in the house, eager to receive his benediction. Among them was one man 107 years old, and another 108. The latter was brought by his sons in a chair, and the venerable man expressed his lively regret, that he was not able to kneel down to receive the episcopal blessing. The Bishop's heart was much affected at the firm faith of these good people, who seem to have been "true Israelites in whom there was no guile." He here received the confessions of some who had kept away from the sacraments for thirty-seven years!

On the 11th, he left Florissant and crossed the Mis-

---

* Father Marie Joseph Dunand, who attended the missions West of the Mississippi river. For some years previous to 1812, the Trappists exercised the ministry on both sides of the Mississippi.

† Journal, July 6.

souri river, sitting in an arm-chair placed in a canoe decorated with flowers. On the other side he visited a congregation,* which he found divided into two hostile parties. He preached to them an earnest sermon on union and charity; and confirmed one hundred and three persons. He went to see two aged ladies; one of whom was 103, and the other was 115 years old. The climate seems to have been at that time favorable to longevity.

He arrived at St. Charles on the 18th; and on the 21st went to *Portage aux Sioux*. Here he confirmed fifty-four persons on the 28th; after which he returned to St. Charles.

This congregation he also found in a sad state; "it had been at war with its pastor for two years."† He here confirmed sixty-seven, on the 31st of July. He labored with great zeal to restore peace to this community; and his efforts were crowned with consoling success. All murmurs ceased, and the people expressed a willingness not only to support their pastor, but also to build for him a suitable residence.

On the 3d of August, the Bishop returned to St. Louis. He says: "This congregation is in a state of extreme indifferentism; my sojourn here will be almost useless."‡ Several young men presented themselves for confession, in order to be re-married in presence of

* The name of this congregation is not given in the Journal; perhaps it was that of *Dardennes*.

† Journal, July 31. The pastor of this place, and of the neighboring missions, was the Trappist Prior, above mentioned, who seems to have had very little tact in managing congregations.

‡ Journal, August 3.

the pastor; their sentiments of contrition did not appear to be very striking.* He here confirmed seventy-two persons, and preached to the Americans in English. These were so much pleased with his sermon, that they sent a deputation to express their satisfaction.

Governor Clark,† the former associate of Lewis in the discovery of the Columbia river, paid him every possible attention. He invited the Bishop to his house, and prevailed on him to baptize three of his children, as well as an orphan girl residing in his family. The Bishop stood God-father, and Mrs. Hunt God-mother of the children.

We take occasion from the Bishop's visit to St. Louis, to furnish a few facts regarding the early history of this now important city; which became an episcopal see in 1827, and an archbishopric in 1847.

St. Louis was founded in February, 1764. The site was selected by Laclede, in the preceding December: he previously visited St. Genevieve. After the cession of Upper and Lower Louisiana by France to Spain in 1763, St. Louis and the other settlements West of the Mississippi were placed under the spiritual jurisdiction of the Bishop (or Archbishop) of Havana;‡ until the

---

* Journal, August 7. *Mais ou est la contrition de leur fautes?*

† He was Governor of the Missouri Territory; and was a relative—we have been told a brother—of General George Rogers Clark; with whom the Bishop had become acquainted, on his journey to Vincennes in 1792, and who had on that occasion shown him so much polite attention.

‡ We have been unable to ascertain at what precise date the Bishop of Havana became an Archbishop. His title, as given in the Registers of St. Louis at an early date, is *Bishop of St. Jago, Cuba.*

erection of the see of New Orleans, in 1793. These missions appear to have been attended, for a time, by the French clergymen stationed on the Illinois side of the river; who were under the jurisdiction of the Bishop of Quebec, until the establishment of the see of Baltimore, in 1790. With the sanction of the ordinary in Havana, or through an express provision made by the Holy See, the Bishops of Quebec and Baltimore, through their local Vicars General, held respectively jurisdiction over the Catholics living in Upper Louisiana, until the year above named.

The following list will exhibit the succession of clergymen, who held pastoral charge of St. Louis, from its first foundation down to a recent date:

1766-9—Rev. S. L. Meurin, S. J.
1770-2—M. Gibault, pastor of Kaskaskias.
1772—From February to May—F. Meurin again.
1772-5—F. Valentin, O. S. F., the first resident pastor of St. Louis.
1775—In October—F. Meurin came a third time to the town.
1776—F. Hilary, O. S. F., second resident pastor.
1776—1789—F. Bernard, O. S. F., third resident pastor.
1789—1793—Rev. M. Ledru, fourth pastor.
1793-9—F. B. Didier, fifth pastor.
1800-4—Rev. M. Janin, sixth pastor.
1804-6—Rev. MM. Donatian Olivier, of Prairie du Rocher, and J. Maxwell, of St. Genevieve, came occasionally to exercise ministerial functions in the town.
1806-8—Rev. Thomas Flynn.
1808-11—The Trappist Fathers, Urban Guillet, F. M. Bernard, and Marie Joseph Dunand, visited successively the parish.
1811-17—Rev. F. Savine.
1817—Rev. MM. Joseph Rosati, and Henry Pratte.
1818—Rev. Felix De Andreis.
1818—1825—Rev. F. Niex.
1825—1831—Rev. Edmond Saulnier, rector.

1832—1844—Rev. Joseph A. Lutz.*

The parish of St. Charles, which, as we have seen, was also visited by our prelate, was of a more recent date; having been established in 1792. Its first pastor was the Rev. M. Lusson; who was succeeded by the Rev. MM. Acquaroni, B. Richard, M. Joseph Dunand, and F. Charles Vanquickenborne, S. J.† It is at present attended by the Jesuits.

On the 14th of August, the Bishop left St. Louis and crossed the river to Illinois. On the opposite shore, there was assembled a large escort of carriages and horsemen, who conducted him processionally to Cahokias. Here, on the 21st, he confirmed fifty-eight persons. On the 23d, he departed for Prairie du Rocher, where he again met M. Olivier, and confirmed sixty-five persons on the 1st day of September.

His incessant labors and constant exposure to the hot sun had thrown him into a fever, under the effects of which he suffered for several weeks. Yet he would not discontinue his apostolic exertions. Though he he was still very feeble from the effects of the malady obstinately clinging to him, and in no condition to continue his visitation, nevertheless he started for Kaskaskias on the 14th of September.

"The church was superb for the country; its length eighty feet, its width forty feet; with a handsome steeple and a fine bell. The evening was spent in blessing the good people."‡ On the 18th, he confirm-

---

* For these details we are indebted to the Rev. EDMOND SAULNIER, at present Chancellor of the Archdiocese of St. Louis.

† *Idem.*

‡ Journal, September 14.

ed seventy, and on the 20th, forty persons, in this congregation. The American inhabitants seemed pleased with his sickness, which gave them a hope that he would be compelled to remain with them some time longer; but they were disappointed.*

On the 21st, he went to St. Genevieve, where he was received with the usual honors. He preached strongly against the violation of the laws of abstinence; and against balls,—"to the great astonishment of the dancers."† He administered confirmation, at three different times, to three hundred and sixty-one persons.

October 5th—19th, he visited an American Catholic settlement at some distance, where forty-five were confirmed.

On his return to St. Genevieve, he preached to the negroes, of whom there were about five hundred in the town and vicinity. Finding that marriage was not common amongst these poor people, he threatened their masters with privation of the sacraments, unless they afforded their servants every facility to enter lawfully into this holy contract. The people of St. Genevieve presented him with a new suit, and $50 in money.

On the 27th of October, he retraced his steps, and rejoined M. Olivier at Prairie du Rocher. Here he was delighted to enjoy a few days of "charming solitude after so much distraction."‡

November 3d, he returned to Kaskaskias; whence, after confirming thirty-six persons, he took his departure for home, on the 8th, by the way of Vincennes.

---

* Journal, September 18.

† Journal—*Ibid.*

‡ Journal, October 28.

He was escorted by sixten creoles on horseback. They safely reached Vincennes on the 12th of November.

As the war was then raging with England, a rumor that the Bishop had been captured by a hostile band of Indians had been circulated, and had occasioned great uneasiness in Kentucky, sometime during his absence. Father David had caused a novena to be said by the seminarians for his safety. That he was exposed to danger, there is no doubt; but Providence watched over his life.

The following rather ludicrous incident, which occurred when the escort were near Vincennes, may have given occasion to the report. We will let the Bishop relate it in his own playful manner, in a letter written from Vincennes to Father David:

"A young man of Post Vincennes, who was in our company, returning home, separated about mid-day from our troupe with two others, without doubt, in order to be the first in arriving (at Vincennes). They were two or three miles in advance; and we did not expect to meet them again till night. What was our surprise at seeing them soon return, * * calling out loudly, that they had fallen in with Indians! We had ourselves heard several shots, but we had thought that they proceeded from these young men, amusing themselves while awaiting our arrival. Their report, which was uniform, the paleness of their countenances, the shots we had heard, and which were certainly fired by persons strangers to our band; above all, imagination so easily excited in times of danger, left no doubt whatever concerning the truth of their statement. On the spot, our troops prepared themselves with the greatest resolution for an attack. The young men counted so strongly on their gallantry, that they did not even reconnoitre the force of the enemy; but with one accord they prepared their arms, deployed into the prairie, and advanced in a trot towards the wood, where they supposed the savages were lying concealed. 'My Grandeur' received the order to remain in the rear:— 'It is for your sake,' said the Captain, 'that we have come; and it is for you that we are going to meet the enemy, to make for you a rampart with our arms and with our bodies.'

"The sensations which I then experienced were very different from what such circumstances would seem well calculated to call forth. My heart was perfectly tranquil, my imagination calm, and what is very singular, I felt a great desire to be in the midst of this little warlike band, to follow their movements and those of the enemy;—to stimulate the courage of the former, and to stay the impetuosity of the latter. Reflecting, however, on my state of life and my character, I believed it was a duty to remain at a distance, and to raise my hands to heaven, like Moses, in prayer for the combatants.

"I was still near my gallant knights,* when a detachment of the enemy's cavalry appeared in sight through the woods. Fancy augmented their number; and it was supposed that a still greater multitude lay concealed in different parts of the wood, in ambush, to cut off all means of escape. Soon the war-cry resounded from the ranks of the enemy; and their troop of horse, which we had seen, charged at full gallop on

* *Preux chevaliers.*

our batallion, who prepared themselves for the shock with great bravery and resolution.

"What a moment! Dear brother in Christ, does not your heart beat at this recital? Do you not imagine, that you already see the muskets of these savages pointed at my heart, or their cruel tomahawk uplifted over my head, to slay and scalp me? Take courage;—this whole army of savages was composed of five or six young men of the Post, who had come out to throw themselves at my feet, to ask my blessing, and then unite with my numerous escort, to render my entrance into the town more brilliant and triumphant!

"In effect, we arrived two hours later, in the midst of the acclamations of all the inhabitants, who had been called together by the ringing of the bells!"

In a Letter to his brother in France, written soon after his return from this long journey, the Bishop speaks of his "episcopal campaign" in the following terms:

"During the episcopal campaign which I have just terminated, I was obliged to travel three hundred leagues (nine hundred miles), to visit ten or twelve thousand Catholics,* most of them French, scattered along the borders of the Mississippi and Missouri. We were sometimes four days at a time traversing immense prairies, exposed to legions of flies and musquitos, who covered both travelers and horses with blood. It is in such journeys as these that I forget all troubles of spirit, and give myself up to my natural gaiety, in order to amuse my companions of travel; and it is here that my health is strengthened.

* This number seems to us a little exaggerated.

"I was received by these French people as an angel descended from heaven; they rendered to my character all due honor. I never went from one village to another, without being escorted by fifteen or twenty persons, among the most respectable in the country. The churches were always full, when I announced the word of God; and I preached every day at least once or twice; on Sundays as far as four times. The confessional was crowded; I remained therein until far into the night; and very often from three o'clock in the morning, persons were waiting for me at the door of my chamber. God has given a special benediction to my words; many conversions have taken place; and Religion, which I thought almost banished from these remote countries, seems to have regained its empire in a manner truly admirable."*

The Bishop remained at Vincennes upwards of two weeks, during which he twice administered confirmation, to forty persons in all. The total number confirmed on this missionary tour was one thousand two hundred and seventy-five. The Bishop estimated that there were one hundred and thirty Catholic families at Vincennes, and one hundred and twenty in Illinois. He had intended to visit Prairie du Chien and Green Bay, in the North-west; but the continuance of the war compelled him to defer the visitation of these remote missions; which could not then be reached without imminent danger.

He left Vincennes November 28th, and arrived in Louisville on the 3d of December. Here he found M. Chabrat, who had been awaiting his return for ten

* Letter, February 3, 1815. French Life—pp. 59, 60.

days. He spent some time at the seminary of St. Thomas, to recruit his strength and to attend to a large amount of business which had accumulated during his long absence. He then visited several of the congregations; among them, those of St. Stephen and St. Charles.

In his Report to his Holiness, above quoted, occurs the following passage:

"Often it has happened that in consequence of sickness or of a voyage beyond the seas, some of my priests were obliged to suspend, or to abandon altogether, the administration of their congregations, sometimes separated from one another by distances of more than a hundred miles. Then it was the Bishop who had to provide for them in person: and God only knows how much this increase in labor, in travel, and in fatigue, put to the proof both my strength and my courage." *

An occasion of this kind occurred in 1815, soon after his return. Early in the spring of this year, the Rev. M. Nerinckx took his departure for Europe; and he was absent from Kentucky for more than two years.†

The Bishop was much perplexed and distressed in mind at the departure of so efficient a missionary, who had already at his earnest request, delayed the journey for three years. While pouring forth his sorrows in prayer on this occasion, he thought he heard a voice sounding forth from the inmost recesses of his soul,—

* Report to Pope Gregory XVI., drawn up at Rome in 1836.

† He returned September 4, 1817, bringing with him the clock now in the old Cathedral at Bardstown, and the two paintings of St. Bernard and the Crucifixion.

"Let ME govern thy Diocese!"* He suddenly became calm, and committed all to the Providence of God.

He now engaged with much cheerfulness in all the laborious details of missionary duty, attending many of the congregations of M. Nerinckx. He was pastor of St. Charles, of Holy Mary, and of St. Bernard, in Casey county; besides attending as chaplain to the infant convent of Loretto. He was absent almost every Sunday, and returned to his home at the seminary only once in about three weeks.

In the year 1816, while discharging these functions of an ordinary missionary, he was drawn into a controversy with a preacher named Tapscott, who had boldly and coarsely asserted "that the Catholics sprang from hell, and into hell they must fall!" Though much averse to controversy, the Bishop believed that the interests of truth required him to accept the challenge of the preacher, who had considerable influence with his sect. They accordingly met at the house of Elias Newton, in the present Taylor county. The concourse was so great, that the orators were compelled to speak in the open air. The Bishop opened the discussion in a discourse of much simplicity and power, on the civil and religious principles of Catholics, in answer to the charges of his opponent. At the close, he offered to answer any objections which might be presented. Though it was Tapscott's turn now to rejoin, he availed himself of this invitation, and demanded that the Bishop should first unfold the doctrine of the Church

* Journal, 1815.

on the power of the keys, and on the Real Presence;—after which he would offer his remarks.

For the sake of peace, the Bishop complied with this unreasonable demand; and explained "those two questions to the best of his power,"—the people listening with breathless attention.

Tapscott attempted to answer, by accusing the Bishop of misquoting the scripture; a charge which was promptly refuted by reference, on the spot, to the sacred volume. The preacher then, getting into a bad humor, boldly accused the sainted prelate of having told a falsehood, in stating that he (Tapscott) had been the first to challenge to the discussion; but the audience, almost entirely Protestant, sustained the Bishop in his contrary statement, which was generally known to be well founded.

To extricate himself from his unenviable position, Tapscott next called on the Bishop to prove that the Catholic was the oldest Church. The prelate answered, that as he had been speaking already for several hours, and his opponent had been comparatively silent, it was now clearly within his province to ask the preacher some questions. But Tapscott would not hear of this proposal, and indignantly withdrew, leaving his adversary master of the field.

Hereupon the Bishop closed the discussion with an exhortation to peace and charity, which was rendered more touching by offering his hand to the preacher; who, however, met his advance with an ungracious refusal. The conduct of the latter filled the audience with indignation; while the bearing of the Bishop won all hearts. The incident made a deep impression on many Protestants, some of whom became converts.

Returning to his chamber, the Bishop poured forth his soul in thanksgiving to God for the words which he had put into his mouth; and he exclaimed: "How happy shall I be, O Lord, if I cause Thee to be known and loved by all those unfortunate sectaries, who are generally such, only because they had the misfortune to be born in heresy!" *

We will close this chapter with the tribute paid to the memory of the illustrious Patriarch of the American Church by two prelates who knew him long and intimately, and who were fully competent to pronounce on his merits. Archbishop Carroll died, in odor of sanctity, on the feast of St. Francis Xavier, December 3, 1815. On hearing of his death, Bishop Flaget has this entry in his Journal:

"This holy man has run a glorious career; he was gifted with a wisdom and prudence which made every one esteem and love him. He had the consolation to consecrate three Bishops; † to see the Jesuits well established; to behold many monasteries and houses of education founded:—great motives these for inspiring consolation and confidence at the hour of death." ‡

In a Letter to our prelate, written from Europe early in 1816, Bishop Dubourg thus refers to the death of the Archbishop:

"The sad intelligence of the irreparable loss sustained by our poor churches in the death of their venerable

* This account is condensed from the Bishop's Journal, 1816.

† We believe *four*—Bishops Cheverus, Egan, Flaget, and Neal.

‡ Journal, 1815.

Founder and our worthy and excellent Father, has reached us here in less than sixty days. What universal grief this death must have occasioned! He has certainly finished a beautiful and glorious career; and we should rejoice for his sake that God has called him to the recompense of his long labors. But for our sakes, and that of our dear churches, he should have been immortal! Happy, however, are we in our misfortune, that his see is filled by a worthy successor, the heir of his zeal and of his virtues." *

* This Letter, without date or name of place, was written shortly after the prelate left Rome, from some city in France, probably Bordeaux.

CHAPTER VII.

DIOCESE OF NEW ORLEANS—BISHOP FLAGET'S TWO JOURNEYS TO ST. LOUIS.

1817—1818.

Early missionaries in the South—De Soto's expedition—The battle of Mavilla—The "dry Mass"—France and Spain—Founding of New Orleans—One of the first martyrs—Jesuit missions among the *Yazoos*, *Arkansas*, *Alibamons*, and *Choctaws*—The Post of Arkansas—Massacre by the *Natchez*—Death of missionaries—Thrilling adventures and narrow escape—The fate of the *Natchez*—Ursuline nuns in New Orleans—Orphans—Hospital—Indian chief's opinion of the nuns—Results of the missions—See of New Orleans—Its first Bishop—The second Bishop—History of the see—M. Dubourg appointed administrator—Religious Statistics of Louisiana—Proposed new see at St. Louis, and translation of Bishop Flaget—How the plan was delayed—Bishop Flaget's second journey to St. Louis—Preparing the way—Success—Liberal donation—A curious scene—Disagreeable travel—A *danseuse*—Arrival of Bishop Dubourg—Joyful meeting—The steamboat *Piqua*—A Noah's ark—Solemn installation of Bishop Dubourg—Return to Kentucky.

We will devote the present chapter to a summary sketch of two other journeys which Bishop Flaget made to St. Louis, in the fall of 1817, and in the winter of 1817-18. They were connected with the appointment of Bishop Dubourg to the ancient see of New Orleans; and we cannot more appropriately introduce our account of these journeys, than by presenting, from the materials within our reach, a few prominent facts regarding the earliest Catholic missionaries in the South, and the subsequent establishment and history of the see of New Orleans.

The first Catholic priests who visited the portion of North America lying North of the Gulf of Mexico, were the Dominican missionaries who accompanied De Soto in his adventurous expedition through Florida and a part of our Southern States,—sometime before the middle of the sixteenth century. The French and Spanish expeditions of discovery and conquest were invariably attended by Catholic missionaries, whose office it was to soften the horrors of war, and to extend the boundaries of Christianity, by converting the savages.

The enterprise of De Soto, though conducted with great courage and skill, proved disastrous. The missionaries appear to have made but few converts. In the battle of *Mavilla*, fought October 18, 1540, they lost their sacred vestments, as well as the bread and wine they had prepared for offering up the holy sacrifice.

"In this engagement," says Irving, "the Spaniards lost all their baggage and private effects. What gave them the greatest concern, however, was the loss of a little portion of wine and wheaten flour, which they had carefully treasured up for the performance of Mass. All the sacerdotal dresses, also the chalices and other articles of worship were destroyed; but the loss of the wheaten flour was irreparable. Consultations were held between the ecclesiastics and the laymen, whether bread made of maize might not be adopted in case of extremity; but it was decided that the use of any thing but wheat was contrary to the canons of the Church. From thenceforward, therefore, on Sundays and saints'-days, they prepared an altar, and the priest officiated, arrayed in robes of dressed deer skin, fashioned in imitation of his sacerdotal dresses; and they performed all the parts of the ceremony, except the consecration of bread and wine. This constituted what the Spaniards called a 'dry Mass.'"*

De Soto penetrated to the Mississippi, which he crossed near the 35th degree of north latitude,—not far from the Southern boundary of Tennessee. He ascended the river as far as the present town of New Madrid. The object dearest to his heart, and one which he earnestly recommended to his followers with his last breath, was the conversion of the savages. He died on the Mississippi, on the 21st of May, 1542.

France and Spain were engaged in a lengthy contest for the possession of Louisiana and the Southern portion of what is now the United States. The discovery of the Mississippi, by the French Jesuit, Father Marquette, in 1673; the exploring of it to its mouth, and the subsequent disastrous expedition, by the adventurous, but unfortunate La Salle; the establishment of French colonies in Louisiana, in the beginning of the eighteenth century; the final settlement of the question between those two great Catholic powers of Europe; and the acquisition of Louisiana by the United States in 1803;—are all topics familiar to those of our readers who are conversant with our different American histories. Full details on them do not properly lie within our present province. We must con-

* Conquest of Florida—p. 282.

tent ourselves with furnishing a few prominent facts in the religious history of this portion of our country; dwelling specially upon the early missions among the various Indian tribes of the South and South-west.

The Jesuit Fathers took a conspicuous part in these missionary enterprises, of which New Orleans was for a long time the centre and the head-quarters. Here resided the Superior General of the missions; and from this point, the Fathers were sent out to preach to the various tribes living near the borders of the Mississippi, and to some even who were roaming far in the interior. New Orleans was founded in 1718, and became the seat of government in 1721; there were then not more than five hundred persons in the whole colony.

We are not acquainted with the precise year in which those Indian missions first commenced, but they began soon after the establishment of the French settlements. We read that, at an early period of the French colony, probaby during the first years of the eighteenth century, M. *De St. Come*, a missionary, suffered martyrdom, while zealously laboring among the *Sitimachas*, a fierce tribe living on the river *Manchat* (or Manchac), below Baton Rouge.*

Early in 1727, the ship *Gironde* was daily expected to arrive at New Orleans from France; having on board Fathers Tartarin and Doutreleau, with a colony of Ursuline nuns.†

On the 25th of May, 1727, Father Du Poisson departed from New Orleans in a small boat, to ascend the

* Father Du Poisson's Letter, quoted *infra*. He suffered, we believe, in 1717.

† *Ibid.*

Mississippi as far as the mouth of the Arkansas. He was accompanied by FF. Souel and Dumas. He was destined to labor for the conversion of the Arkansas* tribe of Indians, living within the limits of the present State of Arkansas. Father Souel was going to live among the Yazoos,† lower down on the Mississippi, near the mouth of the river Yazoo; Father Dumas was to ascend the river as far as the settlements of Illinois. Father De Beaubois was then Superior General of the missions in New Orleans.‡

The traveling missionaries suffered much from the excessive heat, the inconvenience of their small and crowded boats, the overflow of the Mississippi, and the myriads of mosquitoes, which gave them no rest day or night, and which F. Du Poisson thought must have been a continuation of the Egyptian plagues,—to try the patience of Christians. On the 4th of June, they arrived at Baton Rouge; § and on the 13th at Natchez. The French colony ‖ here was at this early date in a flourishing condition; but was soon, alas! to meet an awful fate! M. Philibert, a Capuchin friar, was then curate of Natchez.

F. Souel stopped at the mouth of the Yazoo, where he was cordially welcomed by the savages. The two other missionaries reached the mouth of the Arkansas

---

* Written by him *Akensas*.

† Written *Yatous* by F. Du Poisson—but *Yasous* by F. Le Petit.

‡ A few days later Father De Guienne was sent to the *Alibamons*, and Father Le Petit to the *Chasses* Indians. *Ibid.*

§ Or *Red Stick*—so called from a tree painted red, marking the boundary between two neighboring tribes. *Ibid.*

‖ The place was originally called *Fort Rosalie*.

on the 7th of July. F. Dumas continuing the next day his journey to the Illinois, F. Du Poisson proceeded alone to the villages of the Arkansas, which lay scattered along the Arkansas, some miles above the mouth of White river.

There was here a French Post recently established. F. Du Poisson was well received by the Arkansas tribe. On his arrival, they asked, "How many moons the Black Chief would remain with them?" When the interpreter answered, "Always;" the immediate reply was: "You are deceiving me." But on being assured that such was the truth, and "that they should always have him with them to teach them to know the GREAT SPIRIT, as had been done among the Illinois:" the Indian chief exclaimed: "My heart laughs when you tell me this."*

---

* Letter of F. Du Poisson, written "*At Akensas,*" October 3, 1727—among the *Lettres Edifiantes;* and translated in "Early Jesuit Missions in North America,"—p. 232, seqq.

"The Post of Arkansas is a very old station. In Charlevoix's history of New France (Canada), and the *Lettres Edifiantes et Curieuses* of the early missionaries, it is stated, that these were in the habit of ascending the river from Natchez, then called Rosalie, in order to preach the Gospel to the Arks, Kansas, Arkansas, as the Indians on the banks of the Arkansas river were indifferently called. From a personal examination of the Registers and other ancient documents, I have come to the conclusion, that the Post of Arkansas spoken of in these early times, was somewhere lower down on the river than the Post of Arkansas of the present day. The old Post had a fort, with something like fortifications; and in the fort was a chapel: but of all this nothing now remains but a small eminence on which are found the remains of former foundations. The place appears to have been washed away by the river. The Registers anterior to 1764 are no longer extant. In 1764, on the 11th and 12th of March, Father S. L. Meurin, S. J., is record-

F. Du Poisson labored among the Arkansas Indians for two years; during which time he does not appear to have made any general impression on that tribe, whose language it was difficult to learn, and whose debasement was very great. However, he baptized many who were in danger of death, and received several into the Church.

Before the mission had been fully established, he was cut off by a bloody death. He fell among the two hundred French victims who were suddenly massacred by the Natchez Indians, on the 28th of November, 1729. He was, at the time, on a visit to the Natchez colony, to procure some favor or assistance for his beloved *Akensas;* and as the curate, M. Philibert, was absent on a visit to New Orleans, he said Mass there in

---

ed to have baptized nine persons; Don John Baptist de Montclairvaux being at that time Governor of the Post of Arkansas. Subsequently to the date just named, the following names occur in the Registers:

"1772—Father Valentin, O. S. F.

"1786—Father L. Guignes. Don Joseph de la Valiere was at this time Governor.

"1792—Rev. M. Gibault, who, on the 5th of September, 1793, received into the Church James Darst and Anne Sheffer, his wife, together with their six children. Don Ignatius de Ling was Governor of the Post in this year.

"1794—Father Flavius, O. S. F., was appointed pastor of the Post of Arkansas by the Very Rev. Patrick Walsh, V. G. of the Diocese of New Orleans.

"1796—Rev. M. Janin. On the 18th of February, 1798, the Register records the marriage (by Rev. M. Janin, pastor,) of Baptist Degle and Susan Bole: the publication of the bans having been regularly dispensed with by the Right Rev. the Bishop of New Orleans, on the request of the Governor, Don Charles de Villemont." *Shepherd of the Valley, March,* 1852.

his place, on the first Sunday of Advent, November 27th, the day before the massacre.

Just as he was preparing to offer up the holy sacrifice on the next morning, with a view to carry the Blessed Sacrament to some sick persons, a gigantic chief seized him, and having felled him to the ground, cut off his head with repeated blows of the tomahawk.

The massacre was general and simultaneous, a few only of the French making their escape in the woods. Only two Frenchmen were spared, a tailor and a carpenter. Such of the women and children as escaped death were reduced to slavery.

This dreadful massacre is ascribed by some to the natural cruelty and treachery of the Natchez; by others to the injustice done to the tribe by the French commander. It was soon followed by that of the French in the Post near the mouth of the Yazoo. Father Souel, the Indian missionary stationed here, fell the first victim, pierced by many balls. This occurred December 12, 1729.

Another Jesuit Father, passing casually at the time, made a very narrow escape. F. Doutreleau, descending the Mississippi from Illinois, stopped at the mouth of the Yazoo on the 1st of January, 1730, to pay a visit to his brother missionary, of whose death he could not be apprised. The Indians feigned friendship; and he began to say Mass. The French *voyageurs*, his companions of travel, were kneeling reverently near the rude altar erected in the woods; the Indians stood quietly in the back-ground. At the *Kyrie Eleison*, a number of muskets were fired; the priest was wounded in the arm, and one of the *voyageurs* fell dead at his side. The rest fled to the boat; but the Father, thinking his hour had come, knelt down to receive his death blow. What was his surprise, however, on finding, that though many muskets were aimed at him, from so near that the muzzles of the guns seemed almost to touch his body, he received no additional wound! Instinctively rising, he darted towards the river, clad in his priestly garments, pursued by the infuriate savages. He soon gained the boat; but, on turning to look after his pursuers, received a discharge of small shot in the mouth; some of the shot being flattened against his teeth! The wound was not dangerous, however; and after almost incredible dangers and hardships, the party arrived safely at New Orleans, to recount their adventures and hair-breadth escapes.

Resting for some months to have his wound healed, during which time he acted as chaplain to the French expedition against the Natchez, the intrepid missionary again set out for Illinois, on the 16th of the ensuing April.*

The whole French population of Louisiana was filled with indignation and terror at the news of the fatal tragedy enacted at Natchez. A terrible retribution was about to fall on the blood-stained savages, who had thus imbrued their hands in French blood. Driven from their lands into the Western wilds, they were at length forced to surrender at discretion in their last strong-hold on Red river. Those who survived were either reduced to servitude on the plantations, or had

* Letter of Father Le Petit, dated New Orleans, July 12th, 1730. *Ibid.*

to fly to other tribes for shelter. As a tribe, the Natchez ceased to exist.

At the time of which we are speaking, there was already in New Orleans a community of seven Ursulines, who devoted themselves to works of education and charity. They had charge of a school, a hospital, and an orphan asylum. The number of orphans under their care was greatly increased by the massacre at Natchez. The French expedition rescued many fatherless children from slavery, and brought them to New Orleans.

"The little girls, whom none of the inhabitants wished to adopt, have greatly enlarged the interesting company of orphans whom the nuns are bringing up. The great number of these children only serves to increase their charity and attentions. They have formed them into a separate class, and have appointed two special matrons for their care.

"There is not one of this holy sisterhood but is delighted at having crossed the ocean; nor do they seek here any other happiness than that of preserving these children in their innocency, and giving a polished and Christian education to these young French, who are in danger of being almost as degraded as the slaves. We may hope, with regard to these holy women, that before the end of the year they will occupy the new mansion which is destined for them, and which they have for so long a time desired.

"When they shall once be settled there, to the instruction of the boarders, the orphans, the girls who live without, and the negro women, they will add also *the care of the sick in the hospital*, and a house of refuge for women of questionable character. * * * So many works of charity would, in France, be sufficient to occupy many associations and different institutions. But what cannot great zeal effect? These different labors do not at all startle seven Ursulines, and by the grace of God they are able to sustain them, without infringing at all on the observance of their religious rules." *

There came at this time to New Orleans a deputation from the Illinois tribe, to condole with their French friends, and to offer assistance against the Natchez and Yazoos. When their chief first saw these nuns, following a troop of orphan girls through the streets, he remarked to them: "You are like the Black Robes, our fathers; you labor for others. Ah! if we had above there two or three of your number, our wives and daughters would have more wit, and would be better Christians." †

At the time of the massacre, F. Baudouin was laboring zealously among the Choctaws; ‡ and F. De Guyenne, among the Indian tribes still farther in the interior, on the confines of the Carolinas. Both these missionaries were now placed in a situation of imminent danger. The Choctaws, though allies of the French against the Natchez, were still feared as treacherous and cruel; while F. De Guyenne had been already so often insulted and threatened, that it was feared he would "be obliged to confine his zeal to the

---

* Letter of F. Le Petit, *sup. cit.*, 1730.

† *Ibid.*

‡ Written *Tchactas.*

French fort of the *Alibamons*,* or to seek a more abundant harvest on the banks of the Mississippi." †

These fears were not groundless. Twenty years later, most of the Indian missions in the South were abandoned, at least temporarily, in consequence of difficulties deemed insurmountable. In 1750, F. Baudouin was residing at New Orleans, as superior general of the Indian missions. For eighteen years he had been living among the Choctaws, but had been lately recalled in consequence of troubles excited among them "by the English." But these difficulties having now apparently ceased, the superior thought of sending another missionary to that tribe.‡

Father Moran had been for many years engaged on the mission among the *Alibamons;* but finding it impossible any longer to exercise the ministry with fruit or in safety, he had likewise been recalled to New Orleans, to take charge of the Ursuline convent, and of the Royal Hospital. The English are constantly represented as being a great hindrance to the success of the Indian missions. Besides other obstacles which they threw in the way of the missionaries, "they were always ready to excite controversy" among the Indians.§

The French settlement on the Arkansas river had been attacked and dispersed by the "irreconcilable enemies of the French,"—the Chickasaws,|| in May,

---

* Probably the *Alabamans.*

† *Ibid.*

‡ Letter of F. Vivier, dated "At Illinois, November 17, 1750."

§ *Ibid.*

|| Written by the French Jesuits, *Chicachats.*

1748; and no missionary could any longer remain with the unfortunate tribe of the *Arkensas*.*

The suppression of the Jesuits, some years later, completed the destruction of missions which they had spared neither labor nor blood to establish and consolidate. Though their success seems not to have been so striking nor so brilliant in the South, as that of their brethren had been in the North, yet they no doubt effected much good, and sent many fervent neophytes to heaven, who else had remained "in the region of the shadow of death," and been lost forever.

By a secret article in the treaty of Fontainbleau, in 1762,† France transferred Louisiana to the King of Spain; who retained the dominion of the province until it was restored to the French republic in the year 1800. In 1803, Mr. Jefferson purchased Louisiana from the French, for fifteen millions of dollars.

During the continuance of the Spanish dominion, the missions were attended by French and Spanish clergymen, who were under the jurisdiction of the Archbishop of Havana. A considerable number of Spaniards now mingled with the original French colonists in Louisiana, and particularly at New Orleans.

If we consider the vicissitudes which mark the history of the French and Spanish colonies of Louisiana, we shall not be surprised to find that the interests of Religion suffered greatly; both from the want of the requisite number of suitable clergymen, and from that of a proper organization and an efficient church govern-

* Letter of F. Vivier, *sup. cit.*

† These secret articles were signed in November, 1762; the treaty was publicly ratified early in the following year, at Paris.

ment. The need of a Bishop on the spot to watch over so extensive a territory, was long and painfully felt.

At length, in the year 1793, New Orleans was erected into an episcopal see by the Sovereign Pontiff. The first Bishop was a distinguished Spaniard,—Don Luis Penalver y Cardenas; "a man of great talents, zeal, and piety, whose administration was marked by an uncommon degree of wisdom, and by a strict attachment to the discipline of the Church."* The Bulls, an authenticated copy of which is preserved in the archiepiscopal archives of New Orleans, bear date, April 25, 1793. They stipulate, that the new Bishop shall receive from the royal treasury of Spain the annual sum of four thousand dollars, for his suitable support.† Two canons were to be attached to the cathedral, who were each to receive, from the same source, the sum of six hundred dollars annually.

Bishop Penalver y Cardenas took formal possession of his see only in the year 1795. He immediately began the visitation of his Diocese, which he prosecuted with vigor and zeal. He required all priests who had charge of congregations to send him annual reports of the condition, both temporal and spiritual, of their respective parishes or districts. He continued to exact this during the six years of his vigilant admininistration. He labored earnestly to eradicate abuses, and to promote piety.

---

* Letter of the Most Rev. Dr. Blanc, Archbishop of New Orleans; to whom we are indebted for the interesting details which follow, up to the appointment of M. Dubourg as administrator.

† *Pro mensa episcopali.*

In 1801, this excellent prelate was transferred to the metropolitan see of Guatemala, in Central America. One of the canons having already died, the administration of the Diocese devolved, for a time, on the surviving one,—the Rev. THOMAS HASSET; who himself died about the year 1804.

Soon after the resignation of the first Bishop of New Orleans, a second was appointed, and consecrated at Rome in 1802. He never, however, reached his see; having died in the eternal city on the eve of his contemplated departure. We are not even acquainted with his name; but it is known that he was a Franciscan, of the convent of the *Holy Apostles* * at Rome. When Bishop Portier was there in 1829, he saw, among the portraits of the deceased members of the convent, that of the *second* Bishop of New Orleans; whose memory was revered by his brethren. From this fact it would appear, that Dr. Dubourg was really only the *third* Bishop of that city.

During the vacancy of the see, considerable confusion existed in the administration, owing chiefly to a conflict in regard to jurisdiction among different claimants to the office of Vicar General. In 1805, after the death of canon Hasset, there existed, for a time, a deplorable schism, which manifested itself chiefly in New Orleans. Strong remonstrances on this sad state of things having been addressed to the Holy See, Archbishop Carroll was canonically charged with the administration of the vacant Diocese, until a permanent provision could be made. One reason for this wise appointment, was founded on the fact, that Lou-

* *Dei Santi Apostoli.*

isiana had already been purchased by the United States government.

On assuming the administration, Archbishop Carroll constituted M. Olivier, then chaplain of the Ursuline convent, his Vicar General with ample jurisdiction. This distinguished ecclesiastic was a brother of the Rev. Donatian Olivier, the venerable missionary of Illinois. Under his wise and prudent administration, the existing difficulties were settled. In 1808, harmony again reigned in the capital of the South. He died about the year 1810; and was succeeded, it is believed, by the Rev. M. Sibourd, who governed as Vicar General until the appointment of Dr. Dubourg, in 1812.

Archbishop Carroll had long and anxiously thought of providing a suitable Bishop for the vacant see, the administration of which weighed heavily on him, in consequence of its importance and remote position. He had successively proposed for this office the Rev. MM. David and Nerinckx; but these learned and pious priests had both, from delicacy of conscience, firmly refused the proffered honor. The negotiations with the Holy See consumed several years, during which Religion suffered greatly at New Orleans.*

At length, in 1812, the Rev. William Dubourg was named the third Bishop of New Orleans; and he was

* Our only authority for stating that the office was tendered to Father David, is an expression of Bishop Flaget in one of his Letters to France, to the effect, that Father David had refused *two* bishoprics in our principal cities. It is believed that he meant the sees of Philadelphia and New Orleans. It is certain that the appointment was offered to M. Nerinckx; whose services Bishop Dubourg subsequently sought to secure for his Diocese.

induced to accept the appointment. By an apostolic Brief, he had been previously selected, as administrator of this Diocese. The Bulls, however, were delayed. M. Marechal, then in France, had written that he expected to be the bearer of them to the Bishop elect; but he returned to Baltimore without the documents. Pope Pius VII., lingering in prison, and worn down by the intrigues and harrassing vexations of his imperial gaoler, firmly declined issuing any more Bulls, until he could be permitted to advise freely with his natural counsellors *—the Cardinals.

In this situation of affairs, Archbishop Carroll strongly urged M. Dubourg to accept at once the administratorship, and to lose no time in repairing to New Orleans. The eminent ecclesiastic yielded to the advice of his superior, and started for the theatre of his labors in the fall of 1812.†

M. Dubourg remained at New Orleans, as administrator, for about two years and a half. During this period, he had a full opportunity to know and feel the heavy responsibility and cruel embarrassments of the post he had accepted. In December, 1814, he wrote to Bishop Flaget a long Letter, in which he painted, in rather dark colors, the condition and prospects of Catholicity in Louisiana.

He estimated the total number of Catholics at about sixty thousand, of whom the great majority were only nominally such. He was, however, consoled by the fervent piety of not a few, especially among the weak-

---

* *Conseilleurs nes.*

† All these particulars are gathered from a Letter of M. Dubourg to Bishop Flaget, dated Baltimore, August 11, 1812.

er sex. Four of his clergy had died in the two years which had elapsed since his arrival; * and only twelve remained,† of whom two were over sixty, and three over seventy years of age.

He proposed to visit Europe the ensuing spring, in order to prevail upon the Holy Father to release him from a burden scarcely any longer bearable; or if this should not be possible, to recruit for the Diocese a new body of fervent priests, whose zeal might renovate the piety of the faithful. He writes: "You wish then to go to Rome,—you will tell me:—Yes! *Monseigneur:* were it necessary, I would go to China, either to be relieved of this terrible burden, or to seek necessary aid to enable me to bear it properly."

He signified also, in this same letter, his intention to propose to the Holy See the "dismemberment" of Upper Louisiana from the see of New Orleans, and the placing of that territory under the jurisdiction of Bishop Flaget. The latter endorses on the back of the Letter, that he considers this plan very feasible and proper. ‡

In the spring of 1815, he sailed for Europe, as he had proposed; and, after spending some time in France, he visited Rome. In an interview with the Sovereign Pontiff, he exposed to his view the condition of sad spiritual destitution in which Louisiana was placed; and he forcibly presented his numerous reasons for declining the appointment to the see of New Orleans.

But his Holiness, moved by the long vacancy of the

---

* *Nos pretres meurent comme mouches.*

† *Il m'en reste douze, tant bons, indifferents, que mauvais.*

‡ *Cela me paroit tres a propos.*

see and the pressing wants of the Catholics of Louisiana, insisted on his acceptance; and he was accordingly consecrated at Rome, September 28, 1815.

The new Bishop now proposed to the Holy See, that Upper Louisiana should be detached from his Diocese; that Bishop Flaget should be transferred to St. Louis, as its first Bishop; and that Dr. Gallitzin should take his place as Bishop of Bardstown. His proposition was favorably entertained, though nothing was decided on. Cardinal Litta, Prefect of the Propaganda, wrote on the subject to Archbishop Carroll, asking his counsel. His Letter was dated December 23d, 1815;—twenty days after the death of the Archbishop. In it the Cardinal says:

"But as in Upper Louisiana, the Right Rev. Dr. Flaget, Bishop of Bardstown, is in great fame of sanctity, and as he is most suited for the conversion of the savages who live in the middle of the province of Louisiana, it has seemed very expedient to the Right Rev. Dr. Dubourg, that he should be transferred to a new see to be erected therein." *

M. Bruté was probably acquainted with the contents of this Letter; for he wrote to Bishop Flaget, communicating its substance. A Letter from Bishop Dubourg to the same prelate added, that, according to the plan,

* "Cum autem in Alta Aurelia (Louisiana) magna sit fama sanctitatis Revmi D. Flaget, Bardensis Episcopi, idemque aptissimus sit ad sylvestrium conversionem, qui in media Neo-Aureliœ provincia versantur, hinc valde expedire videtur Revmo D. Dubourg, ut Bardensis Episcopus ad novam erigendam sedem transferatur."

We are indebted for this extract to Archbishop Kenrick, of Baltimore.

the new see of St. Louis was to remain under the immediate jurisdiction of the Holy See; as it was in contemplation to erect a new archbishopric in the West, to which St. Louis would be attached;—a striking instance this of the wisdom and far-seeing sagacity of Rome.*

Bishop Flaget does not appear to have been, at first, averse to the change, concerning which he had already corresponded with M. Dubourg, before the departure of the latter for Rome.

He had in fact, it would appear, himself first suggested the idea to M. Dubourg. In a Letter of the latter to him from New Orleans, dated April 25, 1815, he says:

"In your Letter from St. Louis, you return to your idea of fixing your see there, provided a suitable subject (Bishop) can be found for Kentucky. You propose a Dominican for Kentucky." And again: "I will not fail to present to the Holy See both the pastor and the flock of Kentucky; and I will also submit YOUR PLAN for the erection of a bishopric in Upper Louisiana. From what you tell me, I would be tempted to believe, that a Frenchman would suit best for the new see, and an American for Kentucky; and that you would not be displeased at the change. You should express yourself frankly with me,—I will keep your secret. * * * Nor do I clearly understand what you mean about the location of your see:—it would seem that Bardstown does not appear to you to be a suitable place (for an episcopal see.)"

---

* There was to be established "*une nouvelle metropole a laquelle il* (St. Louis) *doit etre uni.*—Letter written from Europe in 1816, *sup. cit.*

In a letter to one M. Gratiot, of St. Louis, written early in 1815, Bishop Flaget expressed himself as pleased with his contemplated translation to that city. Subsequently, however, he had some misgivings; and we find several entries in his Journal, betraying uneasiness and solicitude on the subject;—which he nevertheless left, as he did every thing else, to the all-wise dispositions of Providence. It was only on the 8th of August, 1816,* that he received definite intelligence, that he was not to be transferred to St. Louis.

The whole plan was frustrated, chiefly in consequence of the bad spirit manifested by a party in New Orleans. This clamorous faction loudly protested against the appointment of Bishop Dubourg; and they even subsequently sent emissaries to St. Louis, to stir up the minds of the people against him;—in which they were, at first, but too successful.

Under these unpleasant circumstances, Bishop Dubourg did not wish to reside in New Orleans; and he had no alternative, but to locate himself, at least temporarily at St. Louis.†

The second journey of Bishop Flaget to St. Louis was occasioned by a Letter from Dr. Dubourg, who requested him to go thither, and "prepare the way" for his entrance therein as Bishop.

This "preparation of the way," was to consist:—1st. In raising, among the Catholics resident there and in

---

* Journal—*Ibid.*

† Correspondence between Bishops Flaget and Dubourg, *passim;* particularly the Letter above quoted. The troubles in New Orleans were settled only in the winter of 1818-19, principally through the agency of Rev. M. Martial.

the vicinity, the sum of $3,000, to defray the traveling expenses of Bishop Dubourg and his *suite* from Europe; 2dly. In obtaining, if possible, a donation of land suitable for the erection of a cathedral and episcopal mansion; and 3dly. In providing suitable salaries for his missionaries. How very difficult all these objects were of attainment, Bishop Flaget had abundant reason to know; yet he promptly decided to make the attempt, to oblige his venerable friend, and to serve the good cause.

Bishop Dubourg had remained two years in Europe, in order to raise funds and to recruit missionaries for his Diocese. Having arranged his affairs, he had lately returned to America, with thirty persons in his *suite*, mostly ecclesiastics. A colony consisting of MM. De Andreis, Rosati, Gonzales, and others, had been sent on previously, and had reached St. Thomas' seminary, November 22, 1816. The Bishop and M. David cheerfully extended to these devoted ecclesiastics the offices of hospitality, notwithstanding their straitened means and want of room. The missionaries remained in the seminary for about a year, studying English, and exercising the holy ministry.*

Bishop Flaget started for St. Louis October 1, 1817, accompanied by MM. De Andreis and Rosati, and the lay brother Blanca, with a Mr. Tucker as guide; and the party performed the entire journey on horseback. They took the route of Elizabethtown, Owensborough,

* A portion of Bishop Dubourg's ecclesiastics remained longer, leaving only in September, 1818. These were mostly the clergymen who came later with the Bishop himself. The above dates are taken chiefly from Bishop Flaget's Journal.

and Morganfield; and crossed the Ohio at Shawneetown. At Kaskaskias, they met M. Olivier, who informed them of the evil disposition already manifested by the Catholics of St. Louis and vicinity. The first overtures, which the Bishop made on the subject at St. Genevieve, were received with much coldness and indifference.

Proceeding by the way of Prairie du Rocher, they arrived at St. Louis on the 17th, and put up at the pastoral residence, which they found in a sadly dilapidated condition. Their accommodations were no better. Rev. M. Pratte, then pastor of St. Louis, had kindly sent the Bishop a bed; the others had to sleep on buffalo robes spread on the floor. The prospects were certainly gloomy.*

In a Letter written at this time, the Bishop thus speaks of his reception and success:

"I went to St. Louis to make the necessary preparations for the reception of Bishop Dubourg. But how much was I astonished to find that they (the people) did not seem more concerned about his arrival, than about that of the emperor of China! Moreover, in what a state was the presbytery! No doors, no windows, no floor, no furniture; the church still worse; the people filled with prejudices against their Bishop, whom they had never seen. But at last I succeeded in reconciling them to the new arrangement: they seemed to rejoice at the thought of having a Bishop: they began to fit up the presbytery," &c.†

A subscription was now commenced, which succeed-

---

* Journal—*Ibid.*

† Letter to Father David from St. Louis.

ed far beyond the anticipations of the Bishop. · A Mr. O'Connor gave the munificent sum of one thousand dollars; and his example had its influence on the rest of the population. The Bishop was waited on by many; among others, by Colonel Benton.*

Having fulfilled his mission, he hastened back, by the same route, accompanied by M. Rosati;—M. De Andreis having remained as pastor at St. Genevieve. His journey homeward was one of the most disagreeable which even *he* had ever performed. The weather was very bad, the swamps were filled with water, and the rivers so swollen, that they could not be crossed without great danger. The company he met in the taverns was also far from being polished, or even ordinarily polite.

At one place in Illinois, he found the room crowded with wagoners, who did nothing but utter continually the most horrible oaths and blasphemies. Fortunately, a negro man came in, who began playing on the violin, left-handed, while a *negresse* danced! The backwoodsmen stopped their swearing, in their admiration of the remarkable fiddler and the novel *danseuse*. Even the Bishop could not refrain from laughing at the grotesque scene, while he blessed God for having thus put an end to blasphemies so revolting; and though he heartily disliked dancing on all occasions, yet he now willingly tolerated it, as the less of two evils.

He arrived at St. Thomas' on the 6th of November, much fatigued with his journey. He found every thing alive here with preparations for the reception of Bishop Dubourg, whose speedy arrival was expected.

* Journal—*Ibid.*

Bishop Dubourg had sailed from Bordeaux on the 1st of July, 1817; and he had landed at Annapolis on the 4th of September. His *suite* consisted of five priests—of whom the present Archbishop of New Orleans was one,—and twenty-six young men, some of whom were candidates for the ministry, and others were destined to become lay brothers to assist the missionaries in temporal affairs. Several of these youths were from Belgium; and among them was the V. Rev. D. A. Deparcq, of our Diocese. A portion of the company started directly for Baltimore with Bishop Dubourg; the rest, with the Rev. M. Blanc at their head, remained at Annapolis, where they were entertained with princely hospitality in the mansion of Charles Carroll of Carrollton, until the end of October.

Preparations were in the meantime made for crossing the mountains. The stage then ran westward only once a week; and no less than three weeks were consumed in transporting the missionary band to Pittsburgh. The Bishop and M. Blanc were in the last division; but after remaining in the stage for two days, during which time it had repeatedly upset, endangering their lives, they finally abandoned it altogether, and performed the remainder of the journey for five days on foot. About the middle of November, the missionary company embarked on a flat-boat; and they reached Louisville on the last day of the month. Here they found the Rev. MM. Chabrat and Shæffer, who had been sent on by Bishop Flaget to welcome them to Kentucky. Accompanied by them and by the Rev. M. Blanc, Bishop Dubourg started immediately for St. Thomas', where he arrived in the evening of December 2d.*

Bishop Flaget was rejoiced to meet his old friend. "I recognized him instantly," says he;—"see! on meeting me, he has the humility to dismount, in order to present me the most affectionate salute that ever was given."† Many and long were the "happy conversations" which he held with his former associate, and now distinguished guest. Bishop Dubourg officiated pontifically, and preached an admirable sermon in the church of St. Thomas,—the only cathedral which the Bishop as yet possessed.

On the 12th of December, the two prelates, accompanied by Father Badin, set out for St. Louis, by the way of Louisville. Here Bishop Dubourg preached in the chapel erected by M. Badin. On the 18th they embarked on the steamboat PIQUA, and on the 20th reached the mouth of the Ohio, where they were detained five days by the ice. Their time was passed chiefly in religious exercises and pious conversations.‡

The following description of the Piqua and its passengers, from the pen of Bishop Flaget, may not be uninteresting to us at the present day, when steamboat building and navigation have so greatly changed for the better:

"Nothing could be more original than the medley of persons on board this boat. We have a band of seven or eight comedians, a family of seven or eight

* These details were furnished by Archbishop Blanc.

† Journal—*Ibid.*

‡ *Ibid.*

Jews, and a company of clergymen composed of a tonsured cleric, a priest, and two Bishops; besides others, both white and black. Thus more than thirty persons are lodged in an apartment (cabin), twenty feet by twelve, which is again divided into two parts. This boat comprises the old and the new testament. It might serve successively for a synagogue, a cathedral, a theatre, an hospital; a parlor, a dining room, and a sleeping apartment. It is, in fact, a veritable *Noah's ark*, in which there both clean and unclean animals;—and what is most astonishing,—peace and harmony reign here." *

They were still at the mouth of the Ohio on the morning of Christmas day. Not being able to say three Masses, they determined to make three meditations. At the conclusion of the second, the redoubtable Piqua resumed her course towards St. Louis. The Bishops and clergy made a kind of retreat on their Noah's ark. On the evening of Christmas day, the boat stopped near the farm of the widow Fenwick, a good Catholic, whom they were happy to visit. M. Badin continued his journey by land from this point, in order to be able to visit on the way many of his old friends, Catholic emigrants from Kentucky.†

The Bishops returned to the boat, where they found the comedians performing a play,—that is, engaged in a general fight among themselves,—until they were separated by the captain. At midnight, on the 30th, they arrived at St. Genevieve; and early next morning,

* Journal—*Ibid.*

† *Ibid.*

they sent a messenger to announce their coming to M. De Andreis.

Two hours afterwards, "about thirty of the principal inhabitants came, with several young men on horseback and a carriage, to escort the Bishops into the town. We went to the presbytery to put on our pontifical robes: twenty-four choir-children with the cross at their head, and four citizens bearing a canopy, conducted us to the church, where after the installation of Bishop Dubourg, on a throne specially prepared for the purpose, we sang the *Te Deum*. The whole day was spent in receiving visits." *

On the first day of the year 1818, Bishop Dubourg celebrated Pontifical Mass at St. Genevieve. The journey was then continued by Prairie du Rocher and Cahokias to St. Louis, where the prelates arrived on the 5th. They were received with great pomp, in the best French style; and Bishop Dubourg was no sooner known than he was universally esteemed and beloved. He professed himself much pleased with the dispositions and sentiments of his new flock,—so different from what he had been led to expect.

Bishop Flaget having now completed his mission, preached his farewell sermon to the Catholics of St. Louis on the feast of the Epiphany; and on the next day he turned his face homeward. He and M. Badin performed the journey on horseback, by the way of Kaskaskias and Vincennes. They were detained three days at the former place, not being able to cross the river in consequence of the running ice; and in traversing Illinois they passed three successive nights in

* Journal—*Ibid.*

the open air of the prairies.* They reached Vincennes on the 27th of January; and after remaining here two weeks, attending to missionary duties, they continued their journey.

On the 21st of February, the Bishop found himself once more at his retired and pleasant home in the seminary of St. Thomas.

---

* *A la belle etoile.*—Journal—*Ibid.*

CHAPTER VIII.

JOURNEY TO THE LAKES AND TO CANADA.

1818—1819.

Bishop Dubourg's kindness—Early religious history of Canada—A golden maxim—The first missionary—First martyrs—The apostle of the Hurons—Glance at the Jesuit missions of the North—Trouble in Detroit—The Bishop departs—Journey through Ohio—Indians—River Raisin—Detroit—Governor Cass and General Macomb—A solemn reconciliation—Falls of Niagara—Montreal—Quebec—The village of the Algonquins—The great Indian treaty of St. Mary's—Colonel Johnson—The Bishop sick with fever—Missionary labors at Detroit and river Raisin—Returns homeward—Swearing boatmen—Pittsburgh—Its early religious history—Cincinnati—Early missions of Ohio—Reception at home.

Bishop Dubourg kindly consented to take charge of the missions of Illinois, scattered along the Eastern borders of the Mississippi. He also offered to the Bishop of Bardstown the services of four of his priests for the missions of Indiana and Michigan, until the latter could be able to make permanent arrangements for the attendance of these districts. Accordingly, on the 25th of April, 1818, we find MM. Blanc and Jeanjean appointed resident missionaries for Vincennes; and MM. Bertrand and Janvier for Detroit.

On the 1st of June, the two first named clergymen

took their departure from Kentucky for Vincennes, escorted by Rev. G. J. Chabrat. Rev. M. Blanc was to have charge of the parish; and the Rev. M. Jeanjean was sent to found a college. But owing to a misunderstanding with a portion of the population—long called *the Vincennes faction*—the attempt to establish the college proved a failure. On learning this, Bishop Dubourg recalled M. Jeanjean, in January, 1819, directing him to repair to New Orleans.

After his departure, M. Blanc was left alone for three months; when the Rev. M. Ferrari, a Lazarist, was associated with him in this mission. In February, 1820, he was himself recalled, and sent to New Orleans.

During his stay at Vincennes, he had built two log chapels; one in Davis county, seven miles from Liverpool—now Washington;—and the other on the Illinois side of the Wabash, twelve miles from Vincennes, where there was a French settlement.*

The mind of Bishop Flaget was greatly relieved by this timely succor; and he was now able to turn his attention towards a far distant, but highly interesting portion of his charge,—the French settlements scattered along the lakes, and the neighboring Indian tribes,—which he had not yet been able to visit. Of his journey to these quarters we propose to treat in the present Chapter.

We find on this subject the following passage in the *Annales de la Propagation de la Foi:* †

"Following the traces of this journey of seven hundred leagues, one would say, that wherever Bishop

---

* These facts were furnished by Archbishop Blanc himself.

† For September, 1850—p. 941. French Life—p. 56.

Flaget pitched his tent, he there laid the foundations of a new church, and that each one of his principal halts was destined to become a bishopric. There is Vincennes, in Indiana; * there is Detroit, in Michigan; there is Cincinnati, the capital † of Ohio; there are Erie ‡ and Buffalo, on the borders of the lakes; there is Pittsburgh, which he evangelized in returning to Louisville, after thirteen months absence;—after having given missions wherever, on his route, there was a colony of whites, a plantation of slaves, § or a village of Indians."

Nearly two centuries had elapsed, since some of the missionary stations which the Bishop was now preparing to visit had been first established; most of them were considerably over a century old. The French who peopled Canada,—or *New France*,—were imbued with no small portion of that missionary spirit so remarkable in the Spanish and Portuguese conquerors of Mexico and South America. The conversion and salvation of the aborigines held as prominent a place in their thoughts, as their physical subjugation to the power of their respective sovereigns. The golden maxim of Champlein, the founder of New France;—"THE SALVATION OF A SOUL IS WORTH MORE THAN THE CONQUEST OF AN EMPIRE,"—was adopted and acted on by all the Catholic pioneers of the new world.

The first missionary among the Indians of the North,

* He did not visit Vincennes on this journey.

† Principal city.

‡ Not yet a bishopric.

§ We believe that, on this excursion, he met with no "plantation of slaves."

of whom we read, was Le Caron, a Franciscan friar. As early as the year 1616, this courageous priest penetrated the wilderness, and preached successfully to the Iroquois and Wyandots, whose wigwams were erected on the rivers running into Lake Huron. The Jesuit missionaries followed, and extended their labors among the tribes dwelling in the far West and North-west; on the borders of Lake Superior, and on the banks of the Mississippi.

For nearly a century and a half, these fearless champions of the cross endured almost incredible sufferings and privations in the discharge of their heroic duties; until every where the wilderness became vocal with the praises of the true God uttered by Indian lips, in all the uncouth idioms of the North-west. A volume would be required to unfold in detail all these edifying missionary enterprises, with their surprising results.* Our limits and purpose will allow us barely to allude to some of the principal persons and epochs in this interesting history.

In 1634, Fathers Anthony Daniel and John De Brebœuf, S. J., established missions among the Hurons. They both cheerfully laid down their lives with their flocks, whom they would not abandon in the hour of peril, though entreated by them to seek safety in flight. On the 4th of July, 1648, one of the Huron missions was invaded by the fierce Iroquois, and Father Antho-

* Those who are curious to pursue this interesting study, are referred to the following works: Bancroft's United States, vol. iii., chapter 20; The Early Jesuit Missions of North America, translated from the *Lettres Edifiantes* by Rev. J. Ingraham Kip; and a valuable work on the same subject by Dr. O'Callaghan, of New York.

ny Daniel was massacred with his faithful children; the first martyr of the North. The same fate befell Fathers John De Breboeuf and Gabriel Lallement, in a similar irruption of the Iroquois, on the 16th of the following March. F. De Breboeuf was justly called THE APOSTLE OF THE HURONS.

The Jesuit missionaries visited Sault St. Marie in 1640. In 1660 they penetrated the wilderness along Lake Superior; where the zealous pioneer, F. Mesnard, after having labored successfully for the conversion of the Indians, perished a wanderer in the woods. In 1665, we find F. Allouez evangelizing the savages on Green Bay; and in 1668, the mission of Sault St. Marie was regularly established by FF. Claude Dablon and James Marquette.

Father Marquette founded the mission of Point St. Ignatius, opposite Mackinaw, in 1671; after which he set out on his famous journey westward, to discover the *Great River*, of which he had heard his red children speak in terms of glowing eulogy. He entered on the waters of the Mississippi on the 17th of June, 1673; and descended the mighty stream in a canoe as far as the mouth of the Arkansas. He then retraced his steps; and, sending a messenger to convey the intelligenee to the Governor of Canada, the humble missionary went to bury his honors in the woods of the North-west, among his beloved savages; where he soon after died. Prairie du Chien was established as a missionary post in 1675.

The French seem to have visited Michigan as early as the year 1610, and missionaries went thither occasionally soon afterwards; but no priest appears to have been stationed at Detroit before 1701. We find Rev. M. De la Halle residing there in 1703, and M. Hubert in 1782. The latter became subsequently Bishop of Quebec.

After the suppression of the Jesuits in 1773, the Bishop of Quebec was compelled to provide for their various missions, so far as his resources would permit. But for the want of a sufficient supply of priests, many of those flourishing missionary establishments gradually languished, and some of them were almost entirely abandoned, or merged into others. After the departure of the Jesuits, the mission of Green Bay was without a priest for twenty-seven years.*

After his consecration in 1790, Bishop Carroll took charge of all those missions of the North and West which lay within his Diocese, embracing the whole of the United States. He sent the Rev. Gabriel Richard to Detroit in 1798, where he remained thirty-four years,—until his death in 1832. From Detroit, this worthy priest occasionally visited Green Bay, and most of the other Northern missionary stations.

Before the year 1817, difficulties, threatening an open schism, had sprung up among the Catholics of Detroit; and on the 24th of February, of this year, Bishop Flaget had issued a Pastoral Letter, strongly denouncing the course adopted by the disaffected faction, and interdicting their church.† The intelligence of this sad condition of affairs gave him much concern, and hastened his departure for Detroit.

---

* These facts are gathered from the works above indicated, and from various articles in the Catholic Cabinet of St. Louis.

† Journal—*Ibid.*

On the 15th of May, 1818, he departed from St. Thomas' for his distant mission. He was accompanied by the Rev. MM. Bertrand and Janvier, and two young men going to Detroit, named Godfroi and Knags. The party performed the entire journey on horseback. They went by the way of Frankfort, Georgetown, and Cincinnati. The night before their arrival at the last named city, they were hospitably entertained by a tavern keeper named Gaines. The Bishop hereupon remarks: "Like St. Francis of Sales, I admire Providence which inspires certain persons to receive travelers for a consideration; for there are circumstances in which the money paid out is as nothing in comparison with the services received." *

He reached Cincinnati on the 19th, and remained there two days; during which he made arrangements for the purchase of a lot and the building of a church, visited several Catholic families, and baptized one child. He was astonished at the rapid improvement of the city; but he was saddened at the thought, that while he saw so many fine temples erected by the Protestants, the Catholics had not even a chapel wherein to assist at the true worship. There were, at that time, but few Catholics in the city.

Continuing his journey, he passed through the beau tiful valley of the Miami, which he greatly admired. "The beautiful country of the Miami! What industry in these Germans! If these good people had as much zeal for the salvation of their souls, they would become great saints." †

---

* Journal, May 18, 1818.

† *Ibid*—May 21.

Passing through Dayton and Springfield, he had the happiness to say Mass at Urbana on the 24th of May. Here he was much perplexed on account of his ignorance of the remaining route, which lay through a country thinly settled. He had recourse to prayer, and committed himself and party to the care of Providence. Fortunately a young officer, named Gwynn, was going to Detroit, and he kindly offered his services as guide. At Solomon's town, May 25th, he met several Indian women, with whom he could not converse, for want of an interpreter. He, however, made the sign of the cross, which they immediately repeated, with joy beaming on their countenances.* The night was passed at Fort McArthur; and on the 26th he reached Fort Finley. Here he found several Catholic Indians, among whom he distributed pictures and beads; and he baptized an Indian girl.†

The Indians expressed their gratitude by the following token: "One of the Indian women, advanced in years, brought me one or two pounds of sugar, giving me to understand that it was a little mark of gratitude from the whole village for the visit I had paid them."

The following description of the tavern at Fort Finley, may serve as a specimen of the privations which the travelers had to endure:

"All the members of this family, without exception, were infected with a cutaneous eruption.‡ The mother, with hands that were disgusting, made up the corn bread which we were to eat; the eldest daughter, on

---

* Journal, May 25. † *Ibid.*

‡ *La gale*--vulgo--*the itch!*

her side, cut the lard which was to serve at supper, and we all drank out of the same vases used by these afflicted persons. There was one sleeping room for fourteen or fifteen persons. The travelers had to spread their covering on a very rough floor, and to sleep the best they could. Thanks to God neither sleep nor appetite failed me in this hotel, and I remarked with pleasure, that my traveling companions were as much privileged as myself." *

The roads were now exceedingly bad, and rendered almost impassable by mud and water. The party encamped on the night of the 27th in the woods.† On the 28th, they arrived at the Rapids of the Miami of the Lakes, and found two towns springing up on opposite sides of the river. Their next station was the river Raisin, where they remained three days, till the last of the month. The Bishop found the church and altar at this place in so wretched a condition, that he could not say Mass; he, however, preached on the 31st, and enjoined a public penance on a man who had married out of the Church. He has this entry in his Journal:

"Took tea with Mr. Anderson, a member of Congress, and a Presbyterian in Religion. I found in his face the imprint of piety; nothing could be more edifying and religious than the conversation of this excellent man. I should be much surprised, if he and all his family do not become Catholics." ‡

At ten miles distance from Detroit, (June 1,) he was

* Journal, May 27.

† *A la belle etoile.*

‡ *Ibid.*

met by an escort on horseback, who conducted him into the city in procession, with great pomp. On the following day he was called on by Governor Cass and General Macomb, who both paid him the greatest possible attention during his stay. He returned their visit; and the Governor promised to extend every aid in his power, both pecuniary and personal, towards the promotion of the missions among the Indians.

He was likewise visited by many of the Indians, who expressed a lively joy at seeing their great Father. From the day of his arrival, the Bishop conceived the purpose of proposing the erection of an episcopal see in Detroit, the condition of whose Catholic population he found greatly improved, from what it had been ten years previously.*

The first object of his solicitude was to heal the schism above alluded to. A difficulty had existed for a long time between a congregation established on the "North-east coast,"† and M. Richard, the pastor of Detroit; and as we have seen, the Bishop had, more than a year previously, interdicted the church of the disaffected party. His efforts for bringing about a reconciliation were now crowned with complete success. He found the "chiefs of the party" in good dispositions.

At his first interview with them, they promised, in the name of the congregation: 1. To remove their dead from the street and lot; 2. To contribute towards the erection of the new church in Detroit; and 3. Not to

* Journal, June 5.

† *La cote de Nord-est"—shore* would, perhaps, be a preferable rendering.

speak of the past, but to bury it in oblivion. On his part, the Bishop promised: 1. To raise the interdict on their church; 2. To permit burials in their cemetery; and 3. To send them a priest once a month.

The preliminaries of the reconciliation having been thus satisfactorily adjusted, and the chiefs of the party having signed his Pastoral in the name of the people, the Bishop determined to render the ceremony of removing the interdict as public and solemn as possible. For this purpose, on Tuesday, the 9th of June, he was conducted to their church in grand procession. The discharge of cannon announced the approaching ceremony. The music of the regimental band mingled with that of the chanters in the procession. Addresses were delivered in English and in French. An affecting public reconciliation took place between the schismatics and their venerable pastor, M. Richard, who shed tears of joy on the occasion. A collection of $500 was taken up on the spot,—which the Bishop considered a substantial omen of a permanent peace.

On the same day, the Bishop dined with Governor Cass; and on the following, with General Macomb. Returning from the house of the latter, the horses took fright on the brink of the river, and he was thrown from the carriage down a precipice into the water. He was not dangerously wounded, but he received a severe contusion on the right shoulder, from the effects of which he never recovered. The first symptom of his approaching dissolution, a few months before his death, was this shoulder turning black.

He was copiously bled by a physician; and on this occasion he records the following pious sentiment:—

"Lord! I have often wished to shed my blood for Thy glory; but, my God, are not these finely conceived resolutions merely speculative, which would end in nothing, or, perhaps, would turn to my confusion, did the occasion present itself to put them in execution? Vouchsafe, then in inspiring me with a sincere wish, (for martyrdom,) to give me also the grace to realize the desire." *

While in Detroit, he preached in English, much to the gratification of the American residents. "After the ceremony, many gentlemen and ladies wished to see me. O my God! What is there in me to rivet the attention of these people!" † This admirable simplicity, combined with the most sincere humility, furnishes a key to his character. He could not perceive in himself the many shining qualities, which all others admired.

For the more effectual instruction of the French Catholics, he and M. Richard adopted the method of holding Conferences; the latter putting questions on religious subjects, and he being the respondent. The people were much moved and edified at this simple and striking mode of imparting religious knowledge. He often adopted this practice, with much fruit, in his subsequent missions; chiefly among the French congregations of the North.

On the 17th June, he left Detroit in a sailing vessel, with M. Bertrand, on his way to Montreal and Quebec. He reached Buffalo on the 23rd, but did not go ashore. On the 24th, he visited Fort Erie and the Falls of Niagara. He greatly admired the sublime spectacle pre-

---

* Journal, June 10. † *Ibid.* June 7.

sented by the falling waters; and he thought of thetorrents of divine grace, which, though stronger than this mighty cataract, yet do not make so deep an impression upon the hearts of men—more impervious to grace than the rocks to the waters. His description and impressions of the mighty waterfall are worthy of being preserved.

"These Falls present the most grand and sublime spectacle, which a mortal can contemplate on earth. No words can express the sensations produced on the soul by those torrents of water, forming a sheet nearly a mile wide, and falling perpendicularly one hundred and fifty feet. The rising vapors, while hiding from your view a portion of the cataract, cause to arise in the imagination ideas of a gulph, of an abyss, which fill you with a religious fear, and seize you with a feeling of solemn awe, never before felt. Until our arrival, the sun had been hidden by clouds, and it continued so for a time, while we were devouring with our eyes a spectacle so astonishing; when lo! on a sudden, the solar rays pierced the clouds, causing us to enjoy the sight of numerous rainbows formed amidst the vapors ascending from the abyss. The masses of water, falling into the depths below, rebound, boiling, from the gulph; and you would believe that you saw, through the vapor, a river of milk flowing on to a great distance. It is impossible for the coldest soul not to become warmed at the sight of this wonder. 'God is wonderful in the highest'—great is the Lord, and exceedingly to be praised! Alas! (said I, to myself,) the torrents of grace, much more extended, and much more voluminous than this cataract of waters falling with so much force before my eyes, are flowing each instant into the hearts of men, and most of those hearts are not more penetrated by them than are the hard rocks upon which these waters fall! Is not this the case with my own heart? O God! do not permit this!" *

On the 25th, he took a steamboat plying between Queenstown and Kingston, preaching in English and French at the latter place. July 2nd, he embarked for Montreal in a vessel twenty-four feet by six. The weather was exceedingly warm, and the navigation of the St. Lawrence was impeded by rapids, very dangerous to the navigator. On the 5th, he arrived at Montreal, and lodged with his brother Sulpicians in the seminary. His heart "was inebriated with joy,"† at being once more in a Catholic city, and in the midst of his brethren.

On the 9th, he took a steamer for Quebec, enjoying on the journey the company of the coadjutor Bishop of Montreal. At Quebec he was very kindly received in the seminary. He passed several days very agreeably and usefully in visiting the several churches and institutions of this ancient city. One of his pilgrimages was to see the relics of those two servants of God, FF. De Brebœuf and Lallement, who had been burnt to death by the Iroquois in 1649.

He could not sufficiently admire the various religious establishments:—"O my God! What pleasure for a Catholic heart, to see so many monuments of piety and and religion in a country so remote! The Seminary, the Sisters Hospitalers—I shall never forget them—the

---

* Journal, June 24. † *Ivre' de joie.*

Cathedral, &c. I have seen too many edifying objects, not to be a gainer." *

He blessed God, that by transferring the government of Canada from the French to the English, he had preserved the Church there from external and internal ruin! "There are no philosophers in the congregation of M. Mignault. In general, the Canadians have preserved much of their ancient simplicity." †

He left Quebec on the 14th, and visited many places; in all of which he was well received, and "loaded with favors and presents." Every where on his journey, he was accompanied by Canadian priests. On the 20th, he returned to Montreal, where he was once more happy in the bosom of the seminary. "My God! how many thanks should I not render Thee, for having always given me a decided relish for the exercises of a seminary, in spite of the distractions in which I am forced to live!" ‡ He visited the charming country house of the Sulpicians, and the churches and institutions of Montreal, and he was forcibly struck with the good comportment of the people at divine worship.

On the 21st, he went to the congregation of St. Ann, to visit M. Malaud, an old schoolmate, whom he had not seen for thirty-one years. Here a large band of Algonquins came to visit him and to receive his blessing. They bore before them a crimson banner, inscribed with the *Ave Maria* of the Sulpicians; and falling on their knees, appeared full of humility and faith. They conducted him to their village; and on his arrival, he was saluted with firing of cannon, while all the inhabitants were on their knees to receive his benediction.

---

* Journal, July 12. † *Ibid.* ‡ *Ibid.* July 20.

At his Mass, on the 28th, the Indians chaunted canticles in two responding choirs, and the Bishop was moved even to tears. Afterwards they amused him with an exhibition of the sports and exercises peculiar to their tribe. He next visited their "superb Calvary," carved in wood. He announced to them his ardent wish to be "in communion of prayers" with them, and to send missionaries to such of their brethren as were within the boundaries of his own jurisdiction. Their night prayers were likewise sung in two choirs.

On his departure, they accompanied him in their pirogues, running races to exhibit their dexterity at the paddle. The Bishop dismissed them with his blessing, and an affectionate parting address, in which he said: "My heart is full of honey, and it is impossible for me to be better pleased with anything I have ever seen or heard." * Returning to Montreal, he took a touching leave of his Sulpician brethren; and departed for Detroit on the 2nd of August. He visited several priests on his way, and passed through Cornwallis and Prescott. On the steamer, he made the acquaintance of the Governor General of Canada, who treated him with great politeness and attention. On the 14th, he arrived at Buffalo, where he remained a week before he could continue his journey. The town had been burnt in the late war, and there was in it no church and no priest.

On the steamer from Buffalo to Cleveland, he was subject to many privations, and annoyed by the bad company into which he was necessarily thrown. The horrid blasphemies with which his ears were hourly saluted, ceased only during a dreadful storm which

* Journal, July 29.

threatened the steamer with shipwreck. He reached Cleveland on the 25th, after a four days' passage. On the 27th, he safely arrived at Detroit.

There was, at this time, a general assembly of the Indians of the North-west, held at St. Mary's, for the purpose of entering into a treaty with the American government. There were present at it about 10,000 Indians of nine different tribes. The Bishop determined to go thither, in order to seek, by all means in his power, to interest our government in the Indian missions; and also, to recover for the Church, if possible, the possessions of the ancient Jesuit missions.*

On the 3d of September, he set out on this benevolent mission, accompanied by MM. Bertrand and Janvier; and he arrived at St. Mary's on the 9th. He was immediately waited on by Governor Jennings, Judge Park, and other distinguished persons, who showed him every attention. Colonel John Johnson, the oldest Indian agent, was specially kind to him; and did every thing in his power to procure him comfortable accommodations. The Bishop pressed upon his attention the importance to the interests of the government itself,—to say nothing of higher considerations,—of the Indians having Catholic missionaries, and desired him to exert his influence with the different tribes to induce them to apply to the Governor for such instructors. How far he was successful in this and in the other objects of his mission, we are not informed. But we have no doubt that his representations carried with them great weight; and that pro-

* Journal, September 3.

bably some of the later Indian missions owed no little of their success to the influence which he then exerted.

Col. Johnson could not forget the impression the prelate then made on his mind, and he still speaks of him in the highest terms of eulogy. He writes as follows, on the Bishop's presence and bearing at the treaty:

"The death of this venerable prelate of the Catholic Church, which lately happened at Louisville, Kentucky, at an advanced age, reminds me of times and seasons during my long intercourse with the Indian tribes of the North-west—a race which dire necessity has compelled to seek new homes in the far West. The largest and most important treaty held with the natives, since that of Greenville, in 1795, by General Wayne, was the one concluded at St. Mary's, in 1818—thirty-two years ago. Bishop Flaget was in attendance at this treaty during the whole time of its continuance, a period of about seven weeks. The Indians present on the occasion numbered about ten thousand, consisting of Miamies, Potowattamies, Chippewas, Ottawas, Delawares, Shawanoese, Wyandotts, Senecas, and Kickapoos. It fell to my lot, as the oldest agent in the service acting under the authority of the commissioners of the United States, to make all necessary arrangements for the treaty. This included, of course, the comfortable accommodation of the good Bishop. I procured him a horseman's tent, a sufficiency of blankets, a man to attend to his wants, sent him breakfast and supper from the officers' mess, he dining regularly with us at the public table. By invitation, the Bishop performed divine service and preached every Sabbath. Many of the sub-agents, interpreters, and Indians were of the Catholic persuasion, and occupied much of his time in attending to their spiritual wants. His conduct throughout his sojourn with us was so marked by the affability, courtesy, and kindness of his manners, with the dignity of the christian and gentleman, that he won all hearts. Added to this, he possessed a fine proportioned and commanding person; few persons excelled him here, when in the prime of his years. Previous to the departure of the Bishop, it was proposed to raise a collection for him. One hundred dollars were speedily made up, and the undersigned was charged with the delivery of the money. The Bishop peremptorily refused to receive any of it, stating that we had treated him so kindly he was largely our debtor. When departing on horseback, he stopped at my tent, which was some distance from his own, and, dismounting to bid farewell, he took me in his arms. After many thanks for my attentions to him, he said: 'I have nothing better to bestow than the blessing of a Christian Bishop;' and, after imparting that in the most affectionate manner, he bade me adieu. I have never seen him since." *

At the time of the treaty, St. Mary's, with its surrounding Indian encampment, presented a singular spectacle; bringing together in a small compass a curious medley of persons and things. Ten thousand Indians, divided out into as many different quarters as

* See his Letter in the Catholic Telegraph & Advocate, February 23d, 1850. The Colonel is mistaken in supposing that the Bishop remained during the whole continuance of the treaty, about seven weeks: he arrived September 9th, and left October 6th, as appears from his Journal—*Ibid.*

there were tribes; bodies of American soldiers encamped at intervals among them; the hall of assembly, where the Talks were held with the various bands of chieftains; the stores, restaurants, and houses for the interpreters: all these, with the constant din and Babel-like confusion, made the little place a scene of remarkable interest to the beholder. The Bishop and M. Bertrand became ill with the fever, which prevailed to a considerable extent in the place; and for several days before his departure he suffered greatly from want of the comforts so necessary to the sick; and which it was scarcely possible to obtain amidst the confusion of that multitudinous throng.

With the malady still on him, he left the encampment, on the 6th of October, and reached Detroit on the 11th. The fever proved obstinate, and he was for some weeks in a very suffering condition from its effects. He was often confined for days to his room, and sometimes to his bed. Yet he did not discontinue his missionary labors; he visited the various neighboring congregations, administering the sacraments, and holding conferences with one of the clergy. On the 1st of November, he gave confirmation to two hundred persons at Detroit.

Being somewhat recovered on the 17th, he started for the river Raisin, where he devoted nearly six weeks to arduous missionary duties. He here gave a course of instruction to the children preparing for first communion, and held conferences for the instruction of the people. Finding that abuses and scandals had crept into this and several of the other congregations, he thought it expedient to exercise the rigor of ecclesiastical discipline against some who had given public scandal. Thus, he publicly excommunicated a man who had married out of the Church, and caused two females—sisters—who had been unfortunate, to do public penance. They were called to the altar-railing; where, kneeling, they humbly confessed their fault, and implored pardon for the public scandal they had given, and bowing down kissed the floor. The Bishop hereupon gave them a fatherly and fervid exhortation; and "the ceremony made many weep."

He returned to Detroit on the 30th of December; and he saw with lively joy that the glorious cross was already planted on the steeple of the new church of St. Ann. He remained in the city throughout the entire winter and spring, until after Easter; making occasional excursions to the neighboring congregations. He now finished a course of spiritual exercises in the church of the North-eastern shore, which had been commenced before his visit to the river Raisin.

This retreat seems to have produced abundant fruits. Old sinners were reclaimed; inveterate enmities were healed by reconciliation; and some scandalous females were admitted to public penance, amidst the tears and sobs of the congregation. Among its fruits, the prelate relates the following: A man who had been a fiddler by profession refused thirty dollars for two nights' playing at balls, "in order to conform to my command; though he was poor, and had a wife and ten children." *

He gave conferences throughout the Lent, himself being always the respondent. This favorite mode of instruction he considered peculiarly well adapted to a

* Journal, February 12, 1819.

people, whose slender opportunities had not allowed them to make much advancement in religious knowledge. Wherever he went, he had the happiness to perceive, operated under his eyes, a thorough reformation of morals, and a new impulse given to Religion. He preached every Sunday in English to an audience mostly Protestant; and he was heard with much respect and attention, but, he feared, "with little fruit." *

On the 14th of April, 1819, he revisited the river Raisin, where he gave a retreat, which was followed by the conversion of some great sinners. He here administered confirmation, and made arrangements for the erection of a new church. In May, he returned to Detroit, and prepared for his journey homeward.

He had now finished his mission; and he was much consoled by the great amount of good God had been pleased to accomplish through his ministry. He estimated the number of Catholics then in Detroit and the vicinity, at between four and five thousand: how many there were in the other congregations which he visited, we are not informed.

On the 29th of May, he bade an affectionate adieu to the clergy and people of Detroit, and, accompanied by some young men for his seminary, took a steamer for Erie, which town he reached on the last day of the month. Thence he traveled by Waterford and French creek to the Alleghany river, which he descended in a keel-boat to Pittsburgh.

The boatmen were much addicted to profane swearing, greatly to the annoyance of the Bishop. One evening on landing, they remarked to him, apologetically,

* Journal—*Ibid.*

that they seldom thought of God. "I believed, on the contrary," rejoined the Bishop, with a smile, "that you thought of him often, as you have His holy name so constantly on your lips!" The men understood and profited by the rebuke, so gently administered.

He remained but two days at Pittsburgh; and he says nothing of the religious condition of the city. He merely remarks that there was a church in which he offered up the holy sacrifice. Here he found the Rev. William Byrne, a sub-deacon, on his way to the Diocese of Bardstown. He also met at this place Mr. Joseph Haseltine, a convert lately from Canada, to whom he administered confirmation, and whom he subsequently had the happiness to ordain priest in Kentucky.

We will avail ourselves of this occasion, to furnish some facts in regard to the early religious history of Pittsburgh and Western Pennsylvania, which have been derived from an authentic source.* Bishop Flaget, it appears, had passed by Pittsburgh on his return from Canada, chiefly with a view to dispose of some property owned by a Mr. Marie, an uncle of Bishop David. The house formerly belonging to this man is yet standing, and it is one of the oldest in the city.

The priest stationed at Pittsburgh in 1819, was the Rev. F. X. O'Brien; and the church of which he was pastor was dedicated to St. Patrick. The building is still standing, though it has since been enlarged by the addition of a transept.

---

* We are indebted to the Right Rev. Dr. O'Connor, Bishop of Pittsburgh, for the interesting summary of facts which follows.

The first mission established in what is now the Diocese of Pittsburgh, was at the place where the Benedictine monastery near Youngstown is at present located. This missionary station was founded in 1789; and with the exception of the French settlements on the borders of the lakes, and along the banks of the Wabash and Mississippi rivers, it was probably the first place where Mass was ever celebrated West of the Alleghany mountains. The Catholics of Pittsburgh were attended for several years from Youngstown. Another mission was established on Sugar creek; and it is believed that Father Whelan, who was subsequently sent to Kentucky, was stationed here for some time.

The Loretto mission was founded by the Rev. DEMETRIUS A. GALLITZIN, about the year 1799. Under the pastoral charge of this learned, pious and devoted missionary, who had sacrificed a princely title and fortune in embracing the Catholic faith, Loretto became an important point in the early missions of Western Pennsylvania. His works yet remain; and his name is held in benediction by the Catholics of that vicinity. He was one of those devoted and truly apostolic men, who laid the foundations of Religion in North America.

The Rev. F. X. O'Brien resided at Brownsville, when he first came to the West; and from that place he attended Pittsburgh, where there was as yet no church. In 1809 or 1810, he went thither to remain as resident pastor. St. Patrick's church was commenced in 1810. About the year 1820, Rev. Mr. O'Brien returned to Maryland; and died, some time afterwards, probably at Annapolis. He was succeeded at Pittsburgh by Father Maguire; who, having remained there alone for some years, was, about the year 1831, assisted by the Rev. J. O'Reilly. The latter clergyman was succeeded in the pastoral charge, in 1841, by the present Bishop of Pittsburgh.

The city of Erie is erected on the site of the old French fort of PRESQU' ISLE,—some remains of which are still to be there seen. There seems to have been no resident priest at this place before the year 1837 or 1838; about which date a small frame church was erected. In 1840, a German church was built, which has since been placed under the pastoral charge of the Jesuits. A spacious church for the English congregation was erected in 1849.

On the 7th of June, the Bishop left Pittsburgh in a keel-boat, and descended the Ohio river to Cincinnati, where he arrived on the 21st of the same month. Here he found that the new church was under roof, and that it had already been used for divine service. It was a frame edifice 55 feet by 25; the lot, about 120 by 118 feet, had been purchased for a small amount, payable in five or six annual installments; and there remained unpaid on the work already done about $100. The congregation was then composed of only five or six families; and the church was situated about two miles out of town. It was moved into the city on rollers about the year 1823, during the absence of Bishop Fenwick in Europe; and it was placed on the site of the present St. Xavier's church.*

The Bishop speaks of the condition and prospects of

* These details were furnished by F. N. D. Young.

Catholicity in the city as follows: "It is a great misfortune that no Catholics come to settle in the neighborhood of this splendid city. At present, there are no other Catholics in Cincinnati than laborers and clerks, and—such as are to be converted. Yet, I think that nothing should be neglected to establish Religion here; for the mercy of God is great, and when He pleases, He can multiply His children." *

Truly has He multiplied His children in Cincinnati; and the Bishop lived to see his anticipations more than realized! Considering its humble beginnings, the progress of Religion in this city and throughout Ohio has been, indeed, marvelous. That city in which, thirty-two years ago, there was but a mere handful of Catholics, is now, thanks to the mercy of God, a full third, perhaps nearly half, Catholic!

The first missionary to Ohio was Father Edward Fenwick, of the order of St. Dominic, who subsequently became the first Bishop of Cincinnati. Residing at the convent of St. Rose, in Kentucky, he made frequent excursions to Ohio; and as the number of Catholics increased, he afterwards devoted the most of his time to this growing mission.

We find very different statements as to the time when Father Fenwick first visited Ohio. The French account of the early missions of Ohio, published at Paris in 1824, says that he first penetrated into that State in the year 1808. A writer in the Catholic Telegraph † fixes the date at 1810; and he tells a somewhat romantic story of the manner in which the pioneer missionary found three Catholic families in the forests,

---

* Journal, June 21. † Volume iii., p. 86.

by hearing at a distance the sound of their axes. Another writer in the U. S. Catholic Magazine judiciously corrects this mistake, on the authority of Bishop Fenwick himself; who, in a Letter written * from Bordeaux to Father Badin then in Paris, expressly states that he first visited Ohio in 1814.†

The fact is, that Bishop Flaget himself, as we have already seen, had discovered those three Catholic families in Ohio, consisting of twenty individuals, when he was on his way to Baltimore, in 1812; and he had promised to send them a Catholic priest, at least once a year. On his return to Kentucky in the spring of 1813, he did not forget his promise. It was he who gave Father Fenwick the information in regard to the existence of Catholics in the neighboring State, and who deputed him to attend to their spiritual wants. The prelate could not have made a better choice. Father Fenwick was admirably suited for the post of pioneer missionary in a new region, through whose waving forests Catholics were at that early day but thinly scattered.

In the year 1815, he visited Cincinnati, Chilicothe, and many other parts of the State. At the close of the following year, he came to St. Thomas', to report the state of the mission to the Bishop. The number of Catholics had meantime so greatly increased, that at least four priests were then needed in Ohio. ‡ In 1817, Father Fenwick reported that he had found at

* Early in August, 1823.

† See three articles in the sixth volume of the U. S. Catholic Magazine, to which our attention was called by the Archbishop of Cincinnati, to whom we are also indebted for other favors.

‡ Journal, December 6, 1816.

Gallipolis many children eighteen years old who had not been baptized. At no great distance from this town, there were sixteen Catholic families.

The Bishop was much afflicted at not being able immediately to meet the pressing wants of this interesting mission; but Father N. D. Young,—ordained December 10, 1817,—was associated with Father Fenwick not long afterwards. He went to Ohio, for the first time, in November, 1818. The two missionaries had to multiply themselves to meet all the calls made on their ministry. They were, under Bishop Flaget, the founders of Religion in Ohio.

In 1819, Father Fenwick reported, that eight clergymen would scarcely suffice for this mission; and that three were needed for Perry county alone. The church of St. Joseph, near Somerset, was established December 6th, 1818; and it was the first erected in Ohio.* This congregation was then composed of only eight or ten families. About a year later, sixty families were attached to it: and there were, moreover, thirty families around Zanesville; thirty in Knox county; and as many in Stark county.†

Our saintly prelate was rejoiced at the blessings with which God was pleased to crown the zeal of the two Dominican missionaries. He ascribed their success, in a great measure, to the circumstance that "they preached little, but prayed the more." ‡

---

* It was originally a log building, erected by the Messrs. Dittoe, on the suggestion of Bishop Flaget. A stone addition was afterwards put up; and the logs having decayed, they were replaced by brick:—so that the church is now partly of stone and partly of brick.

† These statistics are derived from Father Fenwick's correspondence with Bishop Flaget.

‡ Journal, March, 1820.

Bishop Flaget reached Bardstown and St. Thomas' on the 30th of June, 1829. His reception at the seminary is thus related by himself in his Report to the Pope, already quoted:

"Bishop David,* who had been advised beforehand of my arrival, came to meet me at the head of his seminarians. He began to address me a few words, but his tears, more eloquent than any language, prevented him from continuing. Mine followed not less abundantly; we all embraced one another with affection. My heart was so full of joy, that I forgot entirely the sufferings and fatigue inseparable from a journey of at least seven hundred leagues,† of which the greater part had been traversed in the discharge of missionary duties."

---

* Not yet consecrated.

† Nearly 2,100 miles.

CHAPTER IX.

COADJUTOR—CATHEDRAL—SEMINARY—CONSECRATION OF BISHOP FENWICK.

1819—1822.

Scruples of conscience—How solved—Father David—His character—Presented for the bishopric of Philadelphia—Escapes the nomination—Appointed Coadjutor—His objections to accepting—The Cathedral—Laying corner-stone, and solemn dedication—Consecration of Bishop David—The seminary removed—Impressions of a clerical traveler—Arrival of a Propagandist—Correspondence concerning Bishops for Cincinnati and Detroit—Father Fenwick appointed Bishop of Cincinnati, and consecrated—His labors in Ohio blessed—Condition of his Diocese—His zeal, and death—Bishop Flaget's love for his priests—Rev. Mr. Abell—Rev. M. Hosten—Rev. M. Derigaud.

In the beginning of the year 1817, Bishop Flaget began to entertain scruples concerning the propriety of continuing his Journal. The thought occurred to him, that the practice of daily recording his own acts and sentiments was little more than mere vanity and self-love. In this doubt, he applied to his intimate friend and enlightened confessor, Father David; who at once dispelled his scruple, and counseled him to continue the work. From thenceforward, however, the prelate resolved to make a note of his *acts* only, and to omit all pious sentiments and reflections; *—a resolution which, we are very happy to find, he afterwards forgot to observe.

Father David was endowed with solid, rather than brilliant talents; and his profound ecclesiastical learning was ever guided in its application by sound discretion and great good sense. His piety was solid and well grounded, his zeal unbounded, and his willingness to labor commensurate with his earnest desire to do good. He was eminently practical, and he went straight to his point; and withal, he was as humble as a child; always as ready to own his own faults, as he was candid in reminding those under his charge of theirs. All who knew him well, esteemed and loved him. He grew in your opinion upon nearer acquaintance.

He was from the Diocese of Nantes, in France; and was, like our prelate, a Sulpician. As we have already seen, he came to America in the same ship with M. Flaget, in 1792; and from that date they were almost inseparable companions, and intimate friends in Christ Jesus. Content with his offices of simple missionary and superior of the seminary, Father David shrank from honors, aware of their great danger and heavy responsibility; but honors were thrust upon him.

As early as the beginning of the year 1815, Archbishop Carroll had sent his name to Rome, as one eminently suitable to fill the important see of Philadelphia, which was then vacant.† The humble ecclesiastic was alarmed; he wrote to Rome an earnest letter of remon-

* Journal, 1817—*in initio.*

† The Letter of the Archbishop announcing this step was received by Bishop Flaget May 15, 1815.—Journal—*Ibid.*

strance, setting forth, in the strongest terms, his utter unfitness for the place. Bishop Flaget united his efforts with those of his friend, with whose services he could not easily dispense; and their joint influence proved effectual in preventing the appointment.

The following extract from a Letter of the Bishop, written in 1826, would make it appear, that Philadelphia was not the only important see which the humility of Father David prevented him from filling: "My dear Coadjutor, who has been as necessary to me in the administration of my Diocese, as the eyes are to the head, has sacrificed two bishoprics in our great cities of America to be the lowly Coadjutor of the exceedingly poor Bishop of Bardstown." *

The vastness of his Diocese, his frequent absence from home, and his own advancing years, prompted Bishop Flaget to apply for a Coadjutor; and though Father David was a few years his senior, yet, as the health of the latter was still sufficiently robust, the Bishop believed him to be the most suitable person whom he could select. Accordingly, he made the application to Rome, and his petition was favorably received.

The Bulls nominating J. B. M. DAVID Bishop of Mauricastro in *partibus*, and Coadjutor of the Bishop of Bardstown, were dated July 4th, 1817, and they reached Kentucky on the 25th of the following November.† Yet almost two years elapsed before his consecration; during the greater part of which time Bishop

---

* French Life—p. 96. The other bishopric, as was said above, was probably that of New Orleans.

† Journal, *in locis*.

Flaget, as we have seen in the two preceeding Chapters, was absent on distant visitations.

One reason of the delay was the reluctance of Father David to accept the appointment. He entertained serious scruples of conscience on the subject, which he frankly laid before the Holy See. As these reasons for not accepting will furnish us with a clue to his character, and as they are withal edifying, we lay them before our readers.

1. He dreaded the responsibility of the office, which he felt was greatly above his strength. 2. He had himself advised the Bishop to ask for a Coadjutor, and he feared lest he might have had some, at least indirect agency in his own nomination. 3. The reasons set forth in the Bulls for giving the Bishop a Coadjutor,—his age and infirmities, &c.,—applied more strongly still to himself, as he was both older and more infirm than Bishop Flaget.

Cardinal Litta, Prefect of the Propaganda, replied in the name of the Holy See, and strongly advised him to accept; alleging that those clauses, usual in such documents where the appointment of a Coadjutor is in question, were not intended to be interpreted in their strictest and most literal acceptation, and that, moreover, the Pontiff healed whatever deficiencies might be supposed to exist in the premises.

The scruples of the newly elect were dispelled by this authoritative advice and declaration; but his poverty was such that he had not the means to provide immediately what was necessary for his consecration; and this was another reason for the delay. In a letter to his friends in France, he frankly stated this reason,

14

and asked for assistance. This holy poverty, so sincerely cherished by him, and so often extolled as one of the evangelical counsels in his discourses, he carried with him to the grave; leaving nothing behind him at his death, but a few books and manuscripts,—and the sweet odor of his virtues.

Though nearly nine years had elapsed since his appointment to the see of Bardstown, the Bishop had as yet no cathedral, to which the other churches of his Diocese might look up as to a mother, and in which the sublime offices of our holy Religion might be suitably performed. Among his many solicitudes, that connected with the supplying of this important want was not the least.

We have seen, that he thought anxiously on this subject very soon after his arrival in Kentucky. In his poverty, and amid the many pressing needs of his Diocese, it seemed rashness to engage at that time in an undertaking so far above his means. He had a great horror of debt, and he justly thought that Providence did not call on him to involve himself in inextricable pecuniary difficulty.

In 1816, Mr. John Rogers, an able architect from Baltimore, proposed to him to embark in the undertaking, alleging and endeavoring to prove its practicability. The reluctance of the Bishop was at length overcome by the forcible representations of MM. David and Chabrat, who counseled him to trust largely in divine Providence; and he at length gave his consent.

"That which has occupied us most," writes Father David,* "is the building of a cathedral at Bardstown.

* Letter dated November 20, 1817—*sup. cit.*

Though the Bishop had conceived this design immediately on his arrival, he had not, however, yet ventured on its execution: but Providence has at length overcome all obstacles in a wonderful manner. A good Catholic carpenter from Baltimore has offered his services for this purpose; and the amount of the first subscription was found to be from twelve to fourteen thousand dollars. Bardstown alone, which scarcely equals in size one of our large villages in France, subscribed five thousand dollars."

The result of the subscription cheered the Bishop, who considered it a mark of the approval of heaven. Yet he writes: "I keep myself within the limits of a holy indifference as to success. I would heartily wish to live at the see which Rome has established; but still more I wish, that Thy will, O God, should be done! 'That no flesh may glory in thy sight;' but that all glory be given to thee!" *

The corner-stone of the cathedral was laid July 16, 1816; and Father David preached on the occasion, to a very large audience, a luminous discourse, explanatory of the impressive ceremonial. Four priests from St. Rose, and all the seminarians, were in attendance. Two years afterwards, the edifice—a fine structure in the Roman Corinthian style—was almost completed. On the 7th of August, 1819, the Bishop removed to Bardstown, with his Coadjutor elect. He left St. Thomas' with regret; and he often visited the place afterwards, to bury himself in deeper solitude. He found his apartment in Bardstown "too handsome and

* Journal, 1816.

too vast for a Bishop, who should regard himself as one of those of the primitive Church." *

On the following day the cathedral was solemnly consecrated, in conformity with the rites prescribed in the Pontifical; Bishop David preaching during the consecration, and Rev. Mr. Abell at the Mass. The collection taken up amounted to ninety dollars. There was an immense concourse present at the imposing ceremony;—the first of the kind ever performed in the West.

On the feast of the Assumption, a week later, Bishop David was consecrated in the new cathedral by Bishop Flaget, who was assisted by the Rev. MM. Nerinckx and Wilson, O. S. D. The consecration sermon was preached by Rev. M. Chabrat. This was the first episcopal consecration which took place west of the Alleghany mountains.

Bishop David changed nothing in his rigid manner of life, with the exception that he now became still more exact and laborious. In spite of the new cares and responsibility devolved on him, he continued to direct the exercises of the seminary as superior, devoting several hours each day to the duties of this office and to teaching theology. He, moreover, gave a considerable portion of his time to the forming of the new sisterhood of Nazareth, of which he was the founder. When we add that he was for a considerable time chief pastor and organist of the cathedral, and that he visited monthly four stations attached to the cathedral congregation, besides occasionally attending that of St. Thomas, of which he had long been pastor; we will

* Journal—*Ibid.*

probably come to the conclusion, that his time was fully employed, and that he had little leisure for recreation.

On the 21st of September, the seminary was removed from St. Thomas' to Bardstown, now the residence of of the two Bishops. These occupied apartments in the same building with the seminarians; and for many years they ate at the same table, and as far as possible, performed all the spiritual exercises with them. It was a well organized family, in which the fathers lived in the midst of their children. "This day," says the Bishop, "should form an epoch in the history of the Church in Kentucky; for I dare hope that from this house will go forth priests who will sustain and propagate the faith. What embarrassment, however, in providing for temporal wants, under such circumstances! Every thing consists in acting with great liberty of spirit, and in reposing confidence without bounds in God." *

On the Sundays and festivals, the Bishops appeared in the cathedral, surrounded by their seminarians robed in surplices; and all the ceremonies of the Church were performed with great exactness and even splendor. All present were greatly edified by the appearance and deportment of the clergy and young candidates for the holy ministry. The Protestants were also much impressed with the beauty and grandeur of our ceremonial. We cannot do better, while on this subject, than to furnish our readers with the impressions the service as then performed in the cathedral

* Journal, September 21, 1819.

made on the mind of an intelligent clerical stranger, who was at the time on a visit to Kentucky.

"I have just arrived from Kentucky, whither I went to fulfill certain commissions towards the holy Bishop Flaget and some members of his clergy. The prelate showed me his famous establishments and his cathedral. Accompanying me himself on horseback, he made me visit his convents, his seminaries, and his colleges: for we must already speak in the plural number of all these establishments, scattered in the midst of the forest. I avow to you, sir, that if ever I was penetrated with deep feeling, it was while assisting at the Holy Sacrifice in the cathedral on Sunday. Torrents of tears flowed from my eyes. The ceremonies, all performed with the greatest exactness according to the Roman rite; the chant at once grave and touching; the attendant clergy pious and modest:—every thing impressed me so strongly, that I almost believed myself in the midst of one of the finest churches of Rome, which I had before thought could not be equalled any where else in the world. From the bottom of my heart, I poured forth prayers to God for this worthy Bishop, for France, and for those who, by their generosity, had contributed to have the good God so well worshiped in the midst of the waving forests." *

The Bishop himself thus writes on the same subject: "Nothing could be more astonishing, and edifying at the same time, than to see the Bishop officiating pontifically in his cathedral, with deacon and sub-deacon both students of the seminary, surrounded by more

* From Annales de la Propagation, &c., vol, ii., p. 24. Number for May, 1826.

than fifteen young seminarians, tonsured or in minor orders, clad in cassock and surplice, and singing as well as if they had been trained in Paris itself. Many priests have already been reared in the seminary; their piety and talents would render them distinguished even in Europe; and some of them are excellent preachers and very good controversialists." *

Cheered by the hope of soon having priests enough from his own seminary, to supply the wants of his extensive Diocese, and relieved of a portion of his heavy charge by the appointment of Bishop Dubourg, and the kind and timely aid received from him towards providing his most distant missions; consoled, moreover, with the thought, that in his absence Religion could not suffer, with so able and vigilant a Coadjutor as Bishop David, Bishop Flaget was now much more easy in mind, and more happy than he had ever been since his consecration. That kind Providence in which he had always so confidingly trusted, had come visibly to his assistance. But ten years of his episcopal career had passed, and already every thing wore a new aspect.

Two events, which occurred in the year 1821, contributed much to enhance the consolation with which his soul already abounded. The first was the arrival in his Diocese of a young priest from the Propaganda, (September 23d,) with whose first appearance he was greatly pleased,† and whose piety, zeal, and extensive theological attainments, proved an invaluable treasure to him for many years. This young ecclesiastic, shortly afterwards permanently attached to the Diocese, is too

* From Annales, &c.—p. 40.

† Journal, September 23, 1821.

well known to all our readers to require being named by us in these Sketches.

The second joyful occurrence of this year was the intelligence, that Father EDWARD FENWICK had been appointed first Bishop of Cincinnati. The Bishop had long and anxiously thought on the subject of proposing the erection of this and other sees in the West. He and Bishop Dubourg had been for some time engaged in correspondence on the subject. New bishoprics were needed at Cincinnati, Vincennes, and Detroit; as Bishop Flaget had written to Bishop Dubourg on the 30th of December, 1819.* The reply of the latter was received in the following April. Great difficulty existed in settling on the precise sees to be proposed; still greater, in finding suitable persons to fill them.†

At first, it had been determined to propose the Rev. Dr. Gallitzin for the see of Cincinnati; but when this worthy clergyman was made acquainted with the intention of the two prelates, he wrote to Bishop Flaget, peremptorily declining the appointment, and alleging such reasons, prompted by his humility and the circumstances in which he found himself placed, as caused them to abandon the idea of farther insisting on his being nominated.

They then agreed in presenting Father Fenwick for Cincinnati, and the Holy See acted with promptness on the recommendation. They probably, at the same time, united in recommending the distinguished Jesuit, Father Grassi, for Detroit. In a letter to our prelate, Bishop Dubourg writes as follows: "M. Inglesi writes to me from Rome, that the nomination of M. Grassi

* Journal—*Ibid.* † *Ibid.*

for Detroit has met with difficulties; but not so that of Father Fenwick for Cincinnati. M. Sibourd will not be my Coadjutor," &c.*

The Bulls erecting the see of Cincinnati, and nominating Father Fenwick its first incumbent, dated 19th June, arrived in Kentucky, October 13th, 1821; while the zealous apostle of Ohio was buried in its forests, seeking, according to his own phrase, after "the stray sheep." He was surprised on learning that he had been thought of in connection with so responsible an office. He at first expressed great reluctance to accept, but was finally induced to yield to the pressing wants of that mission, and the reasons alleged by those to whom he applied for advice.

The new Diocese comprised the State of Ohio; and its first Bishop was likewise charged with the spiritual administration of the territories of Michigan and the North-west, until new bishoprics could be founded therein. It is not a little remarkable, that an effort should have been made to locate the new see at Somerset, instead of Cincinnati; and it is perhaps still more so, that Bishop Dubourg should have preferred Chillicothe to either of the above cities, as being more central.† It was owing principally to the strong representations and great personal influence of Bishop Flaget, that Cincinnati was eventually selected. The result has proved the wisdom of the advice given on the subject by our enlightened and saintly prelate; whom the Holy See rightly judged to be better acquainted with the state of affairs than any one else.

---

* Letter, August 9, 1821.

† In a Letter on the subject to Bishop Flaget, in 1820.

Dr. Fenwick was consecrated by Bishop Flaget, assisted by FF. Wilson and Hill, at St. Rose, on the 13th of January, 1822.* Bishop David preached the consecration sermon. Towards the end of the ensuing March,† he departed to take possession of his see. That he was worthy of the place, his subsequent life amply demonstrated. He labored "in season and out of season;" and at the close of his administration, his Diocese presented an aspect totally different from what it had been at the commencement of his episcopal career. Besides his brethren of the order of St. Dominic at St. Rose, he was enabled to enlist many others in the service of the new missions. Among these was the Rev. F. Resé, a Propagandist, afterwards first Bishop of Detroit.

Father Hill, a Dominican, and a convert of an illustrious family in England, labored for several years, with devoted zeal and great efficiency, on the missions of Ohio. After sacrificing every worldly consideration on the altar of divine love, he never once faltered in his purpose "to spend and be spent for the salvation of souls." He died, in odor of piety, at Canton, Ohio, September 3, 1828, in the midst of his labors; and he was buried, at his own request, under the eves of the church of which he had been pastor.

Bishop Fenwick had made it a condition for his acceptance of the episcopal office, that the Rev. Father Wilson of St. Rose's convent, provincial of the Dominicans, should accompany him to Ohio, as theologian and Vicar General. Accordingly, this distinguished ecclesiastic and Father Hill went with him to Cincin-

* Journal—*Ibid.*

† *Ibid.*

nati, when he repaired thither to take possession of his See. He was solemnly installed by Bishop Flaget, who delivered one of his most impressive and touching discourses on the occasion. Father Wilson having been compelled to return to Kentucky, about six months afterwards, Father Hill was chosen Vicar General; which office he continued to fill till his death.*

During the early years of his administration, Bishop Fenwick was much distressed at his want of missionaries; and it is not surprising that he used every possible effort to supply the want. For this purpose he applied to the Propaganda, asking for the services of the young propagandist above mentioned; stating that his Diocese had much more need of him than that of Bardstown, which was already, in a great measure, supplied.

When Bishop Flaget heard of this application, he was much distressed, and immediately wrote to Rome an energetic letter on the subject; stating that, though disposed to assist, to the best of his power, the new Diocese of Cincinnati, he could not bear the thought of being deprived of the services of one, so necessary for his support in his declining years.† His protest was successful at Rome.

We will avail ourselves of this occasion to throw together such additional facts connected with the early administration of Bishop Fenwick, as we have been able to gather from the materials within our reach.

After having labored for little more than a year in

---

* Several of these details were furnished orally by the nephew of Bishop Fenwick, the Rev. N. D. Young, O. S. D.

† He entreated, that "D. —— senectutis meæ baculus firmissimus, oculusque acutissimus, apud me remaneat, et ad exitum meum vel Coadjutoris mei, Coadjutor ipse consecretur."

his new Diocese, and having been forcibly struck with the want of every requisite for a complete and solid missionary establishment, he determined to visit Europe, and to lay the condition of his missions before the Holy Father at Rome. He accordingly left Cincinnati on the 30th of May, 1823; and he arrived at Bordeaux in France, on the 6th of August following. The Very Rev. M. Badin was then in Paris, on business connected with the Diocese of Bardstown; and to him the good prelate wrote, a few days after his arrival, setting forth the circumstances under which he had accepted the episcopacy, and the destitute state of his Diocese. We cannot do better than to republish the greater portion of this valuable document, which abounds with interesting facts:

"Having in so many instances of my life experienced the fatherly care and protection of God, the bestower of all good gifts, I confidently hope that the same divine Providence will continue through the remainder of my arduous undertaking to accompany me. It has supplied me, upon loan, with the sum precisely necessary for my voyage to this place, and no more, in order to keep me always in dependence. Our poor backwoods are now so miserable, that I could not have a *sous* (cent) given me, neither by my brethren in the episcopacy, nor by the priests of Kentucky or of my own Diocese. Indeed I esteemed myself happy to borrow, without interest, of a Catholic layman, the sum of about five hundred francs (one hundred dollars), now almost exhausted.

"I am really sorry, my dear sir, that you cannot conveniently join and accompany me to Rome. My object in going is to resign, if allowed, my dignity to better hands and superior heads; if not allowed, to beg for means of subsistence, and all necessary supplies for the mission, especially funds to build a church in Cincinnati, and to pay for the lot I have purchased. I have already raised for my cathedral at present, a wooden chapel, fifty feet by thirty. I had not then a *sous* of money,—all has been done on credit; and a great portion of the expenses remains still to be paid for. The object of my journey is also to procure means for securing, in the vicinity of my episcopal town, the domain of a small tract of land, and a large convenient house, well calculated for a seminary. * * * Moreover, I wish to obtain a Bishop for Detroit, and a Coadjutor for myself, and some good divines, in case my resignation be not accepted.

"I wish you, also, my dear sir, to contribute your mite towards relieving my distresses. I mean, and beg, that you draw up and have printed a short and clear description of my condition, of the extent and wants of my Diocese, of the number and scattered situation of the poor Catholics, &c. When I came first to the State of Ohio, nine years ago, I discovered only three Catholic families from Limestone (Maysville,) to Wheeling. Now the State contains not less than *eight thousand.** There are also ten or twelve thousand in Michigan. Moreover, there are in Ohio two thousand Indians, living on the Seneca River, some of whom are Catholics, and those are obliged to cross Lake Erie, to reach Malden and Sandwich in Canada, in order to have their children baptized, and their marriages celebrated by a

* He means, no doubt, *Catholics*—not *families*.

Catholic priest. In the wilderness watered by the Sandusky river, there are two settlements of white people, one of Catholics, and the other of Methodists, upon the two opposite sides of the river. I intend, if possible, to have two missionaries, traveling continually from place to place, especially devoting their labors and services among the Indians. * * *

"I think we may count two or three hundred converts since I reside in Ohio. Five wooden churches are actually built, and four more are building. The population of Ohio, according to the last census, is six hundred thousand souls. Catholics are to be found in every county; and I have met with many Germans and Swiss. I offer to God many prayers for some zealous and disinterested German priests. I say disinterested, for all missionaries must depend entirely upon divine Providence. Although a Bishop, I have no revenue but the rent of twenty-five or thirty pews in the Cincinnati chapel, which produce, at most, a yearly income of eighty dollars.

"You know a little of my exertions, sacrifices, and labors in Kentucky: that I devoted my whole paternal estate, and all I could collect, scrape up and save; that I debarred myself of comforts and even of necessaries; that I undertook long and painful jaunts to found and promote the establishment of St. Rose; and behold I am now deprived of all right and claim on the Order; being taken out of it—*assumptus ex ordine in episcopatum!* I was obliged by my rule and vows to render an account of all property, even of books and furniture, that I had been allowed to use.

"When I took possession of the Diocese, I had to

rent a house to live in, and to send to market for the first meal we took in the episcopal town—no provision whatever having been made for the maintenance of the Bishop. I had not a *sous*, but what the good people of St. Rose's congregation in Kentucky had given me by subscription,—four or five hundred dollars in paper money, which was depreciated to one half in the Ohio State.

"I had but six congregations, when, eighteen months ago, I first went to reside in Cincinnati; and now there are twenty-two, at least, that I have visited. * *

"You will conceive how great is the want of missionaries in my extensive Diocese, when you learn that I possess only seven priests, and have neither, seminary, professors, nor schools. The Rev. Messrs. Hill and Stephen Montgomery, O. S. D., are charged with the western congregations and all scattered Catholics as far as Vevay in the Indiana,* Fort St. Mary's, Lake Erie, Chilicothe, &c. Rev. Mr. Young, my nephew, and two *confreres* ordained by me, extend their rides and missionary duties in the East to Marietta, St. Clairville, New Lisbon, &c." †

The truly apostolic prelate unconsciously paints himself in this simple, but highly interesting letter. So much devotedness, and so unwavering a reliance on Providence, could not fail of drawing down the divine blessing. Father Badin complied with his request, and published in Paris a statement comprising the above

* In virtue of an arrangement with Bishop Flaget, under whose jurisdiction Indiana was placed.

† Republished, from the London Spectator, (vol. i. p. 350, *seqq.*) in the U. S. Catholic Magazine, (vol. vi. p. 29, *seq.*,) for 1847.

details and making an earnest appeal to the benevolent in favor of the destitute missions of Ohio.

Bishop Fenwick proceeded to Rome, where he was cordially and paternally welcomed by the reigning Pontiff, Leo XII., who generously presented him with a splendid tabernacle, a chalice, candlesticks, and other altar furniture for his cathedral, besides the munificent sum of twelve thousand Roman crowns (dollars.) He also "directed the Cardinal Prefect of the Propaganda to recommend him, not only to the association lately commenced at Lyons, but also to the friends of religion in general, and especially to those whose wealth enabled them to be liberal patrons of the foreign missions. Animated by the example of the sovereign Pontiff and the letters of the Cardinal Prefect, other members of the Sacred College, especially Cardinal Fêsch, uncle of Napoleon Buonaparte, conferred on the amiable prelate the most substantial marks of their regard for himself, and of their sympathy for the destitution of his flock. The king of France, and the wealthy and generous Catholics of his kingdom, as well as those of Sardinia, Belgium, Spain, and Germany, emulated the noble precedent thus given them in the eternal city; and the dejected Bishop, who had landed on the shores of Europe very much in the condition of 'the sower who had sowed in tears,' returned, like that sower, 'with joyfulness,' having gathered a rich harvest." *

As we will not have occasion in the sequel to revert to this subject, we may be permitted to furnish here such additional details, in regard to the history of the

* From the first of three well written articles on the Missions of Ohio, in the U. S. C. Magazine—*sup. cit.*

Diocese of Cincinnati as may be deemed of more interest, up to the death of its first Bishop in 1832.

The ample funds which the prelate collected in Europe were, immediately after his return, judiciously applied to the more pressing wants of his infant Diocese. Among these, one of the most urgent was a cathedral in Cincinnati. The edifice, one hundred feet long by fifty wide, long used for this purpose,* was dedicated to God, under the patronage of St. Peter, on the first Sunday of Advent, 1826. The hearts of the faithful were filled with a holy joy, on beholding this handsome structure, with its splendid altar furniture, reared for the worship of the Most High; and they contrasted it with the humble wooden building, unfinished and unfurnished, in which they had hitherto convened to assist at the holy sacrifice.

New churches were soon erected in almost every portion of the Diocese. The number of Catholics rapidly increased, especially in Cincinnati. This will appear from the following statistics, belonging to the time of the Jubilee: which was proclaimed in the cathedral of Cincinnati on Christmas day, 1826, and terminated there on the following New Year's day; and was during the ensuing year published, with most abundant fruits, throughout the Diocese. In Cincinnati, two hundred persons approached the holy table, during this season of grace, in place of the *eleven* communicants,—the highest number only five years previously!

The Bishop visited the whole Diocese during this year (1827). He was preceded by two zealous mission-

* The present church of St. Xavier.

aries—the Rev. Messrs. Mullon and Young—who prepared the way for the visitation. They gave retreats in the principal congregations; and had the consolation to find their labors crowned with the greatest success. In Lancaster there were sixty communicants; there were four hundred at St. Joseph's, forty at St. Barnabas, ninety in Zanesville, fifty at St. Dominic's, and one hundred in Canton. Besides the reclaiming of many hardened sinners, numerous converts were every where received into the Church.*

We have already spoken of Father Hill. Another zealous Dominican, a native of Spain, deserves special mention, as one of the most laborious and efficient early missionaries of Ohio. The Rev. Raphael Muños, in 1824, obtained permission from his superior, and from the Prefect of the Propaganda, to attach himself to the Diocese of Cincinnati. For several years he devoted himself to this arduous mission, with a zeal truly apostolic. He spared no labor nor pains in instructing the ignorant. He was the father of the poor. After an absence of two or three years in Kentucky, whither he was sent to be prior of St. Rose's convent, he returned to Cincinnati; where he died in the midst of his labors, July 18, 1830, in the fifty-second year of his age. He was a doctor of divinity, and was associated with Father Hill in the office of Vicar General of the Diocese.†

Bishop Fenwick passed none of his time in idleness. For him the sweetest recreation consisted in the discharge of laborious missionary duty. Every where he appeared at the head of his clergy, animating their zeal,

---

* Second paper in U. S. C. Magazine—*sup. cit.*

† *Ibid.*

even more by his example than by his simple but eloquent words, glowing, as they were, with the love of God and of the neighbor. His visitation extended to Michigan and the North-western territory. Here he felt as much at home, while dwelling amidst the wigwams of the savages, as when sojourning among the more polished inhabitants of the towns. Whithersoever he went, he was received with a hearty welcome; and he labored with the zeal of an apostle. The Indians loved and revered him, as a father. God consoled his paternal heart, by the numerous conversions and the abundant harvest of souls he failed not to gather, in every town and village of his extended charge.

At Detroit, he had the happiness to embrace that venerable pioneer missionary of Michigan,—the Rev. GABRIEL RICHARD; who had been stationed there, as resident pastor, since 1799. After thirty-three years of arduous missionary toil, this indefatigable apostle of the North and Northwest, died, like a good soldier, at his post. In September, 1832, he was attacked with the cholera, while attending his parishioners who were seized with this terrible disease; and after receiving the last rites of the Church, he calmly expired on the 13th of that month. He went to receive the reward of his labors in heaven.

The first Bishop of Cincinnati was destined to follow in his foot-steps, and to fall, like him, a victim of charity. He also died of the effects of cholera, while engaged in his visitation; which his zeal would not permit him to interrupt, though he felt that the seeds of death were already sown in his system. He had been taken ill at Sault St. Marie; but, continuing his journey, he died at Wooster, on the 25th of September, 1832. He had said Mass and written two letters on the previous day. At his death, the number of Catholics in his Diocese was estimated at nearly forty thousand; many of whom were converts.

We will close this Chapter with a few examples illustrating a distinguished trait in the character of our holy prelate,—his love for his priests. He always viewed them with a tenderness of feeling equal to that which a parent exhibits towards his children. He rejoiced in their success, and wept with them in their affliction. In time of sickness, he was, as often as possible, at their bed-side, discharging all the duties of a tender nurse. And yet, in cases of sacerdotal delinquency, fortunately of very rare occurence, he could wield the rod of discipline, though it pained him to do so even more than it did the objects of his just chastisement.

In July, 1820, the Rev. Mr. Abell was grievously sick in Breckenridge county, and his dangerous illness was lingering. The Bishop immediately left all things, and flew to his succor. He remained with him for six weeks, affording him every possible consolation and service, and, as he tells us, feeling as much agony in his sufferings as the patient himself.* At length, to the inexpressible joy of the prelate, Mr. Abell, whose case had been pronounced desperate by the physicians, slowly recovered.

Another instance is exhibited, in his attendance on the Rev. M. Hosten, a young Belgian priest of great promise, whom he had recently ordained. In this case,

* Journal—*ibid.*

however, to his unutterable grief, the patient died. Rev. M. Hosten was ordained September 24, 1820, with several others ; and in June of the following year, he was destined for the mission of Louisville, of which place he was the first resident pastor. He was installed in his new mission by the Bishop himself, on the 17th of August.

But the ways of God are inscrutable. This zealous clergyman had scarcely entered upon his missionary duties, when he was suddenly called away from this world. Having left all to follow Christ, he was probably already ripe for heaven. While devoting himself day and night to the visitation of those sick with the prevailing typhoid fever, he caught the disease himself, and died of it, on the 30th of October following. The Bishop was with him for several days before his death, attending to all his wants, and solacing his soul with the last sacraments, as a preparation for eternity.

Several years later, he fulfilled the same office of parental nurse towards the Rev. M. Derigaud. This worthy priest had come to America with the Bishop in 1810 ; and on their arrival in Kentucky in the following year, he had entered the seminary. Though then thirty years of age, he completed his studies, and was ordained January 1, 1817. He was employed on the missions, and in the college of St. Joseph ; was, for a time, superior of the preparatory seminary at St. Thomas ; and finally presided over the new brotherhood, established by the Bishop in 1826.

In the spring of the ensuing year, he removed with the brothers, about eight in number, to St. Bernard's, in Casey county. His health having been long delicate, he did not survive many months.

The Bishop, who loved him tenderly, was inconsolable at his dangerous illness. Earnestly did he pray for his recovery, should such be the holy will of God. He went to see him, and remained with him till he breathed his last. He then had his remains removed to St. Thomas'; where they were solemnly interred.

In his Journal, the Bishop has written a high eulogy of this good priest, saying, that he had never in his whole life given him a moment's trouble or uneasiness.*

To secure a support for his missionaries in their old age, the Bishop once proposed a plan, which the event proved was impracticable. It was, that his clergy should hold all things in common, like religious orders; and that the superabundance of some should supply the wants of others.†

We close this Chapter with an extract from the holy prelate's Report to the Pontiff in 1836, which will be found to bear upon our present subject:

"I come now to speak of my clergy. Oh! may God bless them! May he bless their continual sacrifices and generous devotedness, without which there would be nothing remaining of all that now exists in my Diocese! But, alas! these young priests, whom I love as myself; these priests so zealous and so charitable, become soon exhausted; on them old age and infirmities come prematurely—

---

* Journal, Jan. 17, 1322. He had always given him satisfaction, "*Sans une melange d'amertume.*"

† *Ibid.* Conference, Sep. 2, 1822.

the evident result of their long journeys and painful missions ;—already many are enfeebled, and are left almost without resource. Whither will they go, after labors so glorious ? Alas ! I know not ; and this it is which causes my desolation ! "

CHAPTER X.

VISITATIONS—ADMINISTRATION—NEW BISHOPRICS.

1819—1826.

Pastoral solicitude—*In cœlo quies*—Journey to Vincennes—Amusing incident—Visit to Tennessee—Religious statistics—Preacher Vardiman—Protestant liberality—*Dressing* a preacher—Another journey to Vincennes—Administration—Clerical retreats and conferences—Loving the laws of the Church—Matrimonial dispensations—Public penance—Two anecdotes—Reconciling enmities—Management of temporals—Two visits by Bishop Dubourg—Correspondence on new bishoprics—At St. Louis and Pittsburgh—Dr. Gallitzin—New Archbishopric in the West—Bishops of Boston and of New York—Bishop Dubourg leaves America—His character—The Propagation of the Faith—*Inglesi.*

THE solicitude of all the churches weighed heavily on the mind of Bishop Flaget. No sooner does he return from one journey, than he is compelled to start out on another. Repose—he looked for none this side of heaven. His motto was: IN CŒLO QUIES—IN HEAVEN REST.

Our limits will not permit us to enter into all the details of his numerous visitations; nor would this be either useful or interesting to our readers. From some remarks already made on the subject in a previous Chapter, we may be able to estimate the general character of those episcopal missionary excursions. They were all much alike; animated by the same devoted zeal, and utter disregard of every personal comfort.

But our narrative would be incomplete, without some mention of the longer and more important journeys, which the Bishop performed for the visitation of his still immense Diocese. Hence we shall, in the present Chapter, give a brief account of an excursion he made to Tennessee in 1821; and of two journeys to Vincennes in 1819—1823:—taking them up in the order of time.

Though Bishop Dubourg had sent two priests to Vincennes in 1818, yet this was understood as only a temporary accommodation; and the Bishop of Bardstown was still charged with the missions of Indiana. The last priest from the Diocese of New Orleans, who labored in this State, was the Rev. M. Dahmen; and he was withdrawn November 1, 1821.* The Bishop, as we shall see, was reduced to great straits in providing a pastor for Vincennes.

On the 19th of November, 1819, the Bishop started for Louisville, on his visitation to Indiana. He was accompanied by the Rev. Mr. Abell, lately ordained. On the 22d, he left New Albany, and on the 25th, we find him at Washington; where there were then only twelve or fifteen Catholic families, including those in the neighborhood. He was in Vincennes on the following day, and remained there till the 6th of December. He here divided his time between the settlement of temporal affairs, and the usual duties of the holy ministry. Rev. Mr. Abell preached several times, to the great delight and edification of the English portion

* Journal—*Ibid.*

of the inhabitants. Having given confirmation, the Bishop started for home, by the way of Princeton, Evansville, and the lower part of Kentucky. He does not give us any information concerning Evansville; but at Princeton, he found a few Catholics, whose faith was very weak.

A ludicrous incident occurred during this or a subsequent journey through Indiana, which we may as well relate in this place. It may serve to amuse our readers, to indicate the social progress of Indiana at that early period, and to relieve somewhat the heavier topics treated of in these Sketches.

The Bishop and Mr. Abell put up for the night at a way-side house of entertainment, which was a one story log cabin, with a garret, or *loft*, approached by a ladder. The prelate and his companion lodged in this garret, the floor of which was covered with loose boards; while the family and some wagoners occupied the lower room. The Bishop had an alarm-watch, and he set it so as to go off at four o'clock,—his usual hour for rising. In the morning the watch created quite an *alarm* among the occupants of the lower floor. Several sprang to their feet in fright; when a more knowing, or a more drowsy wagoner calmed them, with the complimentary explanation: "Lie still, you fools! it is only the old priest's watch which has *busted!*" *

On this journey he also visited Harmony, Indiana, then flourishing under the administration of the founder, Mr. Rapp. He lamented that so much industry and energy were wasted on objects—to say the least—

* It is almost needless to say, that this anecdote is *not* found in the Bishop's Journal.

of a merely temporal nature.* It was afterwards sold to Owen, who organized there a society from which Religion, individual property, and indissoluble marriage were excluded. When the Bishop passed by the place ten years later, the establishment had been broken up: †—so true is it, that civilized society cannot subsist, without having Religion as its basis.

On the eve of Christmas day, the Bishop reached Bardstown; and he celebrated a grand Pontifical Mass in his cathedral on that great festival of the Church.

In March, 1820, Rev. MM. Nerinckx and Chabrat started for Europe; and the Bishop being compelled to take charge of many of their congregations during their long absence, as he had previously done during the first journey of M. Nerinckx, could not find time to leave Kentucky in the course of this year. His time was incessantly employed in discharging the duties of an ordinary missionary.

When Bishop David was preparing for his discussion with the Presbyterian preacher Hall, early in the following year, Bishop Flaget ordered public prayers to be offered up in the cathedral congregation, to obtain victory for the truth; and also as some reparation for the blasphemies, which would no doubt be uttered by the preacher against holy persons and things, especially against the Blessed Sacrament.‡

Tennessee was a portion of his Diocese, which he had never as yet been able to visit. As there were but few Catholics therein, he had delayed visiting them, until other and more pressing calls would be met. F.

* Journal, 1819. † *Ibid*, 1829.

‡ *Ibid.*, January, 1821.

Badin had already made four missionary excursions to this State.*

In the beginning of May, 1821, the Bishop set out on this journey, and proceeded by the way of Breckinridge county, in order to take with him the Rev. Mr. Abell, who was there stationed. They said Mass in Litchfield on the 7th, and on the 8th they were in Bowlinggreen, where they found but five Catholics. They reached Nashville on the 10th, and put up with a M. Mont Brun, a Frenchman, who received them with tears in his eyes. On the following day, the first Mass that was ever offered up by a Bishop in Tennessee, was celebrated by our prelate, in the house of his entertainer. The Blood of the Lamb, now mystically shed on the holy altar, made a potent appeal in behalf of that infant mission.

The total number of Catholics in Nashville and vicinity did not exceed sixty; † and there were not, perhaps, half as many more in all the rest of the State. The prospects for soon establishing a congregation here, were certainly not very flattering. The Catholics were both few and poor. Yet the Bishop was not disheartened, and he resolved to make the experiment.

What was his joy, when he found that his proposal was most favorably entertained, even by the first Protestant citizens of the place! A liberal subscription was taken up, signed by Protestants as well as Catholics. A lot for a church, 70 by 100 feet, was offered by a Mr. Foster, grand master of the Masons. The

* This fact he states himself in a marginal note to Bishop Flaget's Report to the Pope in 1836.

† Journal, May 20.

Protestants of the city vied with one another in showing every polite attention to the Bishop and his companion. The late Hon. Felix Grundy, and his amiable family, are gratefully mentioned by the prelate in his Journal. He was even invited to take tea with a Presbyterian preacher named Campbell.

Many of the first families attended Mass; and a large and intelligent concourse were assembled every evening at the court house, to hear the sermons of the Rev. Mr. Abell. They listened with profound attention to his eloquent exposition and defence of the Catholic doctrine, on confession, on baptism, and on several other points little understood among Protestants.

The notorious Baptist revivalist—Vardiman—was in Nashville at the time; and he took the alarm. He even went so far as to give notice, that *he* would hold forth in the court house on an evening, when it was known that Mr. Abell was engaged to preach therein. The stratagem did not, however, succeed; his friends prevailed on him not to attempt preaching, as great public indignation, already partially aroused by his attempt, would be likely to break upon his head, in such a manner as to injure both himself and his sect.

The Rev. Mr. Abell also preached in Franklin, Tennessee, where there was one Irish Catholic family; and in Columbia, where he made a triumphant answer to a preacher, who had grossly attacked the Catholic Religion. A sermon he delivered in the latter place, on the real presence, made a great impression; and several Protestant lawyers, and others in the place, made him a present of money and a new suit of clothes, in consideration of the very handsome manner in which he had *dressed* the preacher, who appears to have been both ignorant and unpopular.*

On the journey, the Bishop served Mr. Abell's Mass, and they mutually went to confession to each other. They departed for home on the 27th of May.

M. Chabrat returned from Europe, July 18th, 1821, bringing with him M. Champomier for the seminary, some young novices for the religious life, and the bell, weighing about one thousand three hundred pounds, destined for the cathedral. M. Nerinckx returned in the following December, with ten novices for Loretto, some superb paintings for the cathedral, and a number of other articles for the convents and for the missions. His return was hailed with great joy by his congregations, and by the sisterhood which he had founded nine years previously. During the absence of these two missionaries, the Bishop frequently attended sick calls at a great distance; often as far as Louisville, where, for some time after the death of M. Hosten, there was no stationed pastor.

M. Champomier was ordained March 20th, 1823; and two months later he was sent to Vincennes. He was the first priest from the Diocese of Bardstown, who resided permanently in Indiana.

In August, 1823, the Bishop, after having visited with Mr. Abell all the missions lying in the lower part of Kentucky, went again to Vincennes, to settle every

* His name was McConico. While he was in the midst of his harangue against the Catholics, Mr. Abell arrived, and gave notice that he would answer him that evening. The sum presented him was two hundred dollars.

thing connected with the residence there of the newly appointed pastor. In going and returning, he visited Mt. Pleasant, where he confirmed thirty-four persons; also the town of Washington, and two French settlements on the Wabash. He returned in October, reporting that the people of Vincennes ardently desired to have amongst them an establishment of Sisters, to conduct a school.*

On the 12th of August, 1824, that devoted missionary, M. Nerinckx, died, in the midst of his apostolic labors, at St. Genevieve, Missouri; whither he had gone to establish branch houses of his sisterhood. He calmly breathed his last in the arms of the Rev. M. Dahmen, who had a few hours before administered to him all the last Sacraments. He contracted the fever which terminated in his death by exposure to the hot sun, while attending a small settlement of Catholics, about fifteen miles from St. Genevieve, who had not seen a priest for two years. He died like a good soldier, at his post; and he was no doubt "ripe for heaven." †

The Bishop was greatly affected by the intelligence. He delivered in the cathedral a glowing eulogy of the good missionary's life, and held him up as a model of every virtue. Some years previously, he had recorded the following estimate of the character of the deceased, in his Journal:

"If the good M. Nerinckx had done nothing else,

---

* Letter to Bishop David from Union county, Kentucky, October, 1823.

† From Bishop Flaget's Letter to Bishop England, published in the U. S. Catholic Miscellany, December 8, 1824.

but to establish the sisterhood of Loretto in this country, nothing more would have been necessary to assure him of salvation at the moment of death. But when we add to this the immense labors of his apostolate, it is then that we are led to bless Thee, O Lord, for raising up such men in these unhappy times, to serve as models for their cotemporaries." *

Those who are acquainted with the multiplied cares and constant solicitude attendant on the episcopal office, especially in this country, may form some idea how arduous is an administration, which embraces so many subjects, both spiritual and temporal; and which has to deal with so many persons of different, and often incompatible, dispositions and temperaments. When we add to all this, the extreme nervous susceptibility of Bishop Flaget, and that exquisite delicacy of feeling which made it most painful to him to wound, in the slightest degree, the feelings of others, even in the necessary discharge of duty; we will still be better able to appreciate the sufferings he must have endured in administering a Diocese, where every thing was to be formed, and where the materials for the work were often rude and unpolished. From what has been incidentally stated in previous Chapters, some opinion may be formed of the Bishop's administration. We propose now to furnish a few additional facts and incidents illustrative of the same subject.

The first care of his administration regarded his clergy. The wish nearest to his heart was, that they might be "models of the flock," and indued with all the virtues of the apostles. The good work which was

* Journal, 1815.

to extend to the farthest extremities of his Diocese, bringing "the peace of Christ" to the hearts of men, was to begin in the sanctuary itself. The people would be like their priests; and the latter should be holy, in order that the former might become good Christians.

To secure this desirable result, he enacted a decree in September, 1822, that the clergy of the Diocese should meet annually in spiritual retreat; at the close of which, conferences would be held on various subjects connected with the exercise of the holy ministry. These retreats were often conducted by Bishop David; and the Bishop gave great edification, by performing all the exercises at the head of his clergy. They produced the most salutary results; and the clergy went out from them, filled with renewed zeal, courage and energy.

The first synod, or conference, held in compliance with this decree, began at Bardstown, August 5, 1823. Several important subjects were discussed, and some regulations adopted for the uniform administration of the sacraments. Though promulgated to the clergy, these statutes were never, however, published.

At this conference, Bishop David gave an example of candor and humility too edifying to be omitted. Some misunderstanding having existed in regard to the person who was expected to prepare beforehand the matter for clerical deliberation, Bishop David thought he had been slighted. Being naturally of a hasty temperament, he had in consequence indulged in some expressions of impatience. The fault was very slight, and scarcely remarked by the clergy; but on reflection, the contrition of the humble prelate was so intense for the scandal he thought he had given, that nothing short of a public apology, made in the most ample terms before the assembled clergy, could put his conscience at rest! The scene was very touching, and it made a deep impression.

Bishop Flaget loved the laws of the Church, and sought to have them every where respected. Nothing gave him more pain, than to see any of those holy regulations of discipline neglected or violated by Catholics. He granted matrimonial dispensations with great reluctance and sorrow; and when circumstances sometimes compelled him to concede them, he did it with fear and trembling; ejaculating on such occasions: "Give me strength, O my God, to resist such violent and importunate demands:—happy, a thousand times happy, are those who have to give an account only of themselves!" *

He was much distressed at finding so many persons, who wished to marry before making their first communion; † and he most cordially hated mixed marriages, on account of the evils usually following them. "If there is so much disorder on the earth, it is because there is not, perhaps, one marriage in a thousand which is in accordance with the will, and, above all, the spirit of God." ‡

Upon those who married out of the Church, he usually imposed a public penance, more or less severe. Assisting a sick man who had married his first cousin without a dispensation, he required from him,—among other things laid down as a condition for absolution,—a promise to do public penance on his recovery, and to ask pardon publicly for the scandal he had given.

On occasion of an application for a dispensation in

---

* Journal, January 7, 1816. † *Ibid*—1815. ‡ *Ibid.*

this same degree of kindred, he breathed the following prayer, which came warm from his heart: "Vouchsafe, O my God, to enlighten me, that I may do nothing to weaken the discipline of the Church: my only desire is, to be a conscientious depository of faith and discipline, in order to be found after my death among the faithful servants." * This application troubled him so far, as to make him sick. †

Called to visit a sick drunkard, he induced him: 1. To beg pardon for his excesses; 2. To promise to do public penance on recovery; 3. To permit him (the Bishop) publicly to beg pardon, in his name, of the congregation which he had scandalized; 4. To pay his salary, which he had neglected; and 5. To be reconciled to his wife, whom he had ill-treated. ‡

He admired greatly the simple, solemn, and impressive music of the Gregorian chant; and feared lest it might not be sufficiently appreciated after his death: "After the death of the two Bishops, it is to be feared that English and worldly airs will take the place of the the grave Gregorian chant." §

His sternness and severity were only occasional; the habitual feature in his administration, as in his character, was the greatest mildness, sweetness, and charity to all persons, no matter how humble or disagreeable. He strove earnestly, with the apostle, to make himself "all to all, to win all to Christ."

He had a happy tact for spiritual direction, and could give an advice disagreeable to nature in the most pleasant manner imaginable. The following incident, which

* Journal, January 22, 1816. † *Ibid.*
‡ *Ibid*—March 1, 1816. § *Ibid*—March 1825.

he often related, may serve as an instance of this trait of character:

Among his penitents was a very pious and discreet lady, who aspired to high perfection. She found the holy prelate too mild and indulgent, and often begged him to impose on her heavier penances. She frequently addressed him in these words: "Father, try me!" The Bishop said nothing; but some time afterwards, being in need of a suitable veil for the chalice, he purchased the silk, and requested the lady to make it up according to his directions. She joyfully undertook to perform this service, and in a few days brought him the veil prepared in the very best style. She expected a compliment for her diligence and skill in needle-work; but what was her surprise when she saw the prelate receive the article with coldness, and even an air of suspicion! After having carefully examined and measured the cloth, he turned to her, and coolly asked: "Madam! is this all? I purchased such an amount of silk; is it all here?" Her face reddened in an instant, and she exclaimed, in evident passion: "Do you take me for a thief?" The prelate hereupon laughed outright; and, with an arch expression of graceful sweetness, rejoined, imitating her tone: "Father! do try me!" The lady immediately understood the rebuke; and she no doubt derived profit from the severe trial, which proved to her conclusively that she had not as yet attained to perfection.

We may as well relate here another anecdote, which will show that the prelate had frequently need of both gravity and patience in his administration:

An old lady, over whom more than sixty summers

had passed, once applied to him for advice in a matter of grave importance. She had received a proposal of marriage, and she wished to know how she should act on an occasion so critical! Having listened patiently to her case, the Bishop promptly advised her to reject the offer, and to spend her remaining days in preparation for death, which could not be far distant. He entered into an elaborate argument to convince her of the soundness of his advice; and as she heard him with seeming attention and interest, he entertained hopes that he had succeeded. At the close of his discourse, the aged lady rose abruptly from her seat, and turning to him, replied rather sharply: "If such be your advice, I shall not follow it!" She hastily withdrew, leaving the prelate in a curious state of suspense between laughter and annoyance at her strange behavior. She married in effect; but early in the morning after her espousals, she was astonished to find that her husband had escaped with one of the finest horses in her stable! He and the steed were never heard of afterwards; and the good lady had abundant leisure to be convinced that the Bishop had given her good advice.*

He was often eminently successful in healing divisions and reconciling inveterate enmities. His patience and sweetness on these trying occasions won the hearts of the litigants, and they placed themselves entirely in his hands, to be moulded like wax. We will present one or two examples of this.

In 1817, he went to Scott county, chiefly to settle a long-standing dispute and enmity between two of the

* This anecdote was related by the prelate himself, in his own happy manner, which we regret we cannot better imitate.

principal heads of families in the congregation; which had been much disedified and agitated by this unseemly quarrel. On arriving, he and Father Badin were engaged for two whole weeks in examining facts and papers on both sides, without coming to any satisfactory result. The disputants seemed farther than ever from an accommodation. At last, one of them remarked, with some bitterness of tone, that "He wished he had burned all his papers, and never brought up the matter for adjudication."

The Bishop seized eagerly on the hint, and at once earnestly exhorted them both to burn their papers, and to forget the past. They could not resist his touching appeal, uttered with so much fatherly feeling; they immediately promised to act on the advice. The next morning, the Bishop said Mass in the house of one of these men, the other being present. One of them was placed to the right, and the other to the left of the altar; and before the communion, the Bishop turned round and addressed them one of his most fervid exhortations. After Mass, the papers were solemnly burned; the two enemies shook hands; and the feud was terminated,—much to the joy and edification of all present, many of whom could not restrain their tears.*

In 1823, another angry discussion arose in the same congregation, in regard to the management of the church land and property. The Bishop visited the place, accompanied by M. Chabrat. At first, he was insulted by different persons, who wrote him impertinent letters. But by mildness, combined with firm-

* Journal, March 7, 1817.

ness, he soon overcame every obstacle; the whole congregation consented to the arrangement, settled by writings, by which the Bishop was recognized as the *sole* manager of the property, with the right to appoint an agent. Some persons who had threatened to demand back the money they had subscribed for the church and land, burned their papers, and agreed to the adjustment.*

It may be remarked here, *en passant*, that this congregation, once the most flourishing in the Diocese in point of numbers and wealth, has since, by emigration to other parts of the State and to Missouri, so far dwindled down, that it is now one of the smallest. God did not bless the spirit of dissension which had in early times been there so often exhibited.

A similar difficulty, which was, however, soon suppressed, manifested itself about the same time in the congregation of Holy Cross,—the oldest in the State. Here a small, but clamorous portion of the congregation made the absurd demand on the Bishop, that the people should be permitted to elect an overseer for the farm, and that the latter should be empowered to nominate the pastor! The Bishop did not yield to indignation; but by mildly stating the absurdities of the suggestion, the disaffected were won over; and peace again reigned in the congregation.

For the management of temporalities, the Bishop adopted the plan of appointing himself certain pious and respectable members of each congregation to act as trustees; or, as was oftener the case, of sanctioning the appointment of persons selected for this office by

* Journal, February 1823.

the local pastors. These trustees had no control over their clergyman; but they were expected to relieve him of the disagreeable office of asking for his own support, and of all anxiety about temporal affairs.

The church property was deeded to the Bishop, in trust, for the use and benefit of each particular congregation; and subsequently a charter of incorporation was obtained from the Legislature, allowing the Bishop to transmit such trust property, and also real estate owned by himself in fee simple, to his successors in office.*

As was stated in the previous Chapter, Bishop Flaget, as early as December, 1819, had begun a correspondence with Bishop Dubourg on the subject of new episcopal sees at Cincinnati, Detroit, and Vincennes. The only result of this correspondence was the appointment of Father Fenwick to Cincinnati. The chief difficulty consisted in finding suitable candidates. The subject was renewed in 1822. In July of this year, the Bishop of Bardstown received a letter from Bishop Dubourg, who "was in great humor to make new Bishops;" † proposing one for St. Louis, one for Vincennes, and another for Florida. This prelate paid Bishop Flaget a visit in Kentucky during the following September; and they conferred together at length on the subject of the new bishoprics, and on other matters of importance. ‡

Shortly after the departure of his venerable friend, Bishop Flaget wrote to Rome, asking a Bishop for Detroit, and requesting the Holy Father to assign the missions of Illinois to Bishop Dubourg, and those of

* In 1842. † Journal—*Ibid.* ‡ *Ibid.*

Indiana to Bishop Fenwick, until permanent arrangements could be made for them. For reasons with which we are unacquainted, this application was unsuccessful. Rome acts slowly and warily, and only after a thorough knowledge of the *whole* merits of the case. The see of Detroit was not erected until more than ten years afterwards, and that of Vincennes at a still later period. The Bishop was compelled to bear for many years longer a responsibility, the extent and amount of which, he felt, were too great and too much for any one man.

In January, 1823, our prelate was cheered by a visit from the new Bishop of Cincinnati, with whom he conferred on the state of the Ohio missions, already presenting a flattering aspect. In the April following, he had another visit from Bishop Dubourg, to meet whom he went to Louisville. Here the Bishop of New Orleans preached to a large audience in the court house, on the interpretation of scripture and confession ; much to the joy of the Catholics, and the edification of the Protestants. On his return to St. Louis, the prelate took with him additional sisters from Loretto, for the establishment lately erected at Bethlehem. The Rev. D. Mulholland was then pastor of the congregation in Louisville.

In December of this year (1823), the Bishop received the joyful intelligence, that Dr. Joseph Rosati had been named Coadjutor of the Bishop of New Orleans ; and that after the lapse of three years, the Bishop elect would be transferred to St. Louis, as the first Bishop of that city. The intelligence was subsequently confirmed. Dr. Rosati was consecrated Bishop of Tenagria and Coadjutor of Bishop Dubourg at New Orleans, March 25th, 1824; and he became Bishop of St. Louis in 1827.

From the Bishop's correspondence with Dr. Dubourg we gather that it was question of proposing the erection of a new see at Pittsburgh, as early as 1825. On this subject the Bishop of New Orleans writes as follows:

"Should you judge it opportune to demand the erection of a see at Pittsburgh, embracing the territory bordering on the Alleghany (Western Pennsylvania) and a portion of Virginia, I will unite with you:—but 1st. You should define very distinctly the boundaries of the new Diocese; 2dly. The Archbishop and the Bishop of Philadelphia, who are both interested, should be consulted, and should unite in the petition; 3dly. I would propose the Prince Gallitzin as first on the list, and Mr. Maguire as second. I think the first place due to the former, in consequence of his long and useful services, and for the good he has effected in those quarters; and because he has already a large establishment which would be very useful to the new bishopric." *

We do not learn whether the application was actually made to Rome at this time; but we gather from a previous letter of Bishop Dubourg, that he had before petitioned the Holy See to have Dr. Gallitzin appointed a titular Bishop (*in partibus*), as a mark of the estimation in which the Holy See held his distinguished services and great sacrifices in the cause of Religion.†

* Letter dated New Orleans, November 28. 1825.

† Latin letter to Rome, without date, written about the year 1822.

He had also proposed the same eminent ecclesiastic as the first Bishop of Detroit; though in the second place on the list, Father Grassi having been the first.*

While on this subject of new bishoprics, we will mention a few other facts, in which we feel the more free, as the parties concerned are all now dead; and, we trust, gone to their eternal reward.

The Bishops of Bardstown and New Orleans, the only prelates in the West and South until 1822, took a conspicuous part in arranging the preliminaries for the erection of new sees and the appointment of new Bishops, not only for this portion of the Union, but also for the Eastern States. Though the latter prelate was, it would appear, a man of superior talents to, and equal address with, the former, yet he always greatly deferred to his judgment, illumined as he knew it to be, by his great sanctity of life and confirmed spirit of prayer.

As early as 1819, a correspondence was opened between the two Bishops on the establishment of an archbishopric in the West, consequent upon the erection of Cincinnati into a see. Bishop Dubourg proposed that the new archiepiscopal see should be located either at Bardstown or St. Louis.†

In the Latin Letter to Rome, above quoted, he strongly and most energetically urged upon the Holy See the appointment of such persons only, for Bishops in the United States, as were already fully acquainted with our missions, and as would be properly recommended by the American prelates. For the new Diocese of St. Louis, he proposed M. Bruté as the first, and M.

* Same Letter.

† October 21, 1819.

Rosati as the second on the list; and he suggested that the new Diocese should embrace Missouri, Illinois, and the portion of Arkansas north of the river bearing the same name.

Not being in possession of the Letters written *to* Bishop Dubourg by our prelate, we are not prepared to say how far the latter concurred in these recommendations; which were only partially adopted by the Holy See. He probably dissented, in part at least, from the suggestions of his venerable colleague.

Shortly after his consecration in Rome, Bishop Dubourg had applied to the Holy See to dissolve the connexion which bound his see to the province of Havana, and to make him a suffragan of Baltimore. But the application was unsuccessful;—Rome being very slow in changing existing arrangements.* He seems to have remained, and to have considered himself a suffragan of the Archbishop of Havana, so long as he continued in America. As late as the spring of 1826,—a very short time before his final departure,—he wrote to Bishop Flaget, expressing some surprise that he had not been consulted in regard to the erection of the new See of Mobile; but he deemed the probable reason of the omission to have been, that he belonged to the province of Havana. He, however, cordially approved the appointment of Dr. Portier; who was consecrated Nov. 5, 1826.

Bishop Flaget exerted a strong influence in having the Rev. B. J. Fenwick, his favorite pupil at Georgetown, appointed to the see of Boston, and Dr. Dubois

---

* Letter from Europe, written in February or March, 1816—*sup. cit.*

to that of New York.* Bishop Dubourg dissented from him in opinion on these nominations. He had recommended Father Fenwick for New York, where he thought he was much more needed, and might do far more good than in Boston. Even after the appointment of this ecclesiastic to Boston had been made known, he asked Bishop Flaget to unite with him in an earnest petition to Rome, to have the new Bishop transferred to New York; suggesting also, that for a time Boston might still be administered by him, until a suitable Bishop could be chosen for that city. He doubted whether M. Dubois, so long accustomed to colleges, would suit for New York; which required, he thought, an American Bishop, or one whose native tongue was English.†

In May, 1826, Bishop Dubourg left his Diocese, and

---

* This is still farther confirmed by the fact, that Archbishop Marechal addressed to him a letter of fraternal complaint, that he had deprived the archdiocese of Baltimore of the services of two clergymen so distinguished as Drs. Fenwick and Dubois. In his answer to the Archbishop, our prelate urges the necessity of the case, and the general good of the Church. In the same letter, he opposes the nomination of Dr. Chabrat to the See of Vincennes, on the ground that he could not then dispense with his valuable services. He concludes his letter to the Archbishop in this amiable way:

"This is assuredly a long letter, well worthy a sexagenarian. I have sought in it to explain my thoughts, and by no means to give pain. Therefore, should there be in it the least thing calculated to wound your delicacy, I disapprove of it; for no one in the world has for you more sincere and more true sentiments of esteem, respect, and affection, than your all-devoted servant and brother," &c.

This extract, and the substance of the letter, were furnished by the Archbishop of Baltimore.

† Letter, November 5, 1825.

went to Europe on ecclesiastical business.* He never returned; but died Archbishop of Besançon in 1833. His eminent talents, his holiness of life, and his long services on the American missions, had richly entitled him to this promotion. He was one of the most brilliant ornaments of our hierarchy.

After his departure, his Coadjutor, Bishop Rosati, administered the Diocese of New Orleans, until the appointment of another Bishop for that city. The Bulls, appointing him Bishop of St. Louis, and administrator of New Orleans, dated July 14, reached him November 4, 1826.

Bishop Flaget had already written to Rome, asking the translation of Dr. Rosati to St. Louis, and the nomination of the Rev. Leo de Nekere, as successor to Bishop Dubourg at New Orleans. Of the appointment and consecration of the latter, we will speak more appropriately in the next Chapter.

We may as well mention here, that Bishop Flaget not only felt a lively interest in the welfare of Religion throughout the United States, but also took an active part in promoting it by his influence, which was considerable, both at home and with the Holy See. Thus we find that he wrote several Letters to Rome on the Hogan case, in which he fully stated his opinion, and advised prompt, but prudent action, to put an end to the scandal.

We find also, that his solicitude extended occasion-

---

† He reached St. Louis on the eve of Ascension day, May 3, 1826. On the following day he preached; and immediately after Mass went to the steamboat,—to which he would permit no one to accompany him,—on his way to France.

ally beyond the bounds of the Union. Thus in 1824, the Propaganda consulted him with regard to a difference which had existed for some time between the Sulpicians of Canada and the Bishop of Quebec.

We will close this Chapter by mentioning an incident belonging to the period of which we are writing; and which is sufficiently striking, as tending to show that God not unfrequently draws goodout of evil. A man of fine address and insinuating manners, named *Inglesi*, had so far won on the confidence of Bishop Dubourg, as to be sent to Europe by him, with full authority to solicit contributions for his Diocese in his name. This man—a clergyman—proved subsequently how utterly unworthy he was of the trust reposed in him; but while at Lyons in 1822, he suggested the formation of a Society for the aid of foreign missions, and he plead the cause with so much earnestness and eloquence, that soon afterwards the foundations were laid of that famous Association for the Propagation of the Faith, which has since done so much for the advancement of Religion. The proceeds of the first year's collection,—not very large,—were divided between China, and the Bishops of New Orleans and Bardstown. The portion which was assigned to the last named prelate was six thousand eight hundred and ninety-three francs, or about one thousand three hundred dollars. This first distribution took place in 1823.*

* These facts are derived from the correspondence between Bishops Flaget and Dubourg.

CHAPTER XI.

THE JUBILEE OF 1825-7—THE CHOLERA—NEW COADJUTOR.

1826—1834.

Why this Jubilee was solemn—Conferences—Discomfiture of Sneed—Effects of Jubilee—Bishop Flaget consecrates Archbish- Whitfield, and goes to the first Provincial Council—His meeting with Bishop England—Charles Carroll of Carrolton—The Bishop in Court—His speech on the occasion—Offers his resignation—Consecration of Bishop Kenrick—Bishop England in Kentucky—Bishop Flaget's eloquence—He is sad—How consoled—Arrival of the Jesuits—Meets Bishop Rosati at Vincennes—Goes to St. Louis—His resignation accepted—Excitement in Kentucky—He is reinstated—The Cholera—His devotedness—He is seized with the malady—His new Coadjutor consecrated—Consecration of Bishops Purcell, Resé, Bruté, Miles, and De Neckere—Anecdote of Bishop England.

Two circumstances rendered the Jubilee of 1825–7 peculiarly impressive and solemn throughout the world; and one made it especially so in the Diocese of Bardstown. Besides being proclaimed at the stated time,—the close of the first quarter of this century,—it was commemorative of the accession of Leo XII. to the pontifical throne; and it had, for this Diocese, the additional attraction of novelty. It was the first occasion on which the Catholics of the West were ever called upon to unite with their brethren throughout Christendom in solemn thanksgiving and prayer, and in offering a holy violence to the throne of grace : while, by the Keys of St. Peter, in the hands of his successor, the treasures of the Church were freely opened to all, and the fountains of grace were flowing abundantly into the hearts of the fervent and the repentant. This season of benediction marked an epoch in the history of the flock committed to the charge of Bishop Flaget; and its happy results filled the heart of the holy prelate with joy and consolation.

The Holy See allowed the Bishop two years for promulgating the Jubilee in the various portions of his extensive Diocese; while six months were allotted to each congregation for gaining the Indulgence.

The good work began in the sanctuary. The priests who were to announce the blessings of the Jubilee were themselves first to receive its fruits in their own hearts; that being themselves inflamed with divine charity, they might enkindle every where that "fire which Christ came to cast on earth." The exercises for the clergy began at Bardstown on the 1st of September, 1826; and they closed on the 8th,—the feast of the Nativity of the Blessed Virgin.

On the following Sunday, September 10, the Jubilee was promulgated in the cathedral. During the week the attendance was very large, embracing Protestants as well as Catholics. Besides the usual devotional exercises and sermons, a method of instruction was adopted,—new in Kentucky,—which awakened great attention, and produced the most happy results. This was the conference between two clergymen on doctrinal and moral subjects; one asking questions or making objections, and the other answering them. In these conferences, at Bardstown and throughout the Diocese, the Rev. F. P. Kenrick was generally the respondent. This zealous clergyman was taken ill, while preaching the Jubilee in Spencer county in October, 1826; and the exercises were in consequence interrupted for several months. His illness was grievous and lingering, and at one time it was thought to be dangerous; but God preserved him for greater labors.

Even if our limits permitted, it would not be necessary to give in detail the various edifying facts connected with the Jubilee in Kentucky. We will present only a few incidents, and some of the general results.

In Springfield, September, 1827, the missionaries were attacked, at the close of their conference, by the Presbyterian minister of the town,—the Rev. Mr. Sneed. He attempted to do away with the favorable impression made on the Protestant mind by their luminous expositions of Catholic doctrine; and he thought that, by a few remarks, he would easily succeed in demolishing Purgatory, and in proving that the Catholic Church is the great apostacy foreshadowed by St. Paul! His argument to sustain the latter position was singular, and we believe original:—

"St. Paul says 'the mystery of iniquity already worketh;' * but you know, my friends, that Protestantism,—in its present form and shape,—did not exist until many centuries after his time; *therefore*, he must have meant the Catholic Church, or 'popery,' by the 'mystery of iniquity'"! He added that those who believed in the doctrine of Purgatory leaned on a broken reed; and alleged the hackneyed argument about the tree

* II. Thessalonians, ii: 7.

falling, either to the north or to the south, and there lying.

Rev. Mr. Kenrick's reply was to the point, and most triumphant, even in the estimation of Protestants. He took up the preacher's admission with regard to the modern origin of Protestantism, deducing therefrom an unanswerable argument as to the divine character of Catholicity, and the confessedly human invention of Protestantism. He suggested, however, an important amendment to Mr. Sneed's modification,—"in its present form and shape,"—submitting to the audience, that the plural number would have been much more conformable to the truth. This opened a fine field for descanting on the numerous contradictions, the glaring inconsistencies, and the endless variations of the Protestant sects; proving conclusively to every impartial mind, that Protestantism is not, and cannot be the work of God. To the minister's argument from the falling of the tree, he happily rejoined, by reminding him, that a tree, instead of always falling directly to the ground, sometimes *lodges*,—according to the familiar parlance of the backwoodsmen, who formed the bulk of the audience,—and falls finally, in the direction in which it started, only after the interposing obstacles are removed.

The poor preacher was so thoroughly demolished, that on his attempting to rise again to reply, he was literally pulled down and prevented by some of his own party. This incident produced a great sensation at the time, and it was long remembered; hence we have thought it worth preserving.

Some other rencontres of the kind took place during

the preaching of the Jubilee, with similar results. Catholicity was every where in the ascendant, and many Protestants joined the Church. Yet some were rendered only the more obstinate by the manifest triumphs of the truth. The Bishop records in his Journal the saying of one among them,—a Presbyterian,—who answered the overwhelming arguments in favor of Catholicity with the horrible remark: "If an angel, descended from heaven, preached a doctrine similar to that of the Irish priest, I would reject him!" *

Almost all the Catholics of Kentucky approached the sacraments during this season of grace. The oldest sinners were converted. Great numbers of children were prepared for their first communion and for confirmation. The number confirmed was one thousand two hundred and sixteen; while more than six thousand approached the holy table. The heart of the good Bishop was rejoiced. He says:

"With what pleasure have I entered on this apostolic career! And if the consolations I at present feel go on increasing, they will afford me happiness enough for this world. I will say, with the greatest pleasure, 'Now wilt Thou, O Lord, dismiss Thy servant in peace'! at the end of the Jubilee,—provided my debts will have been liquidated at that time." †

Early in 1827, (January 19,) he had the happiness to receive a visit from Bishop Rosati, who ten years before had been an inmate of his seminary at St. Thomas'. His respected guest remained with him for nearly two weeks; which were devoted to the interchange of infor-

* Journal, September, 1827.

† Letter to M. Badin, dated September 29, 1826.

mation and advice in reference to the condition of Religion in their respective Dioceses. So deeply was Bishop Rosati impressed with the sanctity of his revered friend, that on taking his leave he fell on his knees, and refused to arise until he would receive a blessing. Bishop Flaget, taken by surprise, on the impulse of the moment imitated the example of the other prelate; and the scene closed with a mutual benediction imparted to each other, and a parting embrace.* To appreciate fully this incident, one must be acquainted fully with the faith, the humility, and the child-like simplicity and candor of these distinguished prelates.

In January of the following year (1828), Bishop Flaget was invited to Baltimore, to consecrate Archbishop Whitfield. Not viewing this invitation as a mere honor or compliment, but as a call made on him to discharge the highest function of the episcopal office, he at first hesitated whether he would accept. Though his humility persuaded him that he was not worthy to fulfil, so sublime an office, yet, upon reflection, he did not feel at liberty to decline. He accordingly set out for Baltimore, accompanied by the Rev. M. Evremond Harissart; who, with his friend M. Fouché, had arrived from France, nearly five years previously.

The consecration was set for the day of Pentecost; and on Ascension day Bishop Flaget entered into a retreat with the Archbishop elect; in order to purify his heart, and elevate his soul to God, in preparation for the solemn function he was about to perform. He was consoled by the thought, that, eighteen hundred years before, the Apostles were engaged with the Blessed Vir-

* Journal—*ib.*

gin in a similar retreat, in order that they "might be clothed with strength from on high."

Pentecost dawned; and with a most lively faith, and eyes overflowing with devotion, he went to perform the solemn ceremony which was to give a new Archbishop to the Catholic Church in America. "This Sunday of Pentecost," he says, "was the most grand, the most august, the most honorable day, that ever shone on the Bishop of Bardstown." *

His numerous friends in Baltimore welcomed most cordially the venerable prelate; whose joy on the occasion was, however, diminished by the reflection, that so many of his old acquaintances had descended to the tomb since his last visit. Bishop David was still an object of constant inquiry. The arrival of the Rev. Mr Abell from France, where he had passed the last two years, gave him great additional satisfaction.

He made an excursion to Washington, where he visited the Jesuits, the sisters of the Visitation, and Mrs. Mattingly, who had been recently cured by the prayers of Prince Hohenlohe. He also called on the President of the U. States, on Mr. Clay, and other distinguished personages, including Madame Iturbide, ex-Empress of Mexico; by all of whom he was most politely received.

At Frederick, he met his old friend M. Bruté; and at Emittsburgh he was received with open arms by many old friends. He passed several days here most pleasantly. While visiting St. Joseph's, the Mother house of the Sisters of Charity, he records the to him consoling remark, that, in many respects, his own sisterhood at Nazareth would not suffer by comparison with this renowned establishment.

* Journal—*ib.* † *Ibid.*

He returned to Baltimore; where he informs us, his friends were so very kind and hospitable as to give him some uneasiness of conscience on his own account, and in consequence of the trouble to which they so cheerfully put themselves for his sake. "He felt like Dives, passing from one feast to another." * He celebrated pontifically on several occasions, and Rev. Mr. Abell preached.

At length, he tore himself away from his friends in Baltimore, and set out for Bardstown, with some novices for Nazareth.

Soon afterwards he was called to Union county, in the lower part of the State, on a most disagreeable piece of business. He was summoned to appear in Court, to give evidence in a lawsuit instituted by a Mr. Alvey against the Rev. M. Chabrat. He had been twice before summoned to appear in the same cause, but had been unable to attend. The case regarded a moneyed transaction, of which the Bishop had not the slightest knowledge or recollection.

On his arrival at Morganfield, he was treated with every consideration by the lawyers and the court, and was offered a seat within the bar. The first question put to him was: "Why did you not obey the two previous summons of the Court?" The Bishop rose, and bowing to the judge, replied with calmness and dignity, in substance as follows:

He owed it to the dignity of his own office and to his respect for the Court before which he stood, to declare, that he loved the country and respected its laws, to be faithful to which was his pleasure as well as his

* *Ibid.*

duty: that he had, of his own proper will and choice, adopted this government, and was therefore more of an American than those who surrounded him; whose birth in the country was only the result of accident, while he had, on the contrary, after mature deliberation and reflection on the various governments of the earth, freely sworn allegiance to this Republic at the ripe age of thirty-four years, renouncing thereby the government under which he was born, and electing to live and die as a citizen of this. Being placed at the head of a religious society, he had always considered it a duty to preach submission to the laws, and to-day he wished to teach this obedience by example.

Of the first summons, he had been informed but two days before the sitting of the Court, and he could not therefore have arrived in time, even had he made the attempt. When the second was made known to him, he was on the eve of a journey to Baltimore on official duty, which he could not neglect or postpone. Now he appeared, ready to obey the Court and to oblige the person who had asked his evidence; and he would not betray his conscience for the whole world. This person had given a striking proof of confidence in his veracity; since he knew well that his (the Bishop's) evidence could not prove useful to his own cause, without damaging that of his friend M. Chabrat.

After a few questions as to his knowledge of the transaction in question, the Court adjourned; and the Bishop's farther attendance was dispensed with,—the assurance being given him, that his deposition would be taken, in the event that his evidence would be again required. He was treated by all with the greatest deference, and his dignified deportment produced a general and profound sensation.*

He visited several congregations on his return to Bardstown; and he gave the Jubilee in Grayson and Hardin counties, assisted by the Rev. Mr. Kenrick and other clergymen. The exercises were every where attended with the usual consoling success.

In June 1829, the Bishop started on his fifth visitation to Vincennes and Indiana. He was accompanied in this journey by the Rev. Mr. Abell, whom he installed pastor of Louisville on the way. In New Albany, he found only five Catholic families, and eleven more in the vicinity,—at the knobs. He offered up the holy sacrifice in a private house at New Albany,—the first time, we believe, that Mass was ever celebrated there,—and again in a log chapel at the knobs. The Jubilee was promulgated throughout Indiana on this visitation.

At Mt. Pleasant and in the neighborhood, there were about forty Catholic families. At the Jubilee, there were seventy communicants, and thirty-one persons were confirmed. At Black-Oak-Ridge, forty-seven were confirmed.

At Vincennes, the exercises continued for eight days, the Bishop preaching daily. The fruits were very abundant. Three hundred approached the holy table, and ninety-two were confirmed. Rev. Mr. Abell preached with success at Washington. Every where he had to revalidate marriages, which were null. On leaving, the people assembled in great numbers at his lodgings, and received his benediction kneeling. Many

* This account is condensed from the Journal.

accompanied him several miles of his journey, on horseback. He stopped at Henderson, Kentucky, and there offered up the holy sacrifice.

In September of this year (1829), Bishop Rosati called to take him to the first Provincial Council of Baltimore. At Cincinnati, they waited on Bishop Fenwick; and the three prelates proceeded in company to Baltimore; passing through Zanesville, Wheeling, Frederick, and Washington.

Bishop Flaget was much affected at once more seeing his old friends, and still more so, on meeting his brother Bishops, now assembled for the first time.

On being introduced to Bishop England, he kissed his right hand, saying: "Allow me to kiss the hand which has *written* so many fine things." The Bishop of Charleston promptly returned the salutation, observing: "Permit me to kiss the hands, which have *done* so much good."

He celebrated pontifically at the second session of the Council; he was much struck with the majesty of the ceremonial; and he could but contrast these happy days with that early period in the infancy of the Church in America,—thirty-seven years before,—when he was first sent out to Vincennes. His heart rejoiced at this happy commencement of ecclesiastical legislation in the province; which was owing to the sound judgment and practical zeal of Archbishop Whitfield, who acted, we believe, on the suggestion of Bishop England.

At the close of the Council, the Bishops visited in a body the venerable CHARLES CARROLL OF CARROLTON, then ninety-two years of age. The estimable survivor of that intrepid band of patriots, who signed the Declaration of Independence, was much affected at this delicate and well-deserved compliment. He received the prelates with his accustomed courtesy and grace; and he was much rejoiced, when now so near the close of his mortal career, to see that the Church which he loved was visibly keeping pace with the rapid improvement of the country.

It would appear that, about this time, Bishop Flaget entertained serious thoughts of resigning the heavy charge which he had now borne for nearly twenty years. That he wrote to Rome, offering his resignation, and proposing an ecclesiastic of high standing as his successor, will appear from the following incident related in his Journal.

On the 1st of May, 1830, at nine o'clock in the evening, he received a package containing the Bulls of the Rev. F. P. Kenrick. Knowing that this clergyman had been proposed by the late Council to the Holy See for the Coadjutorship of Philadelphia, he still cherished hopes that the documents contained in the unopened parcel might nominate him to the see of Bardstown. "With his heart bleeding," he knelt down and breathed a fervent prayer, committing the affair to God, and resigning himself to His holy will.

His worst fears were realized:—the nomination was for Philadelphia! A deep gloom now came over him; he tried to sleep, but repose fled from his pillow. It was only on the next evening after Vespers,—the vigil of the feast celebrating the invention of the Holy Cross,—that he could find courage to deliver the documents to the Bishop elect. This he did, with the significant remark: "Behold here the certificate of the Cross you will have to carry!" *

Bishop Kenrick was consecrated by Bishop Flaget on the 6th of June, in the cathedral of Bardstown. There were four other prelates present: Bishops Conwell, David, England, and Fenwick. The Bishop of Charleston preached the consecration sermon, with his usual ability and eloquence. Bishop Flaget was much cheered by the presence of this eminent prelate, who remained with him some weeks, and visited most of his institutions. He preached every where with great success.

After preaching at laying the corner-stone of the new church, and for an hour and a half in the Presbyterian meeting house, in Louisville, Bishop England was taken ill; and he was not able to fill the appointments, which had been made for him in Shelbyville, Frankfort, and Lexington. His place was supplied by the Rev. Mr. Elder; and also by Bishop Flaget, who preached more than once to the large audiences assembled to hear Bishop England; while he thought "nobody understood a word of what he said!" †

We may here remark, that the Bishop always placed a much lower estimate on his sermons than any one else. Though his pronunciation of the English was far from being perfect, yet he was endowed with the gift of much natural eloquence. He possessed, in a high degree, that *unction*, which sweetly moves the heart. No one could listen to his earnest appeals and soul-

* Journal—*ibid.*

† This not very consoling reflection, prompted by his humility, is duly recorded in his Journal, *in loco*.

stirring exhortations, without being deeply moved. Few could portray more effectually the beauties of virtue, and the winning sweetness of divine love: few could make a more profound or lasting impression on the hearts of men.

Naturally of a very tender heart and of an exquisite nervous sensibility, he suffered much from disappointments and afflictions; and notwithstanding his habitual faith and conformity to the divine will, he occasionally was plunged into profound melancholy. God thus tries his favored servants; and in this light he accepted all his sufferings.

Shortly after the departure of the Bishops, he was visited by one of these fits of sadness. He felt that his strength was fast failing him, and that he was no longer able to bear the awful burden which had so long rested on his shoulders. "Everybody proclaims me the most happy Bishop of the United States," he says, "on account of the number of my churches and institutions; but God visits me with cross after cross." *

He now wrote again to Rome, imploring the Holy Father to accept his resignation, and appoint some one more worthy and younger to the see of Bardstown.†

In the midst of the trials with which Providence now permitted him to be buffeted, he entered more and more deeply into his own heart; and humbling himself before God, he thought that whatever went amiss in his Diocese was fairly traceable to his own inability, negligence, and sinfulness. The more he reflected on the subject, and the more he consulted with his friends concerning his administration, the more settled became

* Journal, November, 1830. † *Ibid.*

his conviction, that he had run his episcopal career; and that, after twenty years of severe labor as Bishop, God would allow him to return once more to his beloved solitude, there to prepare himself for "a holy and happy death."

But the ways of divine Providence are not to be estimated by any human standard, no matter how elevated. Bishop Flaget had barely reached the middle of his career; twenty years more were to roll over his head as Bishop in the Diocese over which he had been placed.

Several things cheered him amid his afflictions. His truly Catholic heart sympathized in the joys, as well as in the sorrows of the Church in other Dioceses. He was delighted to learn that the firm and mild, yet vigorous administration of Bishop Kenrick bade fair to restore peace and order to the church of Philadelphia, so long distracted by schism.* The intelligence of Father Badin's successful labors among the Indians of the North-west, with whom he had been a missionary for some years, brought likewise much solace to his heart. The conversion of the Indians had always been a favorite object of his aspirations and prayers.

Another occurrence, more immediately affecting his own Diocese, gave him much satisfaction:—the arrival, in the month of June, 1831, of the Jesuit Fathers Chazelle, Petit, and Ladaviere. They came from the province of Lyons, France; and they had been sent out by their superior, to examine the ground, with a view to the establishment of a Jesuit college in Kentucky. The Bishop had always been much attached to

* Journal, 1831.

the order of St. Ignatius Loyola; and he had written to his brother in France, to say how much he would be gratified to have a colony of the society in his Diocese. The brother had communicated the letter to the superior at Lyons, and the result was the journey of the Fathers just named.

Negotiations were opened to give them charge of St. Joseph's college, but these led to no satisfactory result. The Rev. William Byrne, the founder and president of St. Mary's college, after having at first opposed the establishment of the order in Kentucky with his characteristic energy, now, on more mature reflection, suddenly changed his mind, and made a free offer of his institution to the Jesuit Fathers. With a generosity which did him honor, he resigned every thing into their hands, and even offered to assist them, until they would be able to conduct the college entirely with their own members. The offer was gratefully accepted; and after the arrangement had been ratified at Lyons, the Jesuits were regularly established in the Diocese. A whole year was consumed in these negotiations.*

In 1832, the distinguished and eloquent Father Kenny, an Irish Jesuit, arrived in the Diocese. The Bishop prevailed on him to preach a retreat to his clergy. The impression made by the discourses of this truly eloquent man of God was deep and lasting. The Bishop was much consoled, while engaged in this retreat at the head of his clergy. At its close, he solemnly promulgated the Decrees of the first Provincial Council of Baltimore; and he insisted particularly on the observance of certain points of discipline, which,

* Journal, 1831-2.

amidst the difficulties and privations of the missionaries, had been hitherto neglected.

Notwithstanding his repeated efforts, in conjunction with Bishop Dubourg, to have Vincennes erected into an episcopal see, Indiana was still without a Bishop; and the solicitude of its missions, now daily increasing in importance, still devolved on himself alone. To terminate, if possible, this state of things, he arranged a meeting at Vincennes with Bishop Rosati,—to take place in the fall of this year—1832.

While awaiting the time set for his journey to Vincennes, he visited the upper portion of his Diocese. In the midst of his labors, he understood that the cholera had broken out with great fury at Louisville. This dreadful scourge, then making its appearance for the first time in the West, was much more formidable than it became afterwards, when the minds of men grew accustomed to its ravages. The Bishop immediately left every thing, and hastened to Louisville, to aid in assisting the sick and dying. Instead of yielding to fear, he rejoiced at the occasion thus presented by Providence for laying down his life in the holy cause of Religion and charity. He even persuaded himself, that his death at this time would result in benefit to the Church, by inaugurating a better administration for his Diocese.* But God did not demand the sacrifice, he would so willingly have offered up.

On his arrival in Louisville, he found the reverend pastor—Mr. Abell—busily engaged in his sacred functions on behalf of those seized with the disease. Three Sisters of Charity had also come from Nazareth, and

* Journal, 1832.

volunteered their services towards the afflicted; ready cheerfully to lay down their lives, for the love of the neighbor prompted by the love of God. In a few days the malady abated; and the Bishop returned to Bardstown.

Late in the fall, he set out for Vincennes, where he was welcomed by the Bishop of St. Louis. The two prelates, after mature deliberation, agreed to propose to the Holy See for the see of Vincennes, the learned and pious Dr. Bruté, of Emmittsburgh. They associated with his name, as usual, those of two others; one of whom,* in deference to the opinion of some other Bishops, they, in a subsequent letter to Rome, very strongly recommended for the same place.† The choice of the Sovereign Pontiff, as is well known, fell upon Dr. Bruté.

This matter settled, Bishop Flaget wished to visit the various congregations of Indiana, and then return home. But he at length yielded to the persuasions of Bishop Rosati, who represented that the season was too far advanced for such a visitation, and pressed him to pay a visit to St. Louis.

Fifteen years had elapsed since the prelate's last visit to this city; and what a change had come over it in that period! The holy Bishop could but wonder at the rapid improvement of the place; and his soul overflowed with joy at seeing the immense progress which Religion had made there, since the installment of Bishop

* As he is still living, we omit his name. He is a Jesuit, and an American.

† Journal—*Ibid.*

Dubourg. The sight of so many splendid religious establishments reared up in so short a time, filled him with admiration. He visited all his old congregations on both sides of the Mississippi; and was every where received with joy, and with every mark of attention and respect. At the Barrens, he found a colony of Sisters of Loretto from his own Diocese.*

While in St. Louis, he received a letter from Bishop David, containing intelligence both joyful and sad. The Holy See had accepted his resignation; and Bishop David had become Bishop of Bardstown, with Dr. Chabrat as his Coadjutor. But these changes had caused general dissatisfaction among both the clergy and laity of Kentucky. The former Coadjutor loudly protested against his unexpected promotion; and the whole Diocese was seized with grief at the apprehended loss of a Bishop so universally esteemed and loved.

In this emergency, the holy prelate persuaded Bishop Rosati to accompany him to Kentucky, in order to assist, with his counsel and influence, in allaying the storm which had arisen. On their arrival, in December, 1832, they found that the excitement had not been exaggerated. Bishop Flaget was overwhelmed with sorrow. After suitable deliberation, it was decided, in accordance with the advice of Dr. Rosati, that the two Bishops should unite in a petition to the Sovereign Pontiff, begging him to accept the resignation of Dr. David, and to dispose at will of Bishop Flaget and Dr. Chabrat.†

---

* Journal, *in locis.*

† Journal—*Ibid.* Another distinguished prelate was also consulted on this perplexing affair.

Towards the end of May, in the following year, the answer was received from Rome; Bishop David's resignation was accepted, and Bishop Flaget was reinstated. Nothing definite was said about Dr. Chabrat.* Our prelate was now in a worse condition than before, having no Coadjutor. This condition of affairs continued for more than a year.

From the Bishop's correspondence, we gather an occurrence worthy of record, which took place in 1833. Illinois was still under his jurisdiction; and its great northern city, since become an episcopal see, was fast growing in importance. In this year, Bishop Rosati, as Vicar General of the Bishop of Bardstown, sent the Rev. M. St. Cyr to Chicago. With the previous religious history of this city we are entirely unacquainted; at the period in question, it numbered already about one hundred Catholic families.

Bishop Flaget was now destined to pass through another severe ordeal. In the spring of 1833, the cholera broke out, in a very malignant form, at Bardstown and in the neighboring counties. The first persons attacked by the disease were in the family of Mr. John Roberts, a Protestant gentleman residing about eight miles from Bardstown. The cholera suddenly appeared here on Whitsun-Monday. Three servant men and a daughter of Mr. Roberts soon fell victims to the fatal malady. The whole neighborhood was seized with consternation; and no one would go near the house.

At the very first intelligence of the distress in which this unfortunate family was involved, two Sisters of

* Journal—*Ibid.*

Loretto flew to the succor of the afflicted; and they were soon after joined by two Sisters of Charity from Nazareth, accompanied by the Rev. Dr. Reynolds, the present distinguished Bishop of Charleston. These ministering angels of charity, totally regardless of self, devoted themselves day and night to the nursing of the sick and dying. One of them, Sister Benedicta of Loretto, died a few days later, of the disease here contracted.

Bishop Flaget himself lost no time in hastening to the house of pestilence. He remained there for several hours, and baptized a sick daughter of Mr. Roberts. He also administered the last sacraments to a dying servant, who was lying on the floor between two already dead of the disease. To hear his confession, he knelt down, the body of one of the deceased having been first removed to afford him sufficient space. He even wished to remain, in order to assist in burying the dead, whom the neighbors could not be induced to touch. It was only after the most urgent entreaties, and after he had received sufficient assurance that the deceased would be decently interred, that he could be induced to leave the spot. Dr. Reynolds had already persuaded the family to leave their house, and take refuge nearer Bardstown.*

The malady soon after appeared in and about Bardstown, where many fell victims to its virulence. Several members of the family of the Hon. Jno. Rowan died. The Sisters of Charity and the Clergy, with the Bishop

* These details we learn from Mr. J. Charles Gilbert, an eyewitness and an actor in the above scenes. He lived then at Loretto.

at their head, were always found by the bed-side of the dying. Sisters Joanna Lewis, Patricia Bamber, and Generose Buckman, of Nazareth, fell martyrs of their charity in serving the sick. Their names are worthy of special record; though their heroism was but the embodiment of that divine charity, which has, in all ages, been common in the Catholic Church.

The terrible epidemic extended to other places. At St. Mary's college, the Rev. William Byrne, after having assisted for death a dying negro woman, caught the disease himself, and died in a few hours, on the 6th of June. The Rev. Mr. Maguire, a Jesuit father, soon followed him to the tomb.

The Bishop had hitherto moved unterrified and unhurt, amidst the ruins which the pestilence had strewn in its path. The scourge had almost disappeared, and all were thanking God that *he* had escaped;—when he too was suddenly seized with the malady in a virulent form. For three days, there was a violent struggle between life and death; his physicians considered his case almost hopeless;—on the fourth, the crisis had passed, and his robust constitution, with the divine blessing, brought him safely through the ordeal. Convalescent, he almost regretted that the physicians had erred in their judgment.

"Alas!" he wrote, "I regret that their conjectures were not verified; for death would have delivered me from a burden, become now almost insupportable, in consequence of my advanced age and its attendant infirmities; and I have every reason to fear that it will be next to impossible for me ever to be better prepared than I was then for a passage so formidable in itself, and which will become a hundred times more so, when I shall have to render an account of an administration so long and so extensive as that with which I have been entrusted. But let the holy will of God be done, and not mine!" *

In a letter to his brother in France, written ten days later, he speaks of his late illness in the following gay and lively tone:

"For several weeks, I seemed to laugh at the pestilence, being almost constantly in the midst of those who were infected with it, speaking to them, consoling them, and rubbing their hands and feet, when circumstances required this service. In brief, I regarded myself as invulnerable. But the *lord cholera*, † whose march is guided by an omnipotent and invisible hand, laughed at my bravados; he struck to the right and to the left the victims which were marked out for him, waiting patiently for the day, when he could, all at his ease, lower my colors, and make me feel the entire weight of his formidable arm. He could not have chosen better the time for avenging himself of my boastings, and for making me know who he was and what he could do; for it was precisely when he appeared to have retired from the country, that he cast himself upon me, with uplifted arms, and struck me so rude a blow, from the very beginning, that all my friends, and even the physicians, believed me to be in a struggle with inevitable death.

"God be thanked; for several weeks the sight of many victims, who in seven or eight hours had been

---

* Letter in the *Annales*, dated December 5, 1833.

† *Le seigneur cholera.*

immolated by this terrible cholera, had suggested to me so many salutary thoughts on the vanity of the world, on the inutility of its goods, of its honors and its pleasures, that, already thoroughly converted on all these points, I had but to re-pass the history of my youth in the bitterness of my soul, and the numberless mistakes of a spiritual administration, which has lasted for nearly fifty years.*

"This retrospect was, without doubt, calculated to cast alarm into all the faculties of my soul, and to make me adopt the most expeditious and efficacious means to purify, the best I could, my poor heart, more weighed down by the burden of its iniquities, than by that of its seventy years completed. I had, then, recourse on the spot to my old Coadjutor, who has been my intimate friend for forty-five years, and my confessor for nearly thirty. With a soul filled with grief,† and a charity more than human, he heard me, he enlightened me, he consoled me; and, above all, he dispensed me from a thousand details, which would have been necessary for any other confessor less acquainted than himself with my conscience. Having then laid before me the most touching and the strongest motives to excite a lively and sincere sorrow for my sins, and an entire resignation to the sacrifice which God seemed to demand of me, he made me hear those words, so sweet and so consoling to a poor sinner struggling with death:—*Ego te absolvo*, &c. ‡

"From that moment I enjoyed a peace, which the

---

* Since he was ordained priest.

† *Navré de douleur*—a favorite expression of the Bishop.

‡ "I absolve thee," &c.

world could not impart, and which the *lord cholera himself* could not trouble. I left to my confessor the charge of administering to me the last sacraments, at the moment he might judge the most suitable. But a favorable crisis having occurred, at the end of three days I was no longer in a condition to require their reception." *

Many years of apostolic labor were yet in reserve for the holy prelate; he was to lay up still greater treasures in heaven, ere his earthly pilgrimage would be terminated. If trials and dangers prove mens' souls, we possess an index to his character, in the fearless devotedness with which he walked in the midst of the dreadful pestilence, and in the calm serenity, tempered by humility and contrition, with which he awaited his dissolution, when he believed that his last hour had come.

On his recovery, he continued to feel no little solicitude in regard to his future Coadjutor. The negotiations on the subject were long pending; Rome moved slowly and cautiously in a matter of so much importance. At length, on the feast of the Apostles SS. Peter and Paul,—June 29th, 1834,—the Bulls arrived, appointing Dr. Chabrat Bishop of Bolina, and Coadjutor of Bishop Flaget. The consecration took place on the 20th of July, in the cathedral of Bardstown; our venerable prelate being the Consecrator, and Bishop David and the Rev. R. P. Miles, O. P., being the assistants. Many of the clergy of the Diocese were present on this solemn occasion.

---

* Letter to brother, December 14, 1833. French Life—p. 68, *seqq.*

From this date to the time of his death, the mind of Bishop Flaget was less solicitous concerning matters of administration, the details of which he generally committed to his Coadjutor. He now breathed more freely, and became daily more and more intimately united with God in prayer.

In the preceeding year,—October 13th,—the Right Rev. Dr. Purcell had been consecrated second Bishop of Cincinnati; and had been duly inaugurated by Bishop Flaget.* He now invited Bishop Flaget to Cincinnati, to assist at the dedication of the German Catholic Church of the Holy Trinity, which ceremony was to take place on the 6th of October, 1834.

In Cincinnati, our prelate had the consolation to meet also his old and intimate friend, Dr. Bruté, lately nominated first Bishop of Vincennes. On receiving his Bulls, this humble and learned ecclesiastic had written to Bishop Flaget, strongly stating the many motives he had for not accepting the responsible charge; but he had concluded by leaving the final decision of the case to the judgment of Bishops Flaget and Chabrat. † These prelates, of course, had advised him to accept; and he now accordingly waived all further objection.

The splendid new cathedral of St. Louis was to be consecrated towards the end of the same month; and Bishops Flaget, Purcell, and Bruté traveled by stage to that city, to be present on the occasion. The dedication took place with great solemnity on the 26th of October; and on the 28th, Bishop Flaget therein con-

* He addressed the new prelate in strains of moving eloquence, telling him of the heavy cross he was to bear for Christ.

† His letter to our prelate.

secrated Dr. Bruté first Bishop of Vincennes; the Bishops of St. Louis and Cincinnati being the assistant prelates; and the latter preaching the consecration sermon.

We may as well mention here, that about a year before—October 6th, 1833—Bishop Rosati had consecrated Dr. Resé first Bishop of Detroit, in the cathedral of Cincinnati. Thus, in the short space of little more than a year, four new Bishops were consecrated for the West; three of them for sees lying within the ancient jurisdiction of the Bishop of Bardstown, and the fourth, for the coadjutorship of the Diocese itself.

Bishops Flaget and Purcell accompanied the Bishop of Vincennes to his new see, in which they solemnly installed him, November 6th, 1834.* The ceremony over, our prelate bade a tender and final adieu to his old friends and former parishioners, endeared to him by a pastoral connection which had commenced more than forty years previously.

With a lighter heart than he had ever felt before since his own consecration, he now returned to Bardstown. His long-cherished aspirations were realized. The vast territory placed under his episcopal jurisdiction was now narrowed down to the two States of Kentucky and Tennessee, which comprised his Diocese, as originally constituted. The latter State was likewise withdrawn from his jurisdiction, four years later, by the consecration—September 16th, 1838—of the Right Rev. Dr. Miles, as first Bishop of Nashville.

* On the road from St. Louis, the stage broke down, and the prelates were left, for a time, to grope their way amidst the darkness. Bishop Flaget cheered them for the mishap by his gaiety. Sitting on a log, he related pleasant anecdotes. This incident was communicated by Archbishop Purcell.

We conclude this Chapter, by referring to another episcopal consecration, which occured during the period of which we are treating. As we have seen, the Rev. LEO DE NECKERE, a learned and most exemplary Belgian priest, was appointed the fourth Bishop of New Orleans, some time after the resignation of Dr. Dubourg. The humble and modest ecclesiastic for a long time firmly refused to accept the proffered honor. His health was very feeble ; and he was of an amiable, diffident, unpretending and retiring disposition, much beloved by all who knew him.

At length his reluctance was overcome, and he was consecrated by Bishop Rosati, assisted by Bishop Portier and Very Rev. B. Richard, V. G., at New Orleans, June 24, 1830. Bishop England was present, and he preached the consecration sermon. The same prelate, during his stay in the city, delivered a number of his powerful discourses, which created quite a sensation. A letter, written from New Orleans to Bishop Flaget, speaks as follows of one among the effects produced by these sermons :

" Bishop England has done frightful mischief here. Every time that he preached in the evening there were not more than four or five persons present at the theatre ! Mr. Davis, the manager, had chosen the most *piquant* pieces ;—he was left in the lurch to provide for his expenses for illumination and other preparations. He pretended that he was injured in his rights ; and he accused the prelate of having but little charity for his neighbor ! The audience of the Cathedral, and at the church of M. Maenhaut, notwithstanding the great numbers and throng, were hushed in so deep a silence that nothing was heard, save a *rat*, which happened, I know not how, to be caught under the feet of some one, and which cried out for mercy after its own peculiar manner!" *

Bishop De Neckere did not long survive his consecration. He died the death of a saint, September 4, 1833. He was succeeded by the Rt. Rev. Dr. Blanc, the present Archbishop of New Orleans; who was consecrated Nov. 22, 1835.

Dr. Blanc had been stationed successively at Natchez, Point Coupé, and Baton Rouge. He was called to New Orleans by Bishop De Neckere, and appointed associate Vicar General, with the aged M. Richard, in December, 1831. In 1832, he received from Rome the appointment of Coadjutor to Bishop De Neckere; who, without his knowledge, had written to the Pope, demanding him, not as his Coadjutor, but as his successor. Dr. Blanc would not accept the office of Coadjutor, unless on condition that the Bishop should promise to abandon his intention of resigning. Dr. De Neckere having declined to do this, the Bishop elect sent the Bulls back to Rome.

Bishop De Neckere wrote to our holy prelate to engage his interest at Rome towards obtaining the acceptance of his resignation. Bishop Flaget answered in a strain of pleasant raillery, gently twitting his young colleague on the *necessity* of his retiring from the cares of the episcopacy, after having borne the burden for the great space of nearly three years! The timid, but holy Bishop of New Orleans, received in good part this rebuke so politely and so elegantly administered; and he appears to have given over his intention of resigning.

* Letter of M. Martial.

At his death, Dr. Blanc was appointed administrator of the Diocese. In 1834, M. Jeanjean was appointed Bishop of New Orleans; but he promptly declined, and sent back the Bulls. In October, 1835, Dr. Blanc was appointed, and he accepted. *

* These interesting details were furnished by the Archbishop of New Orleans.

CHAPTER XII.

HIS RELIGIOUS AND CHARITABLE ESTABLISHMENTS.

1812—1835.

The tree and its fruits—A rapid sketch—Dominican convent—And college of St. Thomas Aquinas—The Sisters of St. Dominic—Loretto Society—Its statistics—The Bishop's testimony—Sisterhood of Charity—Its origin, objects, and subsequent condition—A consoling feature—The Brotherhood—Mount Casino—Bishop Flaget's anticipations—How frustrated—The election of a Guardian—Schools to be every where established—Letter from the Propaganda—Remarks on Christian education—St. Joseph's College—Its rise and history—The Rev. G. A. M. Elder—St. Mary's College—The Rev. Wm. Byrne—The theological and the preparatory Seminary—A forged Letter—Statistics of the Diocesan establishments in 1825—Recapitulation—Consolation at the hour of death.

It is time for us now to pause, and, before tracing farther the episcopal career of Bishop Flaget, to glance rapidly at the numerous religious and charitable institutions which had already sprung up in his Diocese; most of them under his own fostering care. We cannot else estimate aright the character of the holy prelate. Adopting as a standard the Gospel text,—"by their fruits ye shall know them,"—we shall probably come to the conclusion that he was truly a favored child ot heaven, and that God achieved wonders through his instrumentality.

The blessings which crowned his administration exhibit a remarkable fulfillment of what was uttered by the royal Psalmist, in regard to the just man, whose will is the law of God, and who meditates thereon day and night :—" He shall be like the tree which is planted near the streams of water, which shall yield its fruit in proper time; and the leaf shall not fall off; *and all things whatsoever he shall do shall be prospered.*" *

Such was pre-eminently the case with our holy Bishop. He entered upon his career without any other resource than an unbounded confidence in God ; and in this trust he was not confounded. God raised up for him devoted friends, and zealous co-laborers in the vineyard, upon whose generous efforts he bestowed an abundant blessing. Establishments arose, as it were from nothing, and these became the objects of his own wonder, and of his fervent gratitude to " the Father of Lights, from whom every good and every perfect gift descendeth." †

Our present purpose calls for, and admits of only a few general outlines ; nor would the limits of one Chapter permit many details. We shall pass in rapid review the various institutions successively erected up to the year 1835, following the order of time.

1. The first religious establishment of Kentucky was founded five years before the arrival of the Bishop. As we have already seen, in a previous Chapter, the Dominican convent of St. Rose was founded in 1806. In 1808 a noviciate was established, and several youths were soon admitted as postulants. In 1809, the college

* Psalm, i. † St. James, ch. i.

of St. Thomas Aquinas was organized in connection with the convent, and it continued in successful operation for about ten years. After this period, the services of the Dominican fathers being required on the growing missions of Ohio and Kentucky, the college was closed, for want of suitable professors.

About this time—in 1819,—the monastery of St. Magdalene,* for religious women following the rule of St. Dominic, was founded by F. Wilson. From humble beginnings, it soon attained to a highly prosperous condition, under the fostering care of the present Bishop of Nashville, who watched over its interests for many years. A branch of it was afterwards established in Ohio; where, since 1818, a Dominican convent had already existed.

The Dominicans of St. Rose devoted much of their time to missionary duties in Kentucky, in Ohio, and in Michigan. Of the zealous missionary labors of FF. Fenwick and Young in Ohio, we have already spoken.

Father Wilson died at St. Rose in 1824. In August, 1828, the Rev. F. Raphael Muños arrived at the convent, as prior. He had been commissioned by the General of the Order, to re-establish therein, in its full vigor, the holy rule of St. Dominic; which, amidst the trying circumstances and distracting cares of the missionary life the earlier fathers were compelled to lead, had suffered some relaxation. The Order is now in a highly prosperous condition; and it has lately established a new convent and college at Sinsinawa Mound, Wisconsin; also a new college in Ohio, at St. Joseph's.

2. In the course of his arduous missionary labors in

* Now called St. Catharine's.

Kentucky, the Rev. M. Nerinkx had often deplored the negligence of parents in training up their offspring to knowledge and virtue. He found it difficult properly to prepare children for first communion. He had so many congregations under his charge, that he could scarcely devote a sufficient time to the religious instruction of the youth. Finding that the parents were not themselves, in many cases, sufficiently acquainted with their Religion to impart the necessary knowledge to their children, he thought of founding a sisterhood, under whose direction the young females who were to be the future mothers of family, might be thoroughly instructed in the elementary branches of education, and especially in religious principles.

Providence favored his charitable design. Some pious ladies having presented themselves as postulants, the foundations of the new society were laid April 25, 1812. The convent consisted of a hollow square of log cabins; the chapel occupying a central position on one side of the quadrangle. It was situated near the church of St. Charles, and was called *Loretto*, after the famous asylum of the Holy Virgin in Italy. Besides the object alluded to above, the sisterhood was to take charge of destitute orphans; and its members were taught to love poverty, and to earn their own livelihood by manual labor. They were to cherish a special devotion towards that model and pride of her sex, the pure and holy One,—

"Our tainted nature's solitary boast,"—

the Immaculate MARY, Mother of God made man. They were styled, "The Lovers of Mary at the foot of the Cross." Standing with her near the Cross, they were daily to sympathize with the dying SON and the afflicted Mother, with the pious ejaculations:—"O suffering Jesus! O sorrowful Mary!"

Such was the idea of the sainted Founder, and God bestowed an abundant blessing on his enterprise. The society grew apace, and the most edifying fervor reigned throughout the establishment of Loretto. The mother house was soon able to send out colonies to other parts of Kentucky, and subsequently to found houses in Missouri and Arkansas. Bishop Flaget bore the following testimony to the early piety of the sisterhood:

"These women sought for poverty in everything; in their monasteries, and in the plain neatness of their chapels. The plainness, the cleanliness, the simplicity of their dwellings and of their chapels, excited the wonder of their visitors. * * * They were the edification of all who knew them; and their singular piety and penitential lives reminded one of all that we have read of the ancient monasteries of Palestine and Thebais!" *

We may well conceive how the heart of the good prelate was rejoiced at the successful establishment of so edifying a society. But his joy was turned into sorrow, on receiving intelligence of the death of the pious founder, which occurred at St. Genevieve in Missouri, August 12, 1824. He had gone thither, as we have seen, to visit a branch of the sisterhood established in that State some years before, and also to labor for the conversion of the Indians.

* Letter to Bishop England, published in the U. S. Catholic Miscellany, December 8, 1824.

At his death the society already numbered more than a hundred members, and these had charge of six schools. The Bishop soon afterwards appointed the Rev. G. J. Chabrat superior; and in November, 1824, the mother house was removed to its present situation at the old St. Stephen's,—the cradle of the Diocese.

The new convent and church were blessed June 1, 1826. The Bishop was present and officiated on the occasion. Reminiscences of the first year of his episcopacy, passed amid sorrow and privations at this place, crowded on his mind; and he was much affected, especially while transporting the Blessed Sacrament from the old log chapel,—his first rude cathedral,—to the fine brick church of the convent.*

In 1844, the sisterhood contained one hundred and seventy-nine members; the number at present is probably about two hundred. They have four regular houses, with schools attached to them, in Kentucky, and three in Missouri. The Very Rev. D. A. Deparcq has been for many years the ecclesiastical superior. The original rule of M. Nerinkx having been found by experience too austere for this country, was subsequently considerably modified in several of its details; without, however, substantially affecting the nature and original objects of the society.

3. The same year, 1812, which gave birth to the Loretto Society, likewise witnessed the commencement of another sisterhood, destined also to do much for promoting the cause of religion and education. The society of the

---

* Journal—*ibid.* Several of the above details, particularly the dates, are taken from the same source.

Sisters of Charity in Kentucky was founded by Father David, who presided over it as ecclesiastical superior for about twenty years; until old age and infirmities compelled him to resign the post. It was he who, with the sanction of Bishop Flaget, drew up the admirable body of rules and constitutions by which the society is still governed. They are the same as St. Vincent of Paul laid down for the direction of the Sisters of Charity in France, with such slight modifications as the circumstances of time and place seemed to demand.

After the resignation of Bishop David, the present Bishop of Charleston was for some years the ecclesiastical superior; and he was succeeded by the Rev. Joseph Haseltine, the present incumbent.

The society had a very humble beginning. About a year after the removal of the seminary to St. Thomas', two pious ladies, wishing to devote their lives to God and the neighbor in a religious life, placed themselves for this purpose under the spiritual direction of Father David.* Others soon joined the infant sisterhood; and in June, 1813, the number having increased to six, a retreat was given them by Father David, and at its close an election was held, and a mother superior and other officers chosen by the votes of the members. Bishop Flaget was present at the ceremony, and made a most moving exhortation to the Sisters; and the ceremony closed with the solemn episcopal benediction. Thus was organized a society which has since reflected so much honor on Religion in Kentucky, and accomplished so much good. The objects contemplated by its founder in its establishment,—besides the sanctifica-

* November, 1812.

tion of its own members common to every religious body,—were, first, the exercise of the corporal and spiritual works of mercy towards the poor, the sick, and the ignorant; and, second, the promotion of *Christian* education among the young of the weaker sex.

The members of the society lived for several years in a brick edifice erected on the farm of St. Thomas. In June, 1822, the Sisters removed to the present location of the mother house, well known by the name of *Nazareth.* The farm had been purchased from a Presbyterian preacher named Lapsley; and the first chapel was the room which he had occupied as a study. The erection of a new convent was commenced May 26, 1826; and in December, 1829, the Legislature of Kentucky granted charters of incorporation to both the societies of Nazareth and Loretto.*

In 1844, the number of Sisters, including novices, was seventy-six; and they were then educating nearly five hundred girls, besides having charge of forty orphans in the St. Vincent Asylum, at Louisville. This Asylum, founded in 1832, now contains one hundred and fifteen orphans, under the charge of six Sisters, besides three more who attend to the Infirmary attached.

The number of Sisters and of scholars has also greatly increased in the last eight years. Besides the Asylum, Nazareth has five branch houses, conducting six female academies; all of them lying within the State of Kentucky.

One feature, common to both the sisterhoods above mentioned,—and also to that of the order of St. Dom-

* These dates are taken from the Bishop's Journal.

inic,—is the fact that their members have been mainly recruited from the country itself. This circumstance must have been particularly consoling to the holy Bishop, to whom God thus gave a visible proof of His blessing on the vineyard confined to his care. When it yielded such fruits as these,—many hundreds of pious virgins consecrating themselves entirely to the cause of Religion and charity,—he who watched over its cultivation with so much paternal solicitude could not but feel greatly comforted. Only the Catholic Church can originate that sublime self-devotion, which makes the Christian virgin, and preserves her faithful to the end.

The Bishop was the first superior of both these religious societies; and he watched over their rise and progress with a father's care. We find from his Journal, that he gave the mothers special instructions how they should preside over the communities placed under their control; and that he frequently gave lessons in grammar, and in other branches, to those who were preparing themselves to become teachers.*

4. M. Nerinkx had planned a brotherhood, similar in its objects, to the sisterhood of Loretto. He had even made a commencement of the good work; but his death in 1824 cut short his design, which was never fully carried into execution.

Bishop Flaget had long entertained a similar thought. As far back as 1813, we find him revolving in his mind the best plan for founding such an establishment. On this subject he has the following entry in his Journal:

"To-day, while saying Mass, a distraction,—perhaps a good thought,—came into my mind; which was, that

* This occurred particularly at the school of Gethsemane.

perhaps we could unite together several artisans of different trades, who would consecrate themselves to God by religious vows, and would live in community. Each artisan might receive apprentices ; and all who could work together in common, without interfering with one another, might do so. The rest might work in a separate place ; but always in the same enclosure. There would be regular hours set apart, at which all would assemble for prayer, spiritual reading, &c." *

Thirteen years elapsed before this project could be fully matured, or carried into effect. In the spring of 1826, the foundations of the brotherhood were laid at St. Thomas'. The venerable Founder wished ultimately to organize a society of religious men similar to that of the "Brothers of the Christian Doctrine," in France ; and when it would become sufficiently numerous, to select the most suitable members for assistants to the missionary clergy, in the management of temporal affairs, and in teaching catechism to children and servants.

The brotherhood was placed under the charge of the Rev. M. Derigaud, who directed the early exercises of the members. These bound themselves by vows for only three years. In the spring of 1827 the establishment was removed to Casey county, on a farm belonging to the church. Here the Brothers, about eight in number, built their monastery, which was called Mount Casino, after the famous Benedictine Abbey in Italy. Most of them exercised some mechanical trade. The original idea of the Bishop seemed in a fair way of accomplishment.

* July 4, 1813.

But the ways of divine Providence are truly unsearchable. The superior, M. Derigaud, died shortly afterwards; and the Bishop experienced great embarrassment in finding a suitable successor to that devoted priest. In this emergency, he called the Brothers to Nazareth, to hold an election of a Brother Guardian. We will allow him to unfold his feelings and plans on this, to him very interesting occasion:

"The Sisters, and Mother Catharine at their head, received them with a particular attention. The Mother herself served us at table. * * * I was a hundred times more happy in the midst of these good Brothers, than I could have been, seated at the table of kings. How many beautiful fancies started from my old imagination, on seeing these six Brothers seated at the same table with me, and who represented so well the apostles, simple men like them, seated at the table with their divine master! I saw already in full operation a pious association of various trades; shops erected for completing a building; children sent to them from all parts to learn different trades, to acquire an ordinary education, and, above all, to be instructed in their Religion, and to learn to practice its duties. I saw erected a beautiful and vast chapel, in which divine service would be performed with much gravity, majesty, and fervor. I saw one wing of their monastery consecrated entirely to those men, who, tired of the world, might wish to end their days in a holy and rigorous penance. In another wing, I located apartments for the Bishop and such of his priests as would be happy to recollect themselves for a few days and purify their hearts. What did I not see?" *

* *Bon Dieu! Que ne voyais je pas?* Journal, 1827.

All these fine plans were doomed to come to nought. A Guardian was duly elected; but the brotherhood, for the want of an efficient priest to direct them, soon declined; and at the close of the three years, it was dissolved.* . In this utilitarian age and country, it is difficult to induce men, to whom the world opens so many avenues of industry and of wealth, "to leave all things and follow Christ." It requires a healthy Catholic atmosphere to impart to them that heroic vigor of soul, which is an essential condition for the true religious vocation. Hence what is so common in Catholic countries, is rare in this, where the very air is so tainted with Mammonism.

5. The Bishop desired nothing more ardently, than to see schools for children of both sexes rising up under the shadow of the church in each congregation. He knew and felt, that the religious character of the rising generation will depend upon the manner in which youth are trained up. The question of education he rightly viewed, as one among the most important, if not the most important of all, to the interests of Religion. It appears that he even corresponded on this subject with Rome; for we find that—December 1st, 1820—he received a Letter from the Propaganda, strongly urging him to establish schools for children, and to place them under the superintendence of clergymen. A similar recommendation was likewise made to all the Bishops of the United States, as it had been previously to the Bishops of Ireland.†

---

* Most of the Brothers returned to the world; one of them entered the Dominican order, and is now the Provincial in America.

† This is the substance of the Letter, according to the entry in the Journal—*Ibid.*

This system of parochial schools, wherever it can be carried out, harmonizes well with the spirit and practice of the Catholic Church; and, if fully established, it would be attended with immense advantages to morals and Religion. Education without Religion is a body without a soul; it develops and gives strength to the passions, while it withholds the only effectual influence which can guide and control them for good. In the middle ages, when the Catholic spirit was predominant, schools, under the controlling influence of Religion, were seen almost every where in the vicinity of the churches; and in Catholic countries this is, to a great extent, still happily the case.

In missionary countries, where Catholics are scattered, and intermixed with those who are either bitterly opposed to them, or indifferent to all Religion, great difficulties exist in fully carrying out the system; still its adoption, so far as circumstances will permit, would be fraught with incalculable advantages. In this respect, our German Catholic brethren set us an admirable example, worthy of imitation. Children religiously trained up, never forget the good impressions made on their young minds.

If Bishop Flaget was not allowed by the slender resources of his destitute missions fully to carry out the recommendations of the Holy See, he did at least whatever he could to effect this purpose. We have seen how successful he was in founding academies for girls. Shortly after the receipt of the Letter in question, two flourishing schools for boys arose, which soon afterwards attained to the rank of colleges.

6. St. Joseph's college had its humble commence-

ment, as a day-school, in a basement room of the old seminary at Bardstown, about the year 1820; and St. Mary's was founded in the following year. The Rev. G. A. M. Elder was selected by the Bishop to be the founder and first president of the former; and his intimate friend, Rev. William Byrne, was chosen to fulfill the same offices for the latter. These two clergymen had all the qualities requisite for success in the arduous undertakings assigned them; and God's blessing did not fail to attend their efforts.

The institutions respectively founded by these two devoted priests, after having gone through many vicissitudes and reverses, still continue to flourish, after a lapse of thirty years. The number of youths educated in them during this period has been very considerable. Taking two hundred as the average number in yearly attendance in both,—and this figure is not too high, but rather below what was usual,—we may set down the total number of students who performed therein their studies for a year, at six thousand. They were not only from Kentucky, but from nearly all the States of the West and South.

Among the benefactors of St. Joseph's college, the name of the Rev. M. Martial, the special friend of Bishop Flaget, deserves particular mention. In 1824, he brought up from the South twenty Creole boys for the college; and in the year following, fifty-four accompanied him. These had been students in a southern college, with which he had been previously connected. The present Bishop of Charleston, the Rev. J. M. Lancaster, and the Rev. E. McMahon, were successively presidents of St. Joseph's college.

7. For twenty-eight years the secular clergy had charge of St. Joseph's college; and during a great part of this time, the theological seminary was placed near the college, the seminarians teaching, or performing duty therein, a few hours per day. The Bishops for many years lived in the seminary, and ate at the same table with the young candidates for the ministry. This connection of the two institutions had its advantages, as well as its inconveniences. Experience, however, showed that many of the seminarians had their vocations shaken by being thrown so much in contact with youth of the world; while scarcely a candidate for the ministry was obtained among those who received their education in the college. The Bishop was greatly distressed at this, and he adopted every means in his power to obviate or correct the evil.

For this purpose, he established at St. Thomas' a preparatory seminary for such young men as might give indications of a vocation to the ecclesiastical state. In connection with it, was a Catholic school for boys, who were taught the branches of an ordinary education, and were afterwards encouraged to pursue higher studies, in case they aspired to the ecclesiastical state. This seminary was placed at first under the charge of the Rev. M. Derigaud; and after his death, it continued in operation for several years, but was finally closed.

8. The founding of St. Mary's college, and its remarkable success for twelve years, were attributable to the zeal and indomitable energy of one man. Without money or men to help him, the Rev. William Byrne purchased the farm and erected the buildings; paying the whole cost in tuition. He did more. He formed

himself the teachers who were to aid him in carrying on the college. He originated every thing. And what is more remarkable still, he exercised at the same time the holy ministry in the neighboring congregations. He was always the last in bed, and the first up in the morning; though often in the course of the night he was for many hours absent visiting the sick.

How he found time for all this, excites our wonder. Yet he did it all, and did it well, for twelve years. He was president, chief disciplinarian, principal professor, procurator, missionary;—everything at the same time. And yet his talents were not brilliant, nor had his opportunities allowed him to acquire a very extended education. He began his study of Latin, like St. Ignatius, at the age of near thirty. We can explain his wonderful success only in one way:—God was with him, because he labored solely and entirely for His honor and glory.

As we have already seen, he died a victim of charity, after he had generously given up the college to the charge of the Jesuits. The members of this illustrious order continued to conduct it with success for fourteen years; until, in 1846, they left the Diocese and went to New York, to take charge of St. John's college, Fordham. After their departure, the college fell again into the hands of the Bishop, who conducted it through the secular clergy.

The two colleges of St. Joseph and St. Mary became corporate institutions by an act of the Legislature, and received the privilege of conferring degrees. They both passed through an ordeal of fire,—St. Mary's more than once,—but they both rose again from their ashes, with renewed beauty and splendor.

Bishop Flaget was in Rome when he heard of the burning of St. Joseph's; and he was plunged into a sea of grief at the intelligence. When St. Mary's was burned, a first and a second time, under the administration of its Founder, he, instead of yielding to despondency, rather smiled at the disaster as something trivial; and, with his characteristic energy, immediately set to work to reconstruct the edifice.

In 1825, Bishop Flaget received a letter, purporting to be from Henry Clay, Secretary of State of the U. S. Government, requesting him to furnish the religious statistics of his Diocese. The communication turned out to be a forgery; but in reply to it, the prelate gave a summary account of his various establishments, which we republish, in a condensed form, as going to show the condition of his institutions at that date:

1. Diocesan Seminary at Bardstown—Nineteen seminarians, who also teach in the college—cost of the building, $6,000.

2. Preparatory Seminary at St. Thomas—Fifteen young men, two priests and five teachers. To this is annexed a *school for boys*, with thirty students, who pay annually $35 in federal money, mostly in produce—cost of buildings at St. Thomas, $11,400.

3. St. Joseph's College—Will cost $20,000, when completed.

4. Cathedral—Not yet finished—has already cost $22,600.

5. St. Mary's Country School—Cost $4,000—charge per session $6 for tuition, besides board paid in produce—very popular—has one hundred and twenty boys—"application must be made twelve months in advance to secure admission."

6. Sisterhood of Loretto—One hundred Sisters—convent of Loretto of brick, cost $5,000—all their branch houses made of logs—five schools in Kentucky—in 1823, sent out a colony to St. Genevieve.

7. SISTERHOOD OF NAZARETH—Sixty Sisters—sixty boarders in Nazareth academy—three other schools in Kentucky, and one at Vincennes, Indiana—school of Nazareth becoming popular, and patronized throughout the whole Western country.

8, SISTERHOOD OF ST. DOMINIC—Established in 1821—Fourteen Sisters and twenty-nine boarders.

9. The Bishop's salary is about $200 per year, derived from pew rents of the cathedral.

Of a recent important change in the administration of St. Joseph's, and of the founding of a new college and free school in Louisville, as well as of several other institutions, we will speak more appropriately in a subsequent Chapter. We will close this by mentioning an incident which we find recorded in the Bishop's Journal. It will show how much confidence was reposed in him by Protestants as well as by Catholics:

In November, 1826, the citizens of Harrodsburgh, chiefly Protestants, offered the Bishop a fine college edifice, a large farm, and a spacious lot for a convent; on condition that he would establish Catholic institutions in their town, similar to those in and near Bardstown. Other towns also held out flattering inducements for the same object. But the Bishop had not the means nor the men for carrying on so many institutions; and he was in consequence compelled to decline the offers made him.

Thus we have seen four colleges,—two of which yet remain;—three religious sisterhoods, conducting a large Female Orphan Asylum, an Infirmary, and eleven flourishing academies for girls; a brotherhood; and two religious orders of men, devoting themselves to education and the missions; all growing up and prospering under the encouraging auspices of Bishop Flaget.

To these institutions were subsequently added several others,—besides those above alluded to,—to which we will refer in the proper place.

May we not believe that the holy prelate had much to console him in the midst of the weighty labors and wearing anxieties of his long administration? Did not God visibly bless his disinterested exertions to promote His glory? How much good may be accomplished by ONE DEVOTED MAN, intent singly on laboring for God! What consolation do not such reminiscences as these shed on the else gloomy hour of death!

When Bishop Flaget thought he was dying of cholera, he no doubt looked back, with great comfort of spirit, on all these institutions which he was leaving behind him, to continue the good work he had begun. He does not, indeed, tell us so; in his humility he speaks chiefly of his sins, and of his awful accountability to God for his long administration; but the holy calm which followed his confession, and the peace of God which then rested in his heart and beamed from his countenance, told the whole story of his exceeding great joy and consolation, much more eloquently than any words he could have uttered.

The holy prelate was destined yet to pass many years upon earth; and we must now follow him through the remaining days of his pilgrimage.

CHAPTER XIII.

HIS JOURNEY TO EUROPE AND RETURN.

1835—1839.

Journey to Europe long contemplated—Gallicanism—*Ruse* of Bishop David—Taking French leave, and sailing for Europe—He is at Nantes and Angers—Visits Rome—Affecting interview with Gregory XVI.—Is charged with a mission in France—Visits the Austrian Emperor and Metternich—Family of Charles X.—Louis Philippe—Travels in France and Sardinia—Charles Albert—Duke de Montmorency—Count de Maistre—Makes the tour of forty-six French Dioceses—Reputation for sanctity—Wonderful cures—Documentary evidence—Fruits of his labors—Consults the Pontiff—The answer of Rome—Resolves to return—Bids a final adieu to France—Goes to die "among his own."

A quarter of a century had now elapsed since Bishop Flaget's last visit to Europe. Often had he contemplated the journey with great satisfaction; but as often had he been prevented by uncontrollabe circumstances from carrying his wishes into execution. It was not that he sought repose, or desired recreation. Though he greatly needed both, yet he expected and wished for no rest in this world. But he thought, that the journey would promote the interests of Religion in his Diocese.

What he most desired, was to visit Rome, and to

offer up the tribute of his respectful homage to the successor of St. Peter. He had always been devoted to the Holy See, with a most filial attachment. The Pontiff was, in his eyes, truly the Vicar of Christ, having *full* charge, under Him,—the great invisible HEAD of the Church,—of *all* the lambs and sheep of the One Fold. He sought not to place artificial bounds to a power, which Christ Himself had not limited, but had made ample enough to meet every want and emergency of the Church.

He was never partial to that theory,—now happily almost exploded,—which is known under the name of *Gallicanism*. It was enough for him to know, that the Pontiff had spoken; the grace of God, enlightening and warming his faith, prompted immediate and willing obedience. The maxim adopted with joyous and unanimous acclamation by the six hundred Bishops assembled in general council at Chalcedon in 451,—PETER HATH SPOKEN BY THE MOUTH OF LEO,—still reechoed in his ears, and found a warm response in his heart.

Bishops, who are consecrated for Dioceses lying beyond the boundaries of Europe, take a solemn engagement on the day of their consecration to visit Rome, either personally or by a suitable deputy, once in every ten years; in order to render to the Sovereign Pontiff an account of their administration. Our holy prelate had hitherto discharged this duty through another, because unable to do it himself.

In 1825, he thought the long-desired time had at length arrived, when he might visit Rome without detriment to his Diocese. Still his delicacy of conscience would not permit him to take the step, without obtaining the previous consent and advice of the Sovereign Pontiff himself. He accordingly wrote to Rome on the subject, and calmly awaited the reply. But he had communicated his intention to his Coadjutor, Dr. David; and the latter was so much alarmed at the heavy responsibility which the departure of the Bishop would devolve on him, that, without his knowledge, he addressed a strong letter of remonstance to the Pope; setting forth, clearly and forcibly, the reasons against the Bishop leaving his Diocese at that time.

While awaiting the answer from Rome, our prelate wrote as follows to his brother in France:

"If I have not yet made the voyage of Europe, it is because my venerable Coadjutor, in spite of his great learning, has not been able to reconcile himself to taking upon his shoulders my responsibility. I have not wished to sadden him. I believed, nevertheless, that my sojourn in Italy and France would be much more useful to my Diocese, than all I could do here for ten years. I have written to Rome a long letter, in which I have detailed the reasons for and against this pious pilgrimage. In six months I shall know on what to decide." *

His application was unsuccessful at Rome. The reasons alleged by his Coadjutor outweighed his own with the Pontiff. However painful the decision was to nature, it was relished, and cheerfully submitted to, by the principle of grace which ruled within him. In another letter, written to the same brother, a year later, he thus gives utterance to his feelings on the occasion:

* Letter dated November 16, 1825. French Life—p. 99.

"You can scarcely believe how much I have been mortified at the decision of the Pope, who does not deem it advisable that I should visit Rome and my native country. He fears that my Diocese, scarcely yet out of its cradle, might suffer too much through my absence. * * May the holy will of God be done! God be thanked, sacrifices of every kind do not cost me so much now, as formerly. The 'I die daily' of St. Paul, taken in the spiritual sense, constitutes at times my delight. Heaven, and the blessed spirits who inhabit it, are often the objects of my meditations; but when I must enter on the way of Calvary, poor human nature, silly as it is, is greatly hurt, and wages against me a cruel warfare." *

Having subsequently understood the means adopted to prevent his departure, he said to his Coadjutor, with his accustomed amiable gaiety: "Make yourself easy; when I shall again purpose to visit Rome, I will say nothing of my intention either to yourself or to any one else." †

He, in effect, adopted this course, to a great extent, when nine years later, he actually departed for Europe. His old Coadjutor having resigned, and his new one—Dr. Chabrat—having been consecrated, he thought that the propitious day had at length dawned for setting out on his European journey. He, accordingly, privately made all his arrangements for leaving. Having the full consent of his Coadjutor, he felt entirely at ease in reference to the administration during his absence. In the spring of 1835 he departed, so privately, however,

* Letter dated November 28, 1826. French Life—*Ibid.*

† *Ibid.*

that but two or three persons were aware of his intention.

He remained abroad about four years, returning only in the fall of 1839. While in Europe, he was not idle. He was incessantly engaged in missionary journeys and labors. He visited Italy, and the greater portion of France and Austria. Every where he labored for the interests of his Diocese, and for the general good of Religion; and every where his efforts were crowned with the most signal success.

We cannot attempt to furnish all the edifying details of his travels and apostolic labors while in Europe; our limits will allow us to give only what may be deemed most interesting to American readers. These Sketches would be incomplete without some notice of these edifying passages in his episcopal career.

He remained in France about a year, before he was able to continue his journey to Rome. One of his first visits was to Monseigneur de Guerines, Bishop of Nantes. In this city he had discharged the humble office of procurator in the Sulpician seminary, forty-five years previously. He visited eleven parishes of this Diocese, and was every where received with enthusiasm, and venerated as a saint.

From Nantes he went to Angers, where he was lodged in the episcopal palace. His apartments he considered entirely too grand for a missionary Bishop; but he checked all rising vanity by a reminiscence of the poverty of his early childhood, when he was "the little *Benuet* * of Contournat." † The Bishop of An-

---

* Patois for *Benôit*, or Benedict.

† Letter to his brother; December 13, 1835. French Life—pp. 104, 105.

gers presented him a superb soutane. He passed five months in this city, where he was seriously ill for some time with a malady on the lungs, which long baffled the skill of physicians. He next visited Poictiers and some other places; after which, he spent some time with his family at Billom.

Wherever he went, he was received with open arms by the Bishops, clergy, and people. All vied with one another, who should pay him the most honor. All this homage did not shake, however it may have alarmed his humility. He restored all the honor to God, to whom alone he considered it due.

With a simplicity all his own, he thus speaks of the contrast between the pomp with which he now saw himself surrounded, and the humble scenes of his childhood at Contournat and Billom;—we shall see the happy influence which this reminiscence had on his heart:

"It is in vain that they feast me wherever I go; Billom and Contournat present themselves to my mind, and their image furnishes me an inexpressible satisfaction. * * In vain do I find myself associating with Archbishops and Bishops, with mayors and prefects, with marquises and counts; the remembrance of the humble roof, under which I had the happiness to be born, of poor, but very pious parents, puts me back entirely into my proper place. In vain do they overwhelm me with polite attentions and compliments, in prose and in verse, treating me as an apostolic man, as the foreign missionary, &c., &c. * * If I think but one moment of Billom, and the good aunt who nursed me as a mother, all these beautiful eulogies pass over my head, like a light breeze, without affecting it with the least attaint." *

The Bishop was at Avignon, when he wrote the letter, from which the above is an extract. He was on his way to Rome, where he arrived in the fall of 1836.† This was the end he contemplated reaching, when he undertook what he designated his "pilgrimage."

Gregory XVI. then sat on the chair of St. Peter; and the holy prelate lost no time in visiting this excellent Pontiff. He furnishes us with the following simple, but touching account of his first interview with the Pope:

"On the 29th of September, having gone to the palace towards eleven o'clock, A. M., I was without delay introduced into the presence of the Father of all the faithful. Following the usual ceremonial, I made the three prostrations, and at the third I kissed with affection the cross embroidered on his sandal:—it seemed to me that I was kissing the feet of St. Peter himself. At this thought, my heart felt a sensation which I cannot describe; sighs and sobs choked my utterance. According to the ceremonial, I should have remained kneeling until the Pope would give me a sign to rise; but in this audience, altogether friendly and paternal, there was no ceremony to be observed. The excellent Pontiff bowed down, seized me in both arms, and as I was preparing to kiss his ring, he pressed me to his bosom, and embraced me tenderly, saluting me affectionately on both cheeks.

"Such was the impression which these marks of

---

* Letter to brother; August 25, 1836—*Ibid.*

† He reached Rome September 24th. Journal—*Ibid.*

friendship made on my heart, that it was impossible for me to articulate a single word, and I thought I was going to be ill. At this sight the Pope was moved, he pressed me again on his breast, and, with a tender embrace, encouraged me to be calm, bade me sit down by his side, and taking both my hands in his, waited till I would open my heart to him. Throughout this whole scene, my heart was in violent agitation. * * Happily for me, tears succeeded my sobs; they flowed in abundance. At ths juncture, the Pope again embraced me for the third time.

"Having recovered my senses, and feeling now perfectly at my ease, I entered into conversation with this good and excellent Father of the faithful. Our interview, which lasted more than half an hour, was conducted in Latin; and he assured me that he understood me perfectly well.

"As I was speaking to him of my journey to Europe, of the sickness I had suffered at Angers, and the confirmation I had given at Nantes, he stopped me, saying, that he had followed all my footsteps from Havre till my arrival in Rome, that he was satisfied with my conduct, that I was a worthy successor of the apostles, &c. Oh! how agreeable and delicious are such conversations! All the torments one has endured appear now as nothing. No;—I will never forget this interview, so paternal and so delightful. Throughout the day, and at every moment, it was pictured in my thoughts."*

The Pope welcomed him with similar cordiality at

* Journal, *in loco*. The author of the French Life gives a similar account of the interview; but he makes the Bishop *utter* the exclamation about St. Peter, which he only *thought of*, according to his own statement.

several subsequent interviews. He made him assistant prelate at the throne, presented him a full costume of splendid material, and granted him other favors. He took great pleasure in making inquiries concerning the condition of the Diocese of Bardstown, and that of Religion in America generally, descending to the most minute details. He promptly offered to defray the Bishop's expenses while in Rome, and took an interest in procuring him comfortable lodgings.

When the prelate afterwards expressed his intention of leaving the holy city, the Pontiff strongly objected, saying, that he ought not to think of setting out at the approach of winter, and that his age and infirmities would ill comport with his traveling in weather so rigorous. The Cardinals united with the Pope in rendering honor to the venerable missionary. It is refreshing to hear him speak on this subject:

"Probably I shall pass the winter in Rome; and this by order of the Sovereign Pontiff, who does not wish that, at my age, I should undertake long journeys in so rigorous a season. I am a good deal thwarted in my different projects by this command; but when the Father speaks, the son can do nothing but keep silence and obey. * * * At Rome, as at Billom, I receive marks of esteem and even of affection, not merely from the simple clergy and religious, but from the Cardinals themselves, and especially from the Sovereign Pontiff. O my God! how much should I thank Thee for so many favors! For who am I to be known at Rome, and above all, to be there treated with so much honor." *

During his sojourn at Rome, he took up his abode

* Letter to brother; November 24, 1836.

with the Lazarist Fathers at Monte Citorio, where he was visited, with every mark of respect and reverence, by many persons of distinction, both lay and clerical. Here, in compliance with the wish of the Pontiff, he drew up that Report of the history and condition of his Diocese, to which we have already so frequently referred.

From the Bishop's Journal we learn, that he transacted much important business with the Pope; some of which regarded his own Diocese, and the rest, the general interests of Religion.

He presented to Gregory XVI. a petition from the mother house of the Sisters of the Good Shepherd at Angers, praying for the privilege of establishing a branch of their admirable Institute in Rome; where they promised to labor with devotedness for the conversion of the unfortunate among their own sex. The Pontiff received the document with manifest pleasure, and promised to take it into favorable consideration. The petition was granted, and the house has since been established.*

He also presented a petition to his Holiness for the beatification of M. De Montfort. The Pope received it graciously, endorsed it, and sent it to the proper congregation of Cardinals for examination.†

In one of his conferences with the Pontiff, the Bishop spoke of the translation of his episcopal see to Louisville, and exposed all the reasons which induced him to solicit the change. Gregory XVI. would not decide the question immediately, but referred the matter to the congregation of Propaganda, who were to report it back to him with their advice.‡

---

* Journal—*ibid.* † *Ibid.* ‡ *Ibid.*

On the suggestion, and at the instance of several French prelates, the Pontiff now charged Bishop Flaget with a most important mission, on behalf of the pious Association for the Propagation of the Faith. He was directed to visit as many Dioceses of France and Northern Italy as his strength would permit; and there to stimulate the faithful to join the Association. The Bishop cheerfully undertook the mission, and he most faithfully and successfully discharged all the laborious duties connected therewith.

He remained in Rome until after Easter, 1837. After a parting audience with his Holiness, he then left for Vienna, whither business connected with the interests of his Diocese called him. He passed through Viterbo, Assisium, Loretto, Ancona, Bologna and Venice. At Assisium he stopped to visit the famous church of the *Portiuncula*, where the humble St. Francis had so often poured forth his soul in fervent prayer. He delayed three days at the sanctuary of Loretto, to satisfy that tender devotion he had from childhood cherished towards the Immaculate Virgin, Mother of God. He made a retreat here, under the direction of a Jesuit Father. During his stay in this time-honored city of the Virgin, he received distinguished honors from the representative of the Pontiff; who lodged him in the papal palace, and made him sleep in the same bed which had been occupied by the sainted Pius VII., while on his return from his French exile.*

At Vienna he had an audience from the Emperor, and dined with Metternich. He also visited the illustrious exile, Charles X. ex-King of France; and though

* Letter to brother, April 24, 1837.

unwilling to interfere in the politics of Europe, he yet cheerfully yielded to the pious wishes of the family, and invoked a blessing on the head of the young Bourbon heir to the French throne.*

After despatching his business in Germany, he returned to France, to enter upon the arduous duty imposed on him by the sovereign Pontiff,—of aiding the Association for the Propagation of the Faith. He devoted two years to this good work. In this time he made the tour of *forty-six* Dioceses lying in France and Sardinia.

Though now seventy-five years of age, and though he had gone through enough fatigue to have impaired or broken down almost any other constitution, yet his strength did not fail him. He seemed, on the contrary, to have put on again all the energy of his youth. Wherever he went, great crowds gathered to hear the words which fell from the lips of the "old missionary Bishop." He visited not only the episcopal cities of each Diocese, but not unfrequently many of the parish churches; besides the seminaries, colleges, and religious houses. From this fact we may form some idea of the number of times he was called on to preach, to say nothing of administering confirmation and performing other important functions. Many a younger man would have succumbed under the herculean labor.

With burning eloquence, coming warm from the heart, he in every place aroused the zeal of the faithful

* We have often been amused at hearing him relate the coldness with which he was treated by the Court of Louis Philippe, on his return to Paris. At his previous visit the king of the French had shown him every polite atention: at the last he was entirely unnoticed, and invited to no audience!

for the good work; and God crowned his labors with a success, greater even than his own most sanguine anticipations. Thousands, and tens of thousands joined the pious Association; and what was even far more consoling, piety revived, and fervor was aroused under his preaching in the various cities and towns of France.

His example was even more efficacious than his words. No one could look on him, without feeling more deeply impressed than with any sermon. He preached as effectually, when he followed the silent method of St. Francis of Assisium, as when he adopted that of St. Francis of Sales, or of St. Francis Xavier.

In all the cities and parishes, he was received almost as an angel from heaven. People crowded to see him, to receive his blessing, and to commend themselves and their families to his holy prayers. He entered into "union of prayers" with many pious persons, interchanging with them pictures or other tokens of remembrance. Each of his words, every one of his little acts of kindness, was treasured up in the memory, as matter for future edification.

His reputation for sanctity had preceded him to his native country; and it was greatly increased during his abode therein. It was even said and believed, that extraordinary, if not miraculous cures had been effected by his prayers; and ample statements to this effect, with certificates appended, were drawn up and circulated. The humility of the holy prelate would not permit him to believe that he had any positive agency in working miracles, though he could not deny that there was something extraordinary in the cures effected.

We do not venture to pronouce a decided opinion on a subject, upon which the church adopts and enjoins so wise a reserve.* That the power of God is not abridged, and that *the age of miracles has not ceased*, we hold to be an undoubted truth. God surely may operate miracles now, as heretofore, through the prayer or agency of His servants, whenever the good of Religion may be thereby promoted. He has done it in all ages of the Church, from the apostolic days down to the present time. But when it is question of particular miraculous occurrences, the Church has always exercised a most rigid scrutiny into the facts, evidence, and circumstances, before pronouncing a decision.

With these remarks, we will here publish an official and well authenticated document, from the archives of the Bishop of Nantes, which contains the edifying details of the wonderful cure of Mademoiselle DE MONTI, attributed to the prayers of our holy prelate. The paper, we are confident, will be perused by all with interest and profit:

"On the first of June, 1834, Miss OLYMPIA DE MONTI, nineteen years of age, was attacked by a malady which was supposed to be an inflammatory fever. Her illness became so violent, that on the third day she could scarcely breathe. About two o'clock in the morning of that day, the curate of St. Peter's was summoned in great haste, and administered to her the sacrament of Extreme Unction. The physicians became at this period convinced that her disease was a malignant fever; and they had recourse to strong remedies. But, on the

* In this we fully concur with the elegant writer of the French Life.

fifth day, when the fever went off, she fell into such a state of exhaustion, that her life was despaired of. Mr. Audrain, curate of th cathedral, gave her the holy Viaticum, which she received with sentiments of profound piety. A few moments afterwards, she said to those present, that she felt much better.

" Miss De Monti became each day better; and on the seventh she was pronounced out of danger. All anticipated for her a speedy recovery; but on trying to walk, she found that she was unable to stand alone;—nor could she take a step unless she was supported, or rather carried, by two persons. In the month of August following, she became unable to walk even with such support. From that period until August 1835, she was confined to her bed. She was each day placed in an arm-chair; but could remain up only about half an hour in the morning, and the same length of time in the afternoon. From this date she was not able to do even this, and her weakness increased daily. Three of the most celebrated physicians of Paris, and five of Nantes, had been consulted; but they could do nothing to relieve her. The remedies prescribed seemed but to augment her malady. Neither her parents nor herself entertained the slightest hope of her recovery.

" About this time they heard of the miraculous cures which had been effected by the prayers of Bishop Flaget, who was then at Nantes. But they were aware that the holy prelate was unwilling to be spoken to regarding the miracles wrought by his intercession. It was also difficult to obtain the privilege of being visited by the Bishop, as they were then sojourning at the Villa de Grillaud, near Nantes; nor was it possible to have the young lady conveyed thither, in her then prostrate condition. A venerable English Trappist, Father Bernard, was then at the Villa de Grillaud; and to this good religious Miss De Monti's parents expressed their ardent desire to receive for themselves, but especially for their daughter, the Bishop's benediction. Father Bernard promised to do all in his power to engage him to pay them a visit.

"He was successful; and on the 4th of December, at half past ten in the morning, they had the the happiness of receiving a visit from Bishop Flaget. After having obtained his benediction, M. and Madame De Monti remarked to him, that their daughter would be deprived of this happiness, unless he would have the charity to visit her in her room, as she had been confined to her bed for many months. He replied, that he would with pleasure do so, in order to exhort her to resign herself perfectly to the decrees of divine Providence.

"When Madame De Monti had conducted him to her daughter's room, she retired. The Bishop remained fifteen or twenty minutes with Miss De Monti. She afterwards related to her parents that he gave her his blessing twice, and made the sign of the cross on her forehead. Moreover, the holy prelate promised to pray for her intention during nine consecutive days, and recommended to her to recite the Litany of the Holy Name of Jesus, and a prayer to the Blessed Virgin. The good prelate then took leave of her, and left the country house of Grillaud about eleven o'clock.

"After the Bishop's departure, the young lady's parents repaired to her room. She told them, she was persuaded that she would soon be well; but expressed a desire to pass some moments in prayer, in order to give God thanks for this auspicious visit. She was, therefore, left alone with her sister, the Countess De Maquillé. Miss De Monti began to recite the Litany of the Holy Name of Jesus, which she did without being fatigued; though, a few moments before, she was scarcely able to recite a *Pater* or an *Ave*. She has since declared to her parents that she soon felt as if animated by a new life.

"After having repeated the Litany, she said to her sister, that she felt as if she was cured, and that she was strong enough to walk. At the same time, she sat upright in her bed, which so much surprised Madame De Maquillé, that she was near fainting. Miss De Monti, seeing her sister's emotion, asked for her clothes, and bade her be calm. She put on the garments which had been given to her; then rising, without any assistance, seated herself in the chair which Bishop Flaget had occupied during his visit. Then she proceeded to the other end of the room; and, prostrating herself before a crucifix, made a short prayer.

"It was then about half-past one. Madame De Maquillé opened a window, and cried out to those below: 'Olympia is walking.' Upon this announcement, all the members of the household rushed towards Miss De Monti's room. For a long time she could not bear the slightest noise in her apartment; but now the presence of about twenty persons had no effect upon her. All beheld her walking about, without the least assistance.

"She continued walking for some time; then wrote to Bishop Flaget. M. De Monti proceeded to the

21

Bishop's palace, to announce to the two prelates the happy tidings. Falling on his knees before the Bishop of Bardstown, he related the miraculous cure that had taken place. It would be impossible to describe the joy and astonishment of the persons, who were witnesses of this touching interview. The Abbé Vrignaud, secretary of the Bishop of Nantes, went to offer his felicitations to the family of M. de Monti, and to see himself the evidences of this miraculous cure. He saw Miss Olympia walking with perfect ease. She had regained the use of all her members.

"On the following day, the 5th of December, he went again to Grillaud, and there met Drs. Lafond and Padioleau. Miss De Monti had descended from her apartment, and was then in the parlor; she advanced with a firm step to receive them. She had not experienced the least fatigue in coming down the stairs. On the 11th of the same month,—eight days after her recovery, she went to Nantes. The next day she had the happiness of hearing Mass, and receiving the Holy Communion in the chapel of the Archbishop of Nantes.

"During several succeeding days, she received visits of congratulation from her friends, and answered different letters. It cannot be said that her health is improving; because from the day of the Bishop's visit, her cure was complete; as many witnesses testify.

(Signed) F. De Monti.
Olympie de Monti.
Ch. de Commequiers.
De Monti ne'e de Commequiers.
De Commequiers ne'e de Broc.
Euphrasie de Monti, *Contesse de Maquill'e.*

"Certified to be conformable to the original Minutes deposited in the Secretary's office of the Bishop of Nantes; and also by me, as an eye-witness of the first interview which M. Francis de Monti had with Bishop Flaget,—three hours after the miraculous cure of his daughter,—in the presence of ten persons whom the Bishop of Nantes had invited to dinner on the 4th of last December, the eve of the departure of the Bishop of Bardstown for Angers.

Nantes, Feb. 27, 1836.

GELY, *Canon*,

[*Seal.*] V. G. *of Bishop of Bardstown.*"*

* The document, of which the above is a translation, was found among the papers of Bishop Flaget. It is a copy from the original, apparently in the hand-writing of Mademoiselle De Monti herself; and the signatures and certificate appended appear to be original. There is not the slightest doubt either of its authenticity or reliability.

We find also, among the Bishop's papers, another highly interesting document,—likewise a duly certified copy from the original deposited in the episcopal archives of Nantes. It is a lengthy and scientific Report, drawn up by eight eminent physicians "of the Faculty of Medicine in Paris," but practicing their profession at Nantes. On the invitation of the Bishop of this city, they made a minute and careful examination, not only of Miss De Monti's case, but also of *five* others, scarcely less remarkable. Their investigations were very thorough and searching; while their expressions of opinion, on each case, are guarded and moderate. These wonderful cures all took place towards the close of the year 1835, in the city of Nantes or the vicinity. The Report is dated July 15, 1836. It is a carefully drawn paper, covering twenty-three large pages, closely written; and though highly interesting, it is too long for insertion in this place. We translate only the closing paragraph:

"Finally, a last motive which corroborates the opinion we have expressed on the cures of which we have spoken, is the striking

We must now follow our holy prelate through his remaining travels, until his return to his Diocese. At Turin, the Bishop was kindly received by the King, the late unfortunate Charles Albert. He remained some time here, and was entertained with princely hospitality by the illustrious family of the Duke de Montmorency.

After having traversed the greater part of France, Sardinia and Piedmont, he found himself, early in 1839, at Nice on the Mediterranean. Here he was welcomed by the Governor of the place, Count Rodolph de Maistre, a son of the famous writer. He remained under his roof during the entire Lent of this year. This good family overwhelmed him with kind attentions. He needed repose, after his laborious campaign, which had greatly shaken his health and impaired his strength.

He was solicited by many prelates and other persons of distinction, to continue his mission, and by not a few to give up all idea of ever returning to America, and to end his days among his relations and friends in France. On the other hand, he felt anxious about the

---

coincidence which exists among all these facts. The six patients, for a long time the victims of disease over which art had not been able to triumph, present themselves at the feet of a pious Bishop, receive his benediction ; and the most of them find themselves immediately delivered from all their ills. This circumstance, coming to the support of all the considerations which precede, adds much to their value. Hence we do not hesitate to renew here the declaration, that these are not to be viewed as ordinary cures ; but that there intervened in their production certain hidden causes, superior to the province of the medical art, and to the course of nature ; yet, we repeat it, this intervention is not manifest, to the same degree, in all the cases."

affairs of his Diocese, from which he had received letters earnestly asking his speedy return. Embarrassed as to the course he should adopt, and wishing to do nothing but the will of God, he addressed a letter to the Sovereign Pontiff, soliciting advice as to what line of conduct he should pursue under the circumstances. He candidly laid before the Holy See the reasons for and against his immediate return to America, leaving the whole matter to its decision.

The answer of the Pontiff arrived a few days before Easter. He received the package with the most profound respect, and wished to peruse it on his knees. The document breathed the sweet spirit of paternal kindness; while it was marked by the manifold graces of the most exquisite politeness.

After having praised the zeal of the prelate in accomplishing the mission entrusted to him, the Pontiff advises his return to a Diocese, "to which," he says, "many letters received thence, and thy own most ardent love for the flock committed to thy care, recall thee. * * For although thy Church is not without the solace of thy Coadjutor, yet it appears equitable, that after an absence of four years, thou thyself, like a good shepherd, shouldst satisfy the desire of thy flock, and again see them, after so long a time; especially as thy return to America might be again too long delayed, by new obstacles intervening, if the present suitable time for navigation should pass by. Wherefore, unless thy health,—which we hope is re-established,—or some more weighty reason should prevent it, return, venerable Brother, as thou desirest, to thy Diocese; and when it shall be given to thee, to see thy children,* and to

* "Oves,"—literally *sheep*.

speak to them face to face, fail not to testify to them the great good will with which we embrace thee and thy flock, in the bowels of Christ."*

The Bishop's suspense was now at an end, and his decision to return to his Diocese was at once taken. The will of God was made known to him, and he was prepared to obey. The clergyman who was his traveling companion asked him, whether his thus leaving France and his relatives and friends, probably forever, was not extremely painful to him. He promptly replied: "No, no, my dear child; I was already fully decided to do the will of the Pope; and if he had answered that I should neither remain in France nor return to America, but should depart for China, or join the Archbishop of Cologne,†—in case that venerable Confessor could find there a place for me,—I should have departed on the instant.‡

"He often referred to this subject through the day. "O how happy I am," he exclaimed, "to know the will of God!" On another occasion, when his friends expostulated with him for leaving them forever, and offered to write to the Pope, to obtain permission for him to end his days in France, he said: "O no; it is but just *that the first Bishop of Kentucky should go to die among his own.*"§

The Letter of the Pontiff to which we have just alluded, referred chiefly to a petition which had been presented to the prelate to visit several Dioceses out of France; and as in a previous letter permission had

* The entire document, with a French translation, is given in the French Life—p. 126, *seqq.* It is dated March 16, 1839.

† Then in prison.

‡ French Life—p. 125,

§ *Ibid*—p. 135.

been already given him to visit certain Dioceses in the north of France, which he had not yet seen, it was suggested to him that he was entirely free to prolong his stay, until he would have completed the tour of those last named ; and that, moreover, his availing himself of the privilege thus granted would accrue greatly to the benefit of Religion. But the Bishop doubted whether the previous permission had not been withdrawn, by the advice contained in the last letter.

Pressed for his final decision, he said to his clerical companion : " This evening we will go before the Blessed Sacrament, to know the will of God." Having made his visit to the church, he said, smiling : "I will now terminate my mission. We will see Chambery, since I am announced there ; then we will return to Lyons, whither some business calls me ; I will next visit my brothers, for I must absolutely pass one or two months with them,—not, however, all at one time ; I will make some excursions to Clermont ; I will accustom them by degrees to live separated from me. During this time, I will be engaged in collecting some young ecclesiastics for my Diocese ; then I will take my departure about the end of August." *

At Lyons, he had the happiness to meet the Rt. Rev. Dr. Purcell, now Archbishop of Cincinnati, who, but a few days after, accompanied him to Clermont. They arranged to return together to America ; and the Bishop thanked God for the fortunate circumstance, which gave him such good company.

Having failed in his expectation of procuring young ecclesiastics, he hastened his departure. In July, 1839,

---

* *Ibid*—p. 134, 135.

the two prelates, accompanied by the Rev. John M'Gill, now Bishop of Richmond, sailed from Havre; and on the 21st of August they landed safely at New York.

In September, the holy prelate arrived at Bardstown, where he was warmly welcomed by his clergy and people. He came to die among his own children, for whose welfare he had so long and so successfully labored.

CHAPTER XIV

THE LAST YEARS OF HIS EPISCOPACY.

1839—1849.

He makes the tour of his establishments, and visits his Diocese—Travels six hundred miles on horseback—How he spent his intervals of leisure—Anecdote of Bishop David—The death of the latter—His character—Translation of the see to Louisville—Reasons for and against the change—He regrets to leave Bardstown—Arrival of Sisters of the Good Shepherd—How this colony was obtained—Nature and objects of the Institute—Health of his Coadjutor impaired—The Coadjutor visits France, and resigns—His present retreat—The Bishop left desolate—The third Coadjutor is consecrated—The *Nunc Dimittis*—The Jesuits re-enter the Diocese, and take St. Joseph's college—New college in Louisville—Arrival of the Trappists—Character of their institution—Corner-stone of the new Cathedral laid.

THE first months after the return of Bishop Flaget were spent in the agreeable task of visiting his various institutions. He was rejoiced to find, that their prosperity had not been materially affected by his long absence. His children every where welcomed him as a father. He took pleasure in recounting to them the incidents of his foreign travel, and particularly in giving details of what had occurred in his interesting interviews with the Sovereign Pontiff, whose blessing he warmly imparted to them all.

The next subject which engaged his attention, was the visitation of his Diocese. Though now in his seventy-seventh year, and worn down with the labors of a protracted ministry, his resolution did not falter, and he determined to embark in an undertaking apparently so far above his strength. He ardently wished to see all his spiritual children once more before his death; and, in compliance with the intimation of Gregory XVI., "to speak to them face to face," and bestow upon them the paternal benediction of him who sat in the chair of St. Peter.

About two years were consumed in this laborious duty. Accompanied by one or two missionaries, he visited almost all the congregations of his Diocese, now limited to the State of Kentucky. He made the tour principally on horseback; and in each congregation he preached and gave confirmation. He seemed to have again put on the vigor of his younger days; he sat erect in the saddle, and appeared, after a severe day's ride, not to be much more fatigued than his more youthful companions. He traveled thus at least six hundred miles.

In July, 1841, he had made the visitation of all the congregations, except seven or eight. In a letter to France, he thus refers to the subject:

"I have just terminated an episcopal visitation, during the continuance of which we have traveled more than two hundred leagues. * * * What a joy for my dear Catholics, who had not seen me for so many years, and who scarcely hoped ever to see me again, when I found myself once more in their midst! * * * I have yet seven or eight congregations to visit; towards autumn, God assisting me, I will terminate this long, but most consoling visitation." *

His intervals of leisure were spent in his episcopal residence at Bardstown, in company with his actual and former Coadjutor, Doctors Chabrat and David. He passed no idle hours. When not otherwise employed, he was engaged in reading the Holy Scriptures, the history of the Church, the lives of the saints, or other spiritual books.

The following incident, concerning him and Bishop David, will serve to illustrate the admirable simplicity of these two venerable prelates. On opening a box which the Bishop had received from Europe, containing pictures, medals, and beads, Bishop David signified a wish to have some of the articles, for distribution among his friends. Bishop Flaget turned to him, with smiling raillery, and said: "Father David, you are always asking for something, and yet you never give me any thing!" The other rejoined: "I have given you every thing, since I have given you myself." The plea was admitted; and he failed not to receive his suitable portion of the pious objects.†

The sensitive heart of the Bishop was soon to be grieved by the death of his oldest and most intimate friend, his counsellor and spiritual director for nearly fifty years. The health of Bishop David had been declining for some years; and now it was evident that the time for his departure from this world was rapidly approaching. The Sisters of Charity, whose society he had founded, pressed him to come to Nazareth, and

* Letter to the Abbé de George, author of the French Life, July 3, 1841. *Ibid*—p. 142.

† *Ibid*—p. 143.

there end his days in the midst of his children. He accepted the invitation, and from them he received the kindest attentions and the most delicate nursing. He continued to decline for several months, but retained his consciousness to the last. From the hands of Bishop Flaget he received the last sacraments, and calmly expired on the 12th of July, 1841.

In the letter last quoted, written nine days before his death, Bishop Flaget speaks of his illness in the following terms: "My ancient Coadjutor has been struggling with death for more than three months; he has received all the sacraments from my hands: his resignation is perfect, and he rejoices to suffer in this world, to have, as he says, less to endure in purgatory. O! how different is the death of the true disciples of Christ from that of the impious! * * In less than a year, three of my cotemporaries and old friends will have departed from this world; without doubt to prepare the way for me,—by exhorting me every day to hold myself in readiness to rejoin them."

A truer and more sincerely Christian heart never beat in mortal bosom, than that whose pulsations ceased when Bishop David expired. He died as he had lived. Regularity in all the actions of his life had become with him a settled habit—a second nature. Full of burning zeal for the salvation of souls, he never spared himself. In season and out of season, he preached the word; he persuaded, he besought, he reproved in all patience and doctrine. If he was rigid with others, he was much more so with himself; if candid in stating to others their faults, he was at least as much so in acknowledging his own, and in humbling himself for them, both before God and men. No one was too lowly for his patient instruction and tender care; no one too high, to escape the firm, but humble expression of his opinion, whether it was flattering or admonitory. The older clergy of Kentucky who were trained up by him, and all who knew him well, will long hold his name in benediction. His remains repose in the cemetery of Nazareth, and his spiritual daughters have erected a suitable monument to his memory.* He was in his eighty-first year; in the fifty-sixth of his priesthood, and the twenty-second of his episcopacy.

On the day of his death,—though it appears that he had not yet heard of it,—Bishop Flaget, having lately received intelligence of the death of his brother, the curate of Billom, wrote to a member of his family in France, as follows:

"God, in His mercy, wishes that I should prepare for death; for He takes away from me persons who have been much attached to me for more than sixty years: the good Father Bonnet,† my brother, and my old Coadjutor, who is at this moment struggling with death, and who, in three or four days, will be no longer in this world. I bless God for having given me such warnings; in order to detach me more and more from all creatures, and to make me sigh more ardently for heaven, where every thing is holy, every thing is perfect, every thing is happiness, and happiness eternal." ‡

For several years the Bishop had been revolving in

* The classical Latin inscription was written, we believe, by Father Badin.

† A Sulpician of Clermont.

‡ Letter, July 12, 1841. French Life—p. 146.

his mind the project, of having the episcopal see transferred to Louisville. We have seen that, while in Rome in 1836, he conferred with the holy Father on this subject. Bardstown, the cradle of the Diocese, the centre of all the splendid institutions founded under the auspices of our prelate, and for a long time the centre of the Catholic population; was the only point, which could have been at first selected for the location of the see. But in this country, where every thing is constantly changing, a generation often works a revolution in the relative importance of particular localities.

Louisville, which at first was comparatively an unimportant place, having but a mere handful of Catholics, and these mostly indifferent to the practice of their Religion, had now become not only the largest city in the Diocese, but also the seat of a large and fast increasing Catholic population. Its situation on the Ohio at the interruption of navigation, and its central position in the length of the State stretching along that river; above all, the prospect of its still more rapid growth, and the constant influx into it of Catholics from the interior of the Diocese, but chiefly from abroad: it being, in a word, the great centre and commercial emporium of the State, rendered it evidently the most suitable place for the episcopal see.

The Bishop much regretted to leave Bardstown. It had been his residence for more than twenty years; the reminiscences of thirty years of his episcopacy were associated with the place; and the substantial fruits of his labors during that period lay within it, or clustered in its immediate vicinity. There were his fine cathedral, his college and seminary, the convents of

Nazareth and Loretto, the college of St. Mary's,—to say nothing of other institutions.

By long and pleasant association, and by the interchange of mutual offices of kindness, he had become much endeared to the inhabitants of Bardstown, both Catholic and Protestant. All would be deeply pained at his leaving them. But, on the other hand, believing that the interests of Religion would be promoted by the removal of his see, and that its location in the largest city of the Diocese was, moreover, more conformable to the spirit and usage of the Church, he decided to make the change.

The pontifical Rescript authorizing the translation was received by him early in the year 1841; the time for carrying it into effect was left to his own judgment. Finding that the inhabitants of Louisville were all favorably disposed towards the project, and that the Protestants themselves would unite with the Catholics in warmly welcoming him to the city, he set about making the necessary preliminary arrangements, and removed thither, with his Coadjutor, towards the close of the year. His Vicar General * had preceded him some months, in order to prepare the way.

Bishop Flaget was not disappointed in the expectations he had conceived, of the benefits likely to accrue to Religion from the step he had taken, after so much mature deliberation. While Catholicity in the interior was not materially affected by the change, it gave a new impulse to Religion in Louisville. The inhabitants of the city, without distinction of creed, exhibi-

* The present Bishop of Charleston. The Bishop was to have been installed at Christmas; but his illness delayed the ceremony.

ted a commendable liberality in co-operating with him in every good work; they came forward generously to support every appeal made to them on behalf of Catholic charities; and the Catholic population also rapidly increased. On the death of the holy prelate, eight years later, the Catholic population of the city was about one-fourth of that of the entire Diocese.

Personally, the Bishop had no little inconvenience to suffer from the change. In his old age he had to sever ties, which so many years of affectionate association with old friends had drawn around his heart. He had to leave a residence in which he was surrounded by every comfort, to live in a new place, with fewer conveniences, and in the midst of comparative strangers. He had to leave his dear solitude in the country seat near Bardstown, to take up his abode amid the noise and confusion of the city. But he had never been in the habit of counting the cost to himself, when it was question of discharging what he believed to be a duty to others and to the Church.

About a year after his removal to Louisville, the heart of the Bishop was rejoiced by the arrival from France of a colony of religious ladies, belonging to that heroic institute, whose object it is to reclaim to virtue the fallen and degraded of their own sex. These devoted Sisters of Charity of the Good Shepherd reached Louisville December 1st, 1842, from the mother house of Angers. Much as he was gladdened by their arrival, his joy at first was not unmingled with regret; as he had not expected them so soon, and had as yet made no arrangements for their accommodation. But these heroic ladies had already made too many sacrifices in carrying out the painful, but sublimely charitable object of their order, to be deterred by inconveniences comparatively so light. They were lodged for nine months in a house of the Bishop adjoining the academy of Cedar Grove, Portland, where they applied themselves to the study of English; until their monastery in Louisville could be built and prepared for their reception.

While in France, the Bishop, as we have seen, had been detained for some time at Angers by a severe illness. He here became acquainted with the institute of the Good Shepherd; and while he admired the purpose for which it was erected, he was forcibly struck by the uniform cheerfulness and gaiety exhibited by the generous religious, in performing a task so painful to the refined feelings of nature, and so revolting to the sentiments of the world. He expressed an earnest wish to have a colony of the order in his Diocese. The mother general communicated with her council on the subject; and as the intelligence spread through the different communities, so many were found anxious to devote themselves to the distant mission, that the superior was greatly embrarassed in selecting from the numerous candidates the requisite number of five or six for the intended colony. At length it was resolved, that it should be composed of representatives from the different Catholic nations in Europe,—France, Germany, Italy, Belgium, and Ireland;—thus presenting to the new world, torn by conflicting sects, a beautiful illustration of Catholic unity.

On his return to America, the Bishop, after conferring with his Coadjutor as to the resources of the Diocese, feared that he could not then spare the necessary funds for founding the new establishment, without injuring other important interests. Among others, his purpose of soon commencing the erection of a new cathedral in Louisville was the most prominent. The other establishments of the Diocese had been founded, and had gradually grown up, chiefly by the labors of the early members themselves, with little, if any aid from Diocesan funds; this one, could be created only by the resources of the Bishop himself. Accordingly he wrote to Angers, deeply regretting the circumstances, which induced him to ask for some delay in sending the proposed colony.

But the measure had already been resolved on at the mother house; and it was decided to carry it into immediate execution, leaving the question of resources to Providence. The colony was in consequence sent out at once, more in accordance with what was believed to be the ardent wish of the Bishop, than with the advice which prudence had prompted him to give.

The Sisters entered their extensive new establishment, erected entirely at the Bishop's expense, on the 4th of September, 1843.

Their institute was no sooner known, than it was greatly admired by many among the Protestants, as well as by the Catholics. The number of penitents soon became as great as the house designed for their use could accommodate. Liberal presents were made to the infant establishment; their marketing was often furnished gratuitously by Protestants; and the needle-work, their chief reliance for a maintenance, flowed in on them so abundantly, that the institution was soon able to support itself. A large and commodious chapel was afterwards erected; and during the last year, a spacious building was put up, for the separate class of religious Magdalenes, to be composed of such penitents as might give indications of a desire to retire permanently from the dangers of the world, and devote their lives to the religious exercises of the cloister.

About this time, a new trouble of a weighty character afflicted the heart of the good prelate. The health of his second Coadjutor—Dr. Chabrat—had been declining for some years; and now he was threatened with the loss of his sight. In this emergency, after having for some time submitted to a severe and judicious course of treatment from Dr. Gross, one of the most eminent surgeons of the Union, he decided to go to France for farther medical advice. On his arrival in Paris, he applied to M. Sichel, one of the first oculists in Europe; who, while he fully approved the treatment previously adopted by Dr. Gross, gave him but slight hopes of a restoration of sight.

Much to the grief of Bishop Flaget, Dr. Chabrat had, since the first appearance of the malady, entertained serious thoughts of offering his resignation. He had written to Rome on the subject, and received a reply, referring the matter for farther consideration to the approaching Provincial Council of Baltimore, to be held in 1846. The fathers of this Council, after occupying much time in weighing the reasons for and against, finally declined to advise the resignation; and the two neighboring Bishops of Cincinnati and Nashville kindly offered their services during his disability, to aid him in the visitation of the Diocese.

After the Council, the malady continued to increase, and Dr. Chabrat decided again to visit Europe. On his arrival in Paris, the oculist, to whom he had previously applied, at once declared, that unless he resigned his charge and remained in France, he would soon become irretrievably blind. This able physician went himself to Monsignor FORNARI, the papal Nuncio at Paris, and presented the matter in so strong a light, that the latter resolved to write at once to the Holy See, recommending the acceptance of his resignation.

The answer from Rome was favorable. Some time in 1847, Dr. Chabrat was released from his charge as Coadjutor, and he became henceforth simply titular Bishop of Bolina. He has since remained in France; and though not yet stricken with total blindness, his sight has become constantly more and more impaired. He resides at Mauriac, in the house formerly inhabited by his father; and he leads a secluded life, devoted to prayer and preparation for death. His long and arduous labors on the missions of America, must cheer him in his retirement.

These events were a source of most poignant affliction to Bishop Flaget. He had now seen two Coadjutors disabled and compelled to resign at his side, while he still stood up, battling bravely in the arduous missionary field. But his own energies were now fast failing; and he felt himself incapable of attending to the wearing duties of the episcopal office.

To be left thus alone in his extreme old age, with infirmities fast growing on him, was indeed a severe trial, even for one who had already endured so much. During those two years of suspense, when his Coadjutor was mostly absent, and during the additional interval of nearly a year which elapsed from the acceptance of Dr. Chabrat's resignation to the appointment of the new Coadjutor, no one not intimately acquainted with him could estimate aright the amount of acute suffering caused by his exquisite sensibility, wrought upon by his ever-present sense of a responsibility for which he felt himself totally inadequate.

He spent most of this time in prayer; and from his lips audible sighs would often break forth, deploring what he called his utter "nullity," * and the impossibility in which he found himself, from almost continual vertigo in the head, † to think of any serious business. Yet in all things he was fully resigned to the holy will of God; and his ordinary ejaculations at the end of all his prayers and sighs were: "May the good God be praised! ‡ May His holy will be done!" §

At length his suspense was over; his third Coadjutor was appointed. On the 10th of September, 1848, he himself, though extremely feeble, went through the long and solemn ceremony of the consecration, assisted by the Bishops of Philadelphia and Nashville; the Archbishop of St. Louis preaching the consecration sermon. The Bishop of Charleston, detained on the Ohio by low water, arrived only an hour after the conclusion of the ceremony.

This was the last public official act of the holy prelate. Returning to his room, all exhausted with a

---

* *Ma nullité*—was a favorite expression.

† *Ma tête n'y est plus*—was another.

‡ *Que le Bon Dieu soit loué!*

§ *Que sa sainte volonté soit faite!*

labor above his strength, he exclaimed, much affected: "Now can I sing the canticle of holy Simeon—NUNC DIMITTIS—Now dost Thou dismiss Thy servant, O Lord, in peace!"

Providence permitted him to linger on earth for more than two years longer, that he might be consoled by several occurrences; which were well calculated to cheer him, and prepare him to descend to the tomb without uneasiness, and in perfect composure of spirit. The first was the re-entrance of the Jesuits into the Diocese. The Bishop had long wished to place St. Joseph's college under the charge of this illustrious order, to which he was always much attached. When he heard of the restoration of the society by Pius VII., he was at St. Louis on his visitation; and the entry in his Journal shows how his heart bounded with joy at the intelligence. When the Jesuits first arrived in Kentucky, and took the college of St. Mary—in 1832—he also rejoiced, that he, a native of Billom, should have had the happiness to introduce into his Diocese a branch of that society, whose first college in France was founded precisely at Billom, three hundred years before.*

Two months before the consecration of his last Coadjutor,—in July, 1848,—negotiations with the Jesuits of the vice-province of St. Louis had terminated in an agreement, by which they took charge of St. Joseph's college; and they had soon afterwards entered upon the successful management of that institution.

The Jesuits also took charge of the Catholic free school for boys in Louisville, and not long afterwards

* Journal, January, 1832.

erected a spacious edifice for a college, on ground adjoining. This institution was, from its first commencement, in a very flourishing condition. It numbered from a hundred to two hundred students; while in the free school there was an average attendance of about two hundred Catholic boys. The building for the last named school had been erected by subscription a few years before, and it had previously been conducted by two Irish Franciscan brothers.

Another of the joyful occurrences to which we alluded above, was the arrival of a colony of about forty Trappists from the Abbey of Melleray, in France. The Bishop had always been partial to this rigid order; and we have seen, that, more than forty years before, he had made formal application to be received as a member.

The Trappists arrived in Louisville, late in December, 1848; and they immediately proceeded to take possession of their new home at Gethsemane, fourteen miles beyond Bardstown. This place, having about sixteen hundred acres of land attached, had been for many years used as an academy by a branch of the Lorettines. The buildings were of wood, but they were deemed suitable for the temporary use of the monks; and the farm with the establishment had been accordingly purchased some months previously, by two members of the order, sent out to America for the purpose of finding a suitable location.

Apprehending trouble in France, the superiors of Melleray had deemed it prudent to procure, in a distant land, a secure asylum to which they could retire, in case they should be driven from France. With this view, they had applied to the papal Nuncio at Paris, and he had advised them to send a deputation to Bishop Flaget. The result was what we have just stated.

Some time afterwards, an additional colony came out from France; and the present number of members is sixty-two.

These monks belong to the more strict observance of the Cistercian institute, one of the most austere religious orders in the Church.* They devote their lives to manual labor, to perpetual silence, to fasting, and to prayer. Seven hours of each day are spent in the church, and as many are given to manual labor. They never taste flesh, fish, eggs, nor butter. Their penitential austerities would seem almost incredible in this age of boasted progress and enlightenment, as well as of boundless sensual indulgence. Their rigorous lives astonish the worldling, who can appreciate nothing which does not contribute to material progress and enjoyment; they are a matter of admiration for all true Christians, who, enlightened by Christian faith, are able to estimate the awful malice of sin and the absolute necessity of penance. He who Himself led a poor and hard life, and who said to His disciples, "If any one will come after Me, let him deny himself, take up his cross, and follow me," must look down with a smile of complacency on those pious recluses, who, to expiate their own and others' sins, devote themselves, for His love, to this life of severe privations.

Yet, in the midst of their hard labors and penitential austerities, these good monks are remarkably cheerful and happy. The peace of God, surpassing all

* The Carthusians live under a rule perhaps more rigorous still.

understanding, beams constantly from their countenances. They have been hitherto blessed with general good health, notwithstanding the tribute every foreigner has to pay to our unequal climate. They enjoy more real peace of mind, and more heartfelt happiness, than many, who, reposing in the midst of luxury, deride their lives as mere folly and fanaticism.

The house of Gethsemane was commenced under such favorable auspices, and its prospects were so flattering, that when the prior—Father Eutropius—was lately in Europe, he received from the hands of the Sovereign Pontiff, Pius IX., a Rescript, by which the priory was erected into an Abbey, and an election was ordered to be held for choosing the first Abbot. This papal Rescript bore date July 21, 1850.

On his return from Europe, the prior was almost unanimously chosen Abbot; and eight months afterwards, in the fall of 1851, the proper documents approving of the election having come from Rome, the new Abbot was solemnly blessed by the Bishop of Louisville, in the old cathedral of Bardstown.

Adjoining the Abbey, there is a free school for boys lately opened, and already frequented by more than sixty children of the neighborhood. The monks are chiefly agriculturalists; and by introducing the culture of the grape, and other useful improvements, they will no doubt contribute much to—what is most valued in our *enlightened* age of money-making—the material prosperity of the country.

We may well imagine, with what joy our holy Bishop saw thus renewed, amidst the forests of his Diocese, the wonders which had been witnessed in the primitive period of the Church, in the austere lives of the solitaries who peopled the deserts of Nubia, Syria, and Thebais.

On the 15th of August, 1849, the corner-stone of the new cathedral of Louisville was laid, with the usual solemn rites, in presence of an immense concourse of citizens. The Bishop was too feeble to assist at the ceremony; he, however, overlooked the scene from a balcony of his residence; and at the close of the service, with uplifted eyes and hands, but with a weak and tremulous voice, he invoked a solemn benediction on the enterprise, and on the assembled multitude.

Alas! that he did not live to see this great work accomplished!

CHAPTER XV.

HIS DEATH AND CHARACTER.

Finishing his course—The day of eternity—The setting sun—His preparation for death—An incident—His estimate of life—Failing of faculties—What privation gave him most concern—Vertigo—The HEAD of Christ—Forgetting every thing—His favorite expressions and ejaculations—Symptoms of approaching death—He receives the last sacraments—Affecting scene—He "sleeps in the Lord"—His funeral—Description of an eye-witness—Brief sketch of his character—The book of nature—Parable of the hen and chickens—Conclusion.

THE mortal career of our holy prelate was now well nigh run. With St. Paul he could say: "I have fought the good fight, I have finished my course, I have kept the faith; for the rest, there is laid up for me a crown of justice, which the Lord the just Judge will render to me in that day." * The shades of evening were fast gathering around that pure spirit, soon to deepen into the darkness of night; but through these gathering shades and this increasing darkness, the eye of faith already perceived the dawn of a day which should know no night, the bright and unclouded day of eternity, in which he was to receive the reward of his labors.

So holy a life must needs be followed by a holy and happy death: "Precious in the sight of the Lord is

* 2 Timothy, iv., 7, 8.

the death of His saints." His was as glorious even in the eyes of men, as it was precious in the sight of God. Looking at his career with the eye of faith, the portion of it which appears most luminous is that precisely, which to the eye of nature would seem the most shrouded in gloom—the months which immediately preceded his final dissolution. The sun of his life sank calmly to its rest; but as it did so, it lighted up with golden tints the clouds which overhung the horizon, reflecting a mild, but glorious flood of light over the world it left behind.

His whole life may be said to have been one continual preparation for death. He directed all his actions towards this great "moment on which eternity depends." As the event approached, his thoughts turned to it more frequently, and his preparation became more immediate and earnest. To his friends, who often wished him better health and many more years of life, he constantly replied: "O no, pray not for a longer life, but pray for a holy and happy death." This was all he desired and asked for: his most fervent aspiration was to exchange this life of toil and trouble for one of never ending bliss.

The following incident, selected almost at random among many of a similar kind, will serve to show how much he was disengaged from flesh and blood, and how ardently he panted for a heavenly crown:

A clergyman,* a relative of his family, being about to return to France a few years before the prelate's death, on taking his leave, asked him what message he should bear from him to his relatives? "Tell them,"

* The Rev. F. Chambige.

promptly rejoined the holy man, "that I wish most earnestly to go to heaven, where I expect to have the happiness to meet them." This was the only message he could be induced to send.

He had never been attached to this world. His estimate of life, drawn by himself in a letter written to his brother about five years before his own death, was that which he had formed in theory from his early youth; and which now, in his old age, he fully realized and *felt*, as a lesson taught by experience:

"My very dear brother, you will do me a favor by telling me, what you think of the long life you have enjoyed in this world. As for me, mine, which is nearly as long as yours, appears to me but as a dream: for recalling to my memory two or three facts which occurred when I was not more than four years old, and thinking of what happened only last week, these two epochs seem to me to touch each other, and the interval which separates them appears as nothing in my eyes." *

It may be said, without exaggeration, that, especially during the last two years of his life, almost his whole time was given up to prayer. He was even heard frequently uttering prayers during the intervals of sleep. The recitation of the divine office had always been one of his favorite occupations; for several years before his death, this pleasing duty became extremely difficult to him, owing to his impaired sight and failing memory. An ecclesiastic generally aided him in the recitation; but at length, he was compelled to give it up entirely, more than a year previous to his death. He made the

* Letter, December 8, 1844. French Life—p. 161.

sacrifice with great reluctance, and only after repeated assurances from those on whose judgment he relied, that he was not only not bound to say it, but that he was also in a measure bound not to attempt what he could not properly accomplish. He supplied, however, the omission by the recitation of the beads, not merely three times per day, but oftener three times three.

He had always cherished a most tender devotion to the Virgin Mother of God; he had imbibed this feeling at the same pure fountain of living waters from which all the saints of God,—from St. John, the beloved Disciple, down to St. Alfonso Liguori,—had drunk it in so abundantly. He had made it a practice through life to recite a part of the Rosary daily; and now, while unable to perform other devotions which required reading, he gladly availed himself of the occasion to multiply this simple, but touching form of supplication.

Before his sight had failed him, he divided his time between prayer and reading pious books. The holy Scriptures, the Sufferings of Christ, the Following of Christ, and Butler's Lives of the Saints, were his favorites. The last named voluminous work he perused through twice during the last few years of his life, following the calendar of the Church. His conversations frequently turned, easily and gracefully, on pious subjects. He was habitually cheerful, even when suffering most acute bodily pain; and those who visited him always went away with a good impression, and with a higher estimation of virtue. Thus did he diffuse around him "the good odor of Christ."

His cherished subject for meditation was the Passion of Christ. While on his missions, and frequently at home, he used no other book for meditation, save that of the Cross of Christ. In this he read every thing; in this his soul found abundant and wholesome food, and his heart a lively relish and a sincere delight. In this he found the surest solace in his troubles, the safest guide in his doubts and perplexities, and a tower of strength in his multiplied infirmities and sufferings.

He had suffered for many years from a malady in the head, causing an excruciating pain, which was often followed by vertigo. His chief comfort was found in meditating on the Head of our blessed Savior, crowned with thorns for the love of us. A pious young lady of France had sent him a handsome colored engraving of the Head of Christ, thus encircled and pierced with the thorny crown. He had it constantly before his eyes; he turned to it frequently; and when suffering pain, he held it in his hands, pressed it fervently to his lips, and, with a heart throbbing with pious emotion, asked himself how *he* could complain, when his Savior God, though Innocence itself, had suffered without repining, all this excruciating agony!

We will let him speak for himself on this subject, in the letter of thanks he addressed to the person, who had made him the acceptable and opportune present:

"I will tell you, that for many years the Passion of this divine Master has furnished the subject of all my meditations. * * * As, for a long time, I have been incapable of all serious application, my old head being so weak and disorganized, I did nothing but annoy my friends with my continual piteous complaints, rubbing without ceasing my head, which is the seat of my sufferings; but when this HEAD of my divine

Savior, all crowned with thorns, was placed in my hands the very sight appalled me; my lamentations ceased; and I took strongly the resolution to suffer thenceforth without complaint and without sighs, even should my headaches become ten times more painful:—and it is to your precious gift, or rather to your tender devotion for Jesus Crucified, that I am indebted for this resignation, in the midst of my cruel sufferings." *

His faculties were gradually impaired by the approaches of death. His mind became incapable of examining abstruse questions; but whenever his judgment could be brought to bear upon a case clearly unfolded before it, though enfeebled, it was sound to the last. What failed him most, was his memory; he was conscious of it himself, and often playfully remarked: "I forget every thing; could I but forget myself, I would be a perfect man." These, and many other expressions, indicating a profound humility and a perfect resignation to the holy will of God, and breathing a most ardent desire for heaven with a burning love of God, he repeated almost as constantly in his old age, as did St. John the Evangelist his favorite exhortation: "My little children, love one another."

Throughout life, he had been always noted for his ardent devotion to Jesus Christ in the Blessed Sacrament. Whithersoever he went, his first visit was ever to the holy altar, on which the LAMB was reposing. Here he passed many of the happiest hours of his life, in delicious communion with the Savior whom he loved. Daily to ascend the holy altar, and offer up the

---

* Letter to Mademoiselle De la Boissiere, October 8, 1845. French Life—pp. 162-3.

great Sacrifice of the new law, he deemed his dearest and highest privilege.

Six months before his death, he was deprived of this happiness. Unable to leave his room without assistance, his chief concern was for the loss of this blessed privilege. He had himself conducted to a balcony, looking towards the sanctuary of the church; and here, in pleasant weather, he spent whole hours together in prayer to Jesus, on that altar to which he was unable to make a nearer approach. When the benediction of the Blessed Sacrament was given, he caused himself to be warned of the solemn moment by the sacristan, and he bowed down reverently to participate in the blessing.

In August, 1849, the shoulder, which had been injured twenty-one years before at Detroit, suddenly swelled and turned of a livid hue. Apprehensions were entertained, lest mortification might ensue; but the tumor yielded gradually to judicious medical treatment.* Scarcely, however, had it abated, when his limbs became swollen, and every symptom of approaching dissolution appeared in a shape not to be mistaken. The venerable man himself felt that his time was short, and he redoubled the earnestness of his preparation for death.

The cough which had troubled him for many years, especially in the winter, now returned with increased violence. The winter of 1849–50 was very trying to a constitution so much shattered, and now struggling with mortal disease; but it was so robust, even in its ruins, as

* His ordinary physician was Dr. John Hagan, an eminent practitioner.

still to resist for some months the approaches of death. His friends even indulged the hope, that he might survive the attack.

So gradually did he sink, and so gently did death approach its victim, that his attendants, and even himself, did not seem aware of the change daily wrought in his health. The night of February 10th, 1850, was a very restless one for him; a good portion of it was passed in a sleep troubled with delirium; but even while delirious, the holy man seemed constantly engaged in prayer. His children now knew that they were very soon to lose a father on earth; to gain, as they had every reason to hope, an intercessor in heaven. He had often assured them, raising his eyes to heaven, that "if he could once enter into that celestial abode, he would be of much more service to them and to his Diocese, than he could possibly be on earth."

It was not thought prudent to defer any longer the administration of the last rites of the Church; and accordingly, at noon on the 11th, the Bishop Coadjutor, assisted by all the clergy of the city, eleven in number, brought him solemnly the holy Viaticum. He was in the full possession of consciousness, and received the Body and Blood of Christ, and subsequently Extreme Unction and the last benediction for plenary Indulgence, with a fervor and concentrated devotion, which deeply affected all who were present. Unable himself to read the profession of faith, his secretary read it for him, slowly and distinctly; and he followed it, article by article, with absorbed attention, and indications of assent, causing certain passages to be read twice, that he might understand them better, or relish them longer.*

He then said some words expressive of his ardent attachment to his clergy, religious, and people; and at a request from his Coadjutor, he gave, so far as his failing strength would permit, in the regular form, his last solemn episcopal benediction. All in the room were kneeling, with heads reverently bowed down; and tears started to many an eye, at the touching scene of the patriarch blessing his children for the last time.

He rallied somewhat after the reception of the sacraments; his lips still moved in prayer; he caused his favorite book, the Sufferings of Christ, to be read to him. A crucifix lay before him, and he often pressed his lips to it with tender affection. At half after five o'clock in the evening, he calmly expired, without a struggle.

He died, as he had lived,—a saint; and the last day was perhaps the most interesting and impressive of his whole life. Tranquilly, and without a groan, did he "fall asleep in the Lord,"—like an infant gently sinking to its rest.

His remains were laid out in state in the church of St. Louis; and during the interval between his decease and interment, they were visited by great multitudes, both Catholics and Protestants. A gentle smile of peace sat upon his countenance; and it was edifying to look upon those pale but placid features, thus bearing the visible impress of sanctity in death. The Catholic congregations of the city vied with one another in zeal

* Particularly the article, "This true Catholic faith, out of which none can be saved, I now truly possess," &c.

for the privilege of watching in the church during the night.

On the third day, his burial took place, in accordance with the prescriptions of the Ceremonial for the interment of a Bishop. His successor sang a solemn high Mass *De Requiem*, and the Bishop of Cincinnati pronounced the panegyric with his usual eloquence. His old friend and fellow laborer in the early missions of Kentucky—the last survivor of that apostolic band—the venerable Father Badin, was also present, and followed his remains to the grave.

The deceased had always expressed a paternal interest in the success of the establishment of the Good Shepherd, and, in accordance with what was believed to be his own wish, his relics were placed temporarily in a vault within the enclosure of that monastery. Though the weather was very inclement, thousands walked in the funeral procession. The clergy, the orphans, and the children of the free schools, followed immediately after the remains, which were borne by members of the different Catholic congregations, in a coffin richly ornamented with the episcopal insignia and the emblems of death, by the Sisters of the Good Shepherd.

On the completion of the new cathedral, his relics will be solemnly translated to the crypt beneath the high altar.

An eye-witness thus describes the funeral service and procession:

"During the two nights that his remains were exposed in St. Louis' church, the various Catholic congregations of the city solicited the honor to watch over them, through their respective deputations: the first night was assigned to our German brethren, who spent the whole time in prayer in behalf of their departed Bishop: the same duty was performed on the second night by members of the English congregation. On the day previous to the burial, the whole Office for the Dead was chanted in choir, by all the clergy of the city and neighborhood; the Right Rev. Bishop Purcell, of Cincinnati, officiating on the occasion. Thursday, the 14th instant, had been appointed for the final ceremony of the burial service; on that day, the remains were to be interred in a temporary vault, within the enclosure of the Good Shepherd Asylum, this being the place selected by Bishop Flaget himself, with a view to secure to himself the benefit of the fervent prayers of his dear children. Long before the hour appointed for this solemn service, the church was crowded to overflowing by multitudes of all creeds and denominations. At nine o'clock, the funeral service commenced with the Pontifical Mass, sung by Right Rev. Bishop Spalding, attended by Rev. J. Quinn as assistant priest, and the Rev. F. Chambige and J. M. Bruyere, as deacon and sub-deacon. The Holy Sacrifice being concluded, the Right Rev. Bishop Purcell, of Cincinnati, ascended the pulpit, and in a strain of glowing eloquence, portrayed the principal features of a life so rich in good works, and so fruitful in benefits to the Church of God. From the most conspicuous incidents of a long and well spent career, the distinguished orator, like the diver into the deep, drew forth sparkling gems and precious pearls, which he exhibited to the admiration of his attentive audience.

"At the close of the funeral oration, as an homage offered to the last surviving companion of Bishop Flaget, the venerable *Protosacerdos* of the American church, Father Badin, was requested to perform the *last absolution* over the remains of his departed friend. Preparations for the funeral procession were then made.

"It is exceedingly to be regretted, that the unfavorable state of the weather did not permit the carrying into full execution of the appropriate arrangements previously made for this last ceremony. So far, however, as it was possible, the procession was organized as follows:

"1st. The boys of St. Aloysius' free school, followed by the pupils of St. Aloysius' college, under the guidance of Father Emig, S. J. 2d. The boys of the German Catholic schools. 3d. The German Benevolent Societies, with their bands of music. 4th. The Cathedral Benevolent Society. 5th. The clergy, in surplices, preceded by the cross-bearer and his two assistants. 6th. The Bishops of Cincinnati and Louisville, preceded by the venerable *Protosacerdos*. 7th. The remains of the saintly Bishop, carried by deputations from all the congregations of the city, the coffin having been tastefully ornamented with the episcopal insignia and religious emblems, by the Sisters of the Good Shepherd; before the bier marched two Acolytes, bearing the mitre and crozier. 8th. The members of the Bishop's household. 9th. The orphan girls of St. Vincent's Asylum, preceded by the Sisters of Charity. 10th. The pupils of the Female free school, with those of the Presentation school. 11th. The girls of the other Catholic schools of the city, both English and German.

12th. Finally, the members of the three Catholic congregations of Louisville.

"The procession, being formed as above stated, began to move on slowly, with the greatest order and decorum. Neither the cold rain which was falling, nor the unpleasant condition of the streets, nor the crowds of people advancing at the same time, on the opposite side-walks, were able to disturb the imposing funeral march. The solemnity of the funeral pomp was enhanced by the silence which reigned, interspersed occasionally by the solemn chant of the Church, or the mournful dirge struck up by the musical bands.

"Arrived at the gate of the convent of the Good Shepherd, only a small portion of that vast assemblage could be permitted to enter the enclosure, and witness the last ceremony to be performed over the grave. Around the spot where the precious remains of the holy man were to be deposited stood the devoted Sisters of the Good Shepherd, at the head of their fervent penitents, ready to receive the sacred deposit entrusted, for a time, to their care and guardianship. I must not omit mentioning here a very striking evidence of the tender devotion and veneration the bereaved flock of Bishop Flaget bore to the sanctity of their departed father. For a time, it became necessary to yield to the pious wishes of his sorrowing children, all anxious to have some object of piety to touch the venerable remains of their sainted Bishop. In a moment, just as the lid was about to be laid on the coffin, the face of the holy man was literally covered with beads, medals, crucifixes, and other objects of devotion. Every one around the hallowed remains was anxious to keep about him some relic of the venerable man, as a memorial of a life, which, for more than half a century, had shone forth a brilliant pattern of true virtue. The pious devotion of the multitude being at length satisfied, the closing rites were performed, and all returned home with a full persuasion, that if they had lost their father on earth, they had gained an intercessor in heaven.

"On the completion of the new cathedral, the remains of the holy Bishop will be translated into the crypt under the main altar: meantime, they lie in the convent of the Good Shepherd, a fit and suitable tomb for one who has been so eminently a good and faithful pastor of the flock committed to his charge." *

Thus died, in odor of sanctity, the first Bishop who ever labored in the missions of the West. He was in the eighty-seventh year of his age, the fortieth of his episcopacy, and the sixty-second of his priesthood. His "children will rise up and call him blessed."

We need not enlarge on his character. Those who have perused these imperfect Sketches, will be enabled to estimate it for themselves.

His whole life was given to God; and God did but bless and crown His own work, when He prospered all the undertakings of His servant, for promoting His glory and the good of Religion.

The soul of the holy prelate was filled with the love of God; and this was the animating principle of all his actions. His ardent zeal for the salvation of souls, which caused him cheerfully to undergo so many labors and endure so many privations,—on what was it based,

* The Rev. J. M. Bruyere, correspondent of the Catholic Telegraph and Advocate. February 23, 1850.

but the ardent wish to promote thereby the glory of God? He knew and felt, that the most sublime of all occupations, is that which makes men co-operate with God for the salvation of souls ransomed by the blood of His Son.

This principle of divine love was kept alive in his heart by constant prayer. He never omitted his daily meditation, even during the course of his longest and most fatiguing journeys.* Whenever it was at all possible, he daily offered up the holy sacrifice, and passed some time before the Blessed Sacrament. We have seen also, that he never omitted to recite daily a portion of the Rosary. He also frequently perused, with much relish, books of devotion, and treatises on spiritual subjects.

"His conversation was in heaven." His treasure was there; and thither his heart instinctively turned. He possessed a happy tact in directing conversation towards spiritual subjects, without annoying his companions or visiters. Every one perceived at a glance, that "out of the abundance of the heart the mouth spoke." No one was ever thrown into contact with him, without receiving an impression favorable to piety. He was a living example of what St. Paul says: "Piety is profitable unto all things." It influenced his most ordinary actions, and gave them a winning grace and sweet attractiveness, not of this world. Whithersoever he went, a blessing seemed to follow in his footsteps. His daily walk, deportment, and conversation thus

* A standing entry in his Journal, while traveling, was the intimation, at the beginning of each day, in a kind of short-hand, that he and his companions had performed their "spiritual exercises."

continually radiated the light of heaven on the dull scenes of this earth.

The works of the visible creation were for him so many books, in which he read the goodness and surpassing beauty of God. In his Journal, he happily expresses this idea:

"O God! how grand and admirable are Thy works! Grant that they may be for me a BOOK, in which I may read Thy goodness and Thy infinite riches." *

His faith extracted spiritual food from every object and occurrence; and, like St. Francis of Sales, he happily and gracefully turned everything to the advantage of piety. Our pages have already recorded many examples of this trait. We here present another, too exquisite to be omitted. It is taken from a letter to one of his brothers in France, the notary of Billom, dated Nov. 17, 1821:

"My Dear Brother;—this morning, after having performed my spiritual exercises, I walked out of my apartment; not for a change of air, for that which I breathed on the terrace circulated also freely in the chamber, where 'my grandeur' reposed, with as much liberty as it could have done on the plains of the ocean; but rather to relax my members, and to contemplate the grand spectacle which nature presents, when the sun first appears to illumine and embellish it with his rays. This brilliant scene made me forget the cold pervading the atmosphere; and it suggested to me a thousand thoughts, delicious both to the spirit and to the heart.

"I was thus musing, when a hen, a tenant of the place,

* While admiring the beauties of the St. Lawrence River, in descending it, July 2, 1818.

and the mother of a numerous family, came to my side, —not indeed to contemplate the beauties of nature, but to seek after its productions, and to nourish therewith the eleven chickens which followed in her train. In spite of myself she riveted my whole attention; and I could not avoid admiring her prudence and maternal affection. It was not on the side of the north that she took her walks; for there her little ones would have beentoo much exposed to the rigor of the cold. But she walked gravely back and forth, near my enormous chimney, in which wood is burnt by cords,* or in those places which were most exposed to the solar heat.

"She did not limit to this her maternal attentions. Frequently she let fall from her bill the grains which she had gathered, to give them to her young brood; and every five or six minutes, after having selected the softest, and, above all, the warmest place, she gave forth the signal of retreat, and immediately her docile little ones, though wholly taken up in the enjoyment of their liberty, and in picking up here and there the grains which they could find, forgot every thing, left all, to run and fly to their tender mother, to nestle in her bosom, and to hide themselves under her wings.

"At this affecting spectacle, I was naturally led to think of the earnest and pressing invitations which our divine Savior makes to all men; who, very different from these little creatures, instead of seeking refuge in the bosom of their Father and their God, wander after vanity, and lose themselves in the ways of lying. But that which presented itself to my mind with the greatest force, and which excited all the affections of

* *Par cordes et toises.*

my heart, was the resemblance which I thought I saw between your family, and this good and vigilant mother who was moving before my eyes."

In one word, he was possessed, in a high degree, of every christian, sacerdotal, and episcopal virtue. Faults and imperfections he, no doubt, had ; for human nature is at best imperfect and frail ;—but for the smallest faults he did the most ample penance.

In him his Diocese has lost a holy Bishop, and the Hierarchy of the Church in the United States, a brilliant ornament. But though "dead, he yet speaketh." His works remain. Besides the many institutions of charity, and monuments to religion and learning which he reared, he has left behind him, for all future generations, the priceless legacy of his virtues.

May they be long embalmed in our minds, and in our HEARTS !

APPENDIX.

Appendix.

THE CHARACTER AND SPIRIT OF BISHOP FLAGET.

THE second part of the French Life is devoted to Sketches of the Virtues of our holy prelate, drawn from the personal observation of the writer, who was his traveling companion in Europe for eighteen months.* They are written according to a plan not unusual with French biographers, who deem the inward life and spirit of an eminent individual worthy of at least as much study as his public acts. We republish such portions of this portraiture, as have been deemed most interesting to readers in this country; who cannot fail to be edified by the estimate of the prelate's character, made by one who knew him intimately during his last visit to Europe. For the translation we are indebted to a person of known taste and accuracy.

I.

HIS SPIRIT OF PRAYER.

WHILE sojourning in Europe, his time was so engrossed by visits which he was compelled to make or receive, by sermons which he was constantly requested to deliver in parishes, communities, and houses of edu-

* These Sketches are entitled: "MONSEIGNEUR FLAGET: *Etude sur son Esprit et ses Vertus.*"

cation, that his patient condescension was constantly put to most severe trials. But, on all occasions, an unalterable serenity and affability appeared in his words and manner. Those who had the happiness of approaching him, were charmed as soon as they beheld him. His speech,—the expression of his countenance, all bespoke the union of his soul with God. For he began each day by fervent prayers, and by meditation prepared his heart for the duties and struggles of his office. He habitually rose at a very early hour, in order to enjoy uninterrupted communion with God ; and when I repaired to his room, in order to obtain his first blessing, his reception had in it something so paternal and touching, that it was easy to perceive that he had been conversing with the Most High.

Being one day much indisposed, I urged him to sleep later the next day. " O no ! " he replied immediately, with unwonted vivacity, " it is only at that time that I can speak to God as I should. Deprive me not of this happiness."

The life of our Lord Jesus Christ was the habitual subject of his meditations. I once inquired of him, whether he was in the habit of using a book when meditating. " Yes," said he ; " but when I meditate on the passion of the Lord,—and I generally do so,—I have no need of one. I know all that by heart."

More than once I surprised him, while engaged in this holy exercise. It is impossible for me to describe his humble and respectful attitude, or the expression of profound recollection which was stamped on his features. He seemed to have entirely forgotten his fatigues and sufferings ; the presence of God engrossed his thoughts.

But, at the approach of certain festivals, his fervor redoubled. In 1838, he was at Turin during the Christmas solemnities. The missionaries of St. Vincent of Paul having courteously offered him hospitality, he was permitted to repair to a little oratory, where he might adore the Blessed Sacrament. The cold was excessive, and the Bishop was laboring under an indisposition which terminated in a dangerous illness; but he continued to repair to his cherished oratory, where, it was evident to all, he received signal favors. His prayer seemed the overflowing of a heart burning with divine love. At times, profound sighs expressed the emotions of his soul; and, unable to speak, his eyes were bedewed with tears. "God,"—he observed to me, at this period,—"has given me the grace, from my youth, to meditate on those mysteries with an especial relish. To contemplate this divine Savior in the manger, has ever afforded me a singular pleasure. I have interrogated our Americans, in order to ascertain the attentions which are bestowed upon the children of the savages and slaves at the moment of their birth; and I have discovered that they are far better treated than was this divine Infant! Oh! God of love!—and, after that, dare I complain of anything?"

He loved also to reflect on the parable, in which the Sovereign Master compares himself to a vine, of which his disciples are the branches. "I have never," he said, "meditated on this text without profit. Oh! my God, grant that this little branch may ever remain attached to the divine trunk. Ah! my child, it is from this sacred trunk that all life proceeds." These last words were accompanied by one of those expressive looks, he so often cast towards heaven.

It may be said that the remembrance of our Lord, in some of the mysteries of His holy life, was ever present to the mind of the venerable Bishop; and that he thence derived strength and consolation. "Truly," he was wont to say, "when we consider the mystery of the incarnation, we are led almost to rejoice for the sin of our first parents. To have a God for Father and Redeemer! *Felix culpa!*—happy fault!!"

But, of all the mysteries, the one in which he most delighted, was that of the Holy Eucharist;—it is not possible to describe the piety with which he offered up the divine Sacrifice. All present were profoundly impressed by his manner. I remember a distinguished Archbishop, who respectfully carried away the sacred linens of which Bishop Flaget had made use; and the Archbishop's secretary afterwards remarked to me: "I am very sure it was to preserve them as relics." As to his thanksgiving, it may be asserted that it lasted the entire day; for everything reminded him of the happiness he had enjoyed in the morning. He often spoke to me of it, and invited me to think of it also; and, having one day said to him: "My Lord, you would have been happy to repose, like St. John, on the bosom of our Lord Jesus Christ, would you not?" "Alas!" he replied, with that accent of faith which animated all his words, "I might do so every day; for this good Savior comes daily to me. What grieves me is, that I think not sufficiently of Him. I think of Him often, it is true, but I ought never to forget Him." On another occasion, he said to me: "A God who desires to give

Himself to us! No, I see no severity in the sentence which shall condemn such ungrateful wretches. Soon will this condemnation be pronounced: 'Depart from me, ye accursed.'"

The pious Bishop was far from falling into this sin of ingratitude. His heart swelled with the liveliest emotions of gratitude; and I, one day, having spoken in admiration of the happiness which St. Paul experienced in pronouncing the name of Jesus Christ: "Ah," said he to me, with touching pathos, "one cannot love any thing else."

It was not merely at certain stated periods, that Bishop Flaget practiced this holy recollection and spirit of prayer. He never lost sight of the presence of God;—and the different objects he beheld, instead of proving sources of distraction to him, tended to promote recollection. From his American correspondence, it is evident that, for many years, he had contracted the habit of being ever mindful of the presence of God. Some extracts from this correspondence will prove our assertion:

In 1805, the prelate had retired for some time to the country,in order to recover from the effects of a long illness. From his solitude, he wrote thus to his family:—"Often I plunge into the depths of those immense forests, where are seen trees coeval with time. Far away from the noise and confusion of cities, nothing interrupts my solitary walks. Even the sun seems to respect these retreats; for his rays reach me not. Amid this repose of nature, I remember with pleasure what history relates of the ancient Germans,—that they made a deity of the silence of the forests;—and, extending my view higher than those poor barbarians, I adore the Author of this silence, and the Source of all Peace. What pious thoughts have come to my mind! What contempt do I not conceive for the world, and all it contains! Happy, could I only learn to contemn myself, and to desire that others should also contemn me!"

At a later period, the duties of the ministry having led him to the famous Falls of Niagara, he wrote to his brothers as follows: — "This spectacle, perhaps the greatest and most magnificent which the universe presents, furnished me with subjects of meditation, which I shall never forget. After having passed three or four hours in contemplating those volumes of water, which are precipitated with a prodigious velocity, from a height of one hundred and fifty feet, it seemed to me I had been there but a moment;—my eyes still desired to rest upon this scene. But night cast over it her sombre veil, and I reluctantly retraced my way to the hotel. As I walked on, I repeated often to myself: Alas! torrents of grace are daily flowing upon the hearts of men,—and upon mine in particular,—and, like those rocks over which this immense river rolls, we are not penetrated by them; and grace returns again into the infinite abyss whence it proceeds, without having produced any fruit." *

It is said of St. Francis of Assisium, that he loved to behold impenetrable forests, lofty rocks, harvest fields and smiling vineyards, the beauty of the wide extended meadow, the freshness of fountains, the verdure of gardens, earth and fire, air and winds; and that he ex-

* See his fuller, but similar description of the Falls, taken from his Journal—*supra*, Chapter viii—p. 129—*seqq.*

horted them to remain pure in order to honor God and serve Him. Bishop Flaget evinced similarly elevated tastes. Every thing in nature spoke to him of God, and his active mind saw in each creature a motive for praising and blessing the Creator. Thus, when the time of prayer came, he had no effort to make in order to recollect himself; it might rather be said that he then entered into his proper element. Prayer was his life; and it has been already seen that, although age deprived him of all else, it could not take from him this precious treasure.

We may hence affirm that this holy Bishop was truly a man of prayer; and, amid the labors and turmoils of a life constantly agitated, he was able to maintain the spirit of prayer. This it was that enabled him to perform such great actions; for, though of ourselves we can do nothing, if God be with us, we can do all things.

II.

HIS HABITUAL PEACE OF MIND.

THE peace of mind which Bishop Flaget enjoyed reminds me of a beautiful thought, found in the works of the learned Father Saint Jure. This pious author compares the world to an immense sphere, of which God is the centre:—"As when a globe is turning round upon its axis, those parts most distant from the centre move with accelerated velocity, while those that are near partake in some degree of the immobility of that centre; in like manner, in this vast universe, where all creatures are borne along with fearful rapidity, those that remain close to God,—the common Centre of all things,

—partake, in a certain degree, of His unalterable peace and eternal repose."

This doctrine being incontestable, it is evident that the soul of Bishop Flaget must have been ever near to God; for it would be difficult to imagine a peace more perfect than that which he possessed. To be candid, however, it must be acknowledged, that he seemed sometimes agitated by the difficulty in which he found himself to meet the exigencies of his position, by the obstacles he met with in the accomplishment of his pious designs, and the scandals he witnessed; but, even under those circumstances, he soon regained tranquillity of heart, by seeking for it in God.

When it was question of his personal interests or feelings, it was rarely that he manifested either dejection or anxiety. He had beforehand prepared himself for disappointment and contradiction; and he was not, consequently, disconcerted. He sought himself so little, that he seldom experienced much pain in disappointment; and his will was kept in such habitual subjection, that, amidst all trials, his first impulse was to bless the hand that sent them. * * *

He knew how to adapt himself to all situations; and he was contented every where. Towards the close of our journey, I had the weakness to show some disinclination for this wandering life, adding, that I longed to be again in my room. "As to me," said he, "now that I have not a room of my own, I consider myself at home every where."

I can never forget his entrance into the town of Annecy. He had started from Lausanne in the morning; the road had proved much longer than the guide books indicated, and the accommodations greatly inferior to what is generally found on our roads in France; so that, instead of arriving at eight o'clock at night, as the Bishop's secretary had been informed we should, it was midnight when we reached our destination. The hotels were at that time crowded; they had ceased to look for the Bishop at the episcopal palace, and he knew not where to find lodgings. After useless researches, the carriage brought him a second time to the General Hotel; but we were again refused admission, as there was not a room to give us. I then asked the prelate, if he would object to pass the night on a mattress, placed on the floor; to which he replied: "Oh! I do not need even a mattress; I am accustomed to sleep in the woods. If you can procure me an arm-chair and some fire, I shall sleep perfectly well."

But, in addressing him, I had given him the title of "My Lord," and the waiters having heard it, one of them said to me: "Sir, you shall have two beds. The Bishop having descended from the carriage, I remained to attend to our baggage; in a few moments I found him at the kitchen fire, keeping profound silence. I took the liberty of asking him the subject of his reflections. "I was thinking, said he, with a smile, "that St. Francis of Sales is laughing at us in Heaven. 'No doubt,' he says, 'they are expecting to lodge in a superb palace; well! I will give them one after my own fashion!'" Then he laughed heartily, adding, that he was happy I had such inconveniences to experience. Having told him, that he would not be so illy accommodated as I had at first feared, two beds having been offered us, he seemed displeased, saying that no one should be incommoded on his account. But measures had already been taken; and some moments after, we were introduced into a small chamber belonging to the servants, where the Bishop considered himself too well accommodated. The next day, according to his custom, he rose early, in order to disturb no one. He made a seat of his traveling bag; and when I awoke, I found him thus seated, tranquilly reciting his office.

When we proceed to treat of the simplicity and condescension of the good Bishop, we shall dwell more at length on this happy condition of a calm and peaceful soul. In effect, the virtues go hand in hand,—all of them descend from heaven; and when they meet on earth, it is easily seen that they are sisters; for they mutually assist one another, and labor often in the same work, with a touching harmony. We will only add, that Bishop Flaget was one of those men of peace spoken of in the Following of Christ, who are proper to promote the peace of others. On merely accosting him, one felt the influence of that peace which was imprinted on his countenance, which embellished his features, and accompanied all his words.

The language, addressed by him to the students of the little seminary of Iseure, fell with peculiar grace and efficacy from his lips. He said to them: "Be friends of virtue, and when age shall whiten your locks, and you can give to your own hearts the testimony that your lives have been pure and without spot, you will not fear death; you will, on the contrary, regard it as a happiness, because it will open heaven for you."

III.

HIS HUMILITY.

It may be concluded from what has been said, that a virtue thus solidly established, must have had for its foundation a profound humility. This humility, ever exhibited in the life of Bishop Flaget, was grave and dignified, simple and natural; because it was sincere. There was seen in him nothing of that studied manner, or that affected politeness, which is often but a veil cast over pride and self-love. It was not necessary for him to compose himself, in order to speak and act as the humble are wont to do.

One day, I having taken the liberty of remonstrating with him on a certain subject, he replied: "I thank you; if I have been mistaken, it is not at all astonishing; I have been awkward all my life."

He had, on the same day, requested me to make some alterations in a manuscript of his; which I did, as his habit of speaking English rendered him liable to commit errors in writing French; but I requested him to say nothing about it, giving him good reasons for thus acting. "No," said he; "never shall I say that I have done what I have not done." Then he added: "While at Rome, I wrote a little notice, at the request of the Holy Father, which I submitted to the correction of the young ecclesiastic who accompanied me. And, of course, I did not conceal the fact."

At the borough of St. Andeol, a compliment having been addressed to the venerable prelate by the orphans of the Presentation convent, he made the following modest, but touching response: "I, too, my children, was left an orphan at three years of age, and if kind friends had not taken care of me, I should never have received the education, which I owe to divine Providence."

I had traveled with the Bishop for nine months, when I discovered at Toulouse, that he had no stamp for his letters. I then offered to have one engraved for him, and asked him what were the armorial bearings of his family? "I was born of poor parents," he answered, "and have never had any coat of arms." "But now that you are a Bishop,"—— "No; I have never thought of such things;—the cross and a crown of thorns would suit me best, and you can have them engraved on the seal, adding the inscription: IN CRUCE SALUS." I acted accordingly.

"Yes, my child," he observed on another occasion, "I am poor, and was born of poor parents; I have lived in poverty, and hope to die poor." * * *

On the 3d of November following, as the traveling carriage was approaching Belley, closing his Breviary, he said to me: "I have just been reading the legend of St. Charles; this biography frightens me. When I see this saint dying at the age of forty-five, after having done so much, what must I think of myself?" "But," I remarked, "you have traveled more than he did." "Oh! yes, undoubtedly; but all his steps were for God; whithersoever he went, he labored; and, sometimes, I have journeyed over a hundred leagues without meeting a single Catholic." I endeavored to represent to him, that such journeys were more painful than those of St. Charles. "Even so," said he; "but then all must be done for God. Oh! no, my dear child, I have yet much to do in order to become an interior man. It is true, I do not often appear exteriorly angry or agitated; but within my soul there is often much agitation, and I ought to be master of all its impulses. If, for example," he added, alluding to a conversation he had had with me four months previously, "the Bishop of Belley should refuse me, saying: 'Go from my house;' and that, on repairing to the hotel, the landlord should address me thus: 'Oh! behold this Bishop, who has caused himself to be so much talked of,—this pretended worker of miracles; we are well acquainted with you, and want none of your company;' well, I ought to bear all this without complaining, even without thinking it hard!"

Such virtue must confound our pride, for the words we have cited were spoken in sincerity. His heart, as truthful as a child's, abhorred the shadow of a falsehood; but I must not omit to state, that Bishop Flaget had attained this height of virtue, only after long and violent efforts; he called to his aid all the succors of grace. I will even add,—for the consolation of those who may be discouraged because they have gained so few victories over themselves,—those words which he addressed to me in confidence: "Every day, in my meditations, I have a reflection on the love of humiliations; but I acknowledge to you in sincerity, that I have never yet been able to desire them, and to seek for them. At my nightly examination, I am embarrassed; it seems to me that, were I asked: Have you attributed to your merit, to your talents, the honor that has been rendered you? I could answer in the negative; but that, notwithstanding, there was always in my heart a feeling of self-gratulation."

God, no doubt, permitted the holy Bishop to experience those attacks of self-love, in order to increase his merits, by multiplying his combats; for he never shrank from the contest; and to secure the victory, he armed himself, by filling his mind and heart with the pure doctrines of faith. When he wished to make use of them for his defence, he had but to turn within himself, and there he heard an interior voice which repeated to him incessantly, as he one day said to me: "Whatever may be our condition, we are still too well treated; for if we were driven from society, it would be only what we merit. One single venial sin renders us unworthy of the smallest favor."

IV.

THE MANNER IN WHICH HE RECEIVED THE HONORS PAID HIM.

To be humble in obscurity is a rare virtue; for there are so many avenues to pride in the human heart, that this perfidious enemy easily gains admittance therein. But to preserve humility when at the height of glory, and when honors seem to pursue us, is the attribute of noble souls, who have obtained the most exalted virtue. All the saints have not been subjected to this severe ordeal; on the contrary, the greater part of them have lived poor and unknown. But it was agreeable to divine wisdom, sometimes to invest his saints with a mantle of earthly glory, in order thereby to show how immense is the glory prepared for them in eternity.

Bishop Flaget has been thus distinguished. In Europe, he was every where received with extraordinary demonstrations of esteem, respect, and veneration; he was treated not only as an illustrious visiter, but as a saint. To converse with him and receive his benediction, was considered a singular happiness. Priests and laity,—all were anxious to have a place in his remembrance. As to the prelates, it was evident that they regarded him as an apostle, and experienced, in his company, those sentiments of profound admiration, which the presence of a saint produces. But let us examine in what manner the good Bishop received all these honors.

Nothing was seen in him, which would indicate that his self-love was thereby gratified; his countenance was dignified, peaceful and recollected. He did not reject those flattering testimonials of regard; but with calmness, allowed them to fall at his feet. One day as I observed, that such marks of honor might be dangerous to virtue, he tranquilly replied, that when God subjects a soul to such an ordeal, He fortifies it by His grace.

The reception which he received in the palaces of the different Bishops, was most touching. Frequently, the prelates fell on their knees to receive his benediction. At Aire, Bishop Savy, though a paralytic, came, with his clergy, the inmates of his seminary and college, in procession, to meet him. The night of our arrival at Vintimille was dark and gloomy, and in order to reach the episcopal palace, it was necessary to ascend a hill. The Bishop of the place had kindly sent a litter to convey Bishop Flaget to his residence; but it was with difficulty that he could be induced to enter the conveyance.

But the scene was still more touching at the moment of separation, as he was then better known and more appreciated. The Bishops, after having lavished favors upon him, always considered themselves the obliged party; they implored, as a favor, that he would give them his benediction. When leaving Bourges, Bishop Flaget was giving his blessing to the little orphans who had been presented to him, when, to his great confusion, he saw the venerable Archbishop de Villèle kneeling in their midst. This circumstance so much affected him, that he made frequent allusions to it during the day.

Although, as we have before said, Bishop Savy was afflicted with paralysis, he rose when taking leave of the Bishop of Bardstown, saying, in an agitated voice: "I have, my Lord, a favor to ask of you; you have blessed this city; now, I beg you, bless this child, (it was his nephew,) and in him all his family." As he spoke, his eyes were filled with tears. Bishop Flaget was likewise deeply moved, and, perceiving that his friend was kneeling, he knelt also, and in this attitude gave his benediction to all present.

A similar scene took place at Nevers, between himself and Bishop Naudo. I was the only witness of this edifying contest between the modest prelates, each refusing to give to the other his episcopal benediction. Bishop Flaget eventually yielded, on condition that Bishop Naudo would afterwards give him his; but the latter, rising quickly, retired to the other side of the room, while the former kissed the floor on which he had trod, saying: "At least, my Lord, I will kiss the place on which you have walked."

During his travels in France and Piedmont, he was courteously welcomed and entertained by the first families. At Turin, his Excellency, the Minister of Foreign Affairs, treated him with the utmost kindness. Being admitted to the table of His Majesty, Charles Albert, he was placed at the right of the Queen; but there, as elsewhere, he retained the same modesty and simplicity. The desire of pleasing God, at all times, occupied his mind. All that came from men seemed to him of little value. "They do not know," said he, "the heart; of twenty judgments which they form, nineteen are false; but if he, who is the subject of their eulogies, enters into himself, he soon finds enough to humble him. Oh! I hope vanity may never enter into my heart."

The modest Bishop, however, feared the attacks of self-love. He knew that it is an enemy which is never conquered, and he frequently examined himself on this subject, calling to his aid the most moving considerations of faith. He, on one occasion, remarked to me: "I believe that God has in store for me some great humiliations; for, have you ever seen any man receive more honors than I have for some months past? God will doubtless see that, in the end, I shall need to be humbled." Having, in my reply, made use of the word *prison*, he immediately rejoined: "Prison! ah! it would be the greatest happiness for me to be imprisoned. I may be deceived, but it seems to me I should glory in it. That which I fear, is an attack upon my character; for instance, were my reputation blackened by an atrocious calumny, I should be sorely tried. But God," added he, "is infinitely wise; He knows what is most for His glory." On another occasion, he expressed similar sentiments, saying: "Yes, I am persuaded God will send me some great affliction, and I often beg Him to do so; for it is by afflictions that we are purified."

It was truly admirable to observe the perfect liberty and noble independence, which this holy man preserved amid the homages every where lavished upon him. On the contrary, in proportion as they increased, he became more and more disengaged from all that this world can give, and those circumstances which might have been fatal to others, served but to augment in him the love of God. "This journey," he remarked to me, "is extremely useful to me, because it teaches me not to fix my affections on any thing here below. All those fine palaces, those magnificent dwellings, belong not to me; I must soon leave them." * * *

In proportion as God seemed pleased to exalt him, this good Bishop sought to humble himself. He was no doubt gratified to see, that the good work in which he was engaged, received an additional lustre from the honors bestowed on him; but the smoke of human glory passed over his soul, without dimming, in the least, its purity. Divine grace, which seeks only to be diffused, is delighted to enter into the hearts of the saints.

V.

HIS KINDNESS AND GENTLENESS.

It is not sufficient to say that Bishop Flaget was kind; we ought rather to say that he was kindness itself. Nature had bestowed upon him a heart susceptible, tender, and affectionate. During the journey, in which I had the happiness to accompany him, he experienced anxieties and embarrassments of various kinds; but I do not remember ever to have seen him manifest impatience or ill humor. Always forgetful of himself, he was ever ready to oblige others. He was importuned by questions, oftentimes puerile, and which had become wearisome to him from repetition; but he invariably replied with grace and kindness. As I have before said, every one wished to preserve a memorial of him, and in each place where he stopped, he was requested to write his name on small pictures. This he was called on to do so frequently, that it must have become exceedingly annoying; but he never showed disgust or disinclination. I remember a venerable curate, who brought him a very large number of these little pictures, in order to have his signature affixed to them. The Bishop took them with his usual kindness, and afterwards said: "Rather than disappoint the curate, I would sit up all night."

As the prelate was proceeding from Besançon to Vesoul, a boy had got behind the carriage. I, perceiving it, told him to descend; but he answered that he had a sore foot. Our vehicle was small; yet the Bishop insisted upon the boy's having a place, saying: "Oh! we can suffer a little inconvenience for charity."

It was proposed to him to visit an ancient castle near Foix. He was undecided, fearing that this excursion might be merely for the gratification of curiosity. But when I told him that prisoners were there confined, he hesitated no longer, and was happy to have it in his power to address to these poor people some words of comfort.

I had often occasion to remark his exquisite sensibility. When, at the altar, he recited the Collect for friends and benefactors, his heart overflowed with gratitude. The slightest service rendered him, called forth expressions of thankfulness so touching, that they seemed to surpass the benefit. When he received from his Diocese a letter, which expressed the regret his absence caused, or gave him information of some melancholy event, he was sad and almost overcome; but he forbore intruding his griefs on others. As we were walking together one day, he spoke to me of a letter which had greatly affected him. I inquired whether he had just received it: "No," said he, "it reached me yesterday; but I did not wish to sadden others by alluding to my grief."

He was reading, in one of our journeys, the Annals of the Propagation of Faith; but when he came to the account of the martyrdom of the young Abbé Cornay, he closed the book, observing: "It is impossible for me to continue reading, so much am I affected by the sufferings of this young priest." But, a few moments afterwards, his lively faith overcoming his natural sensibility, he added: "Oh! how good is God, to give so young a person such admirable courage!"

While at Turin, he received intelligence which exceedingly grieved him. Bishop Savy, whom he much loved, had had a second attack of paralysis. He sent for me to read the letter which bore the news, saying, with deep emotion: "I could not read it all at once; I had to pause, in order to compose myself. Willingly would I take his sickness, because at my age, and at the end of my career, I am good for nothing; but he is yet young and vigorous. But God knows what is best;

perhaps this worthy Bishop is more useful to his Diocese in his present suffering condition, than if he were in perfect health."

In one of his journeys in America, Bishop Flaget met a French lady who was a Protestant, and who addressed very harsh language to him, in the course of a conversation respecting the revocation of the Edict of Nantes. This lady, at the end of the journey, was unable to pay her traveling bills. The Bishop immediately gave her the sum of which she was in need. His generosity made her bitterly regret the hasty language she had used towards him.

Habituated as was Bishop Flaget to princely receptions, he had, however, on one occasion, reason to complain of the unbecoming manner in which a visit he had purposed making, was announced; but the only vengeance he took, was to write a most tender and affectionate letter to the offending party.

VI.

HIS FIRMNESS.

But, though thus mild and gentle, the Bishop was inexorable on points of duty. He condescended to every request which demanded only a personal sacrifice; but when the glory of God required that he should refuse, he became inflexible.

I seem now to hear the impressive language of this venerable old man, as, on a certain occasion, he spoke to me on the subject. I had been deputed to ascertain public sentiment with regard to a journey some persons desired him to make, for the interests of the Propagation of Faith. I inquired of the prelate, if he himself would oppose any obstacle to this enterprize. "But," said he, "I must first have the command of the Pope." "Of course," I rejoined; "but were he to give the command, would you be willing to perform the journey?" "Oh!" replied the holy man, "if the Pope were to command me to proceeed to Botany Bay, I should go without reluctance. My dear child, I seem weak and yielding, and in some circumstances I confess I am so; but if conscience requires me to do a thing, nothing stops me. I have traveled a hundred leagues, in order to promulgate an interdict against an unhappy priest, who had obliged me to pronounce against him the censures of the Church."

In conversing with the prelate about his project of returning to America, I was often struck with his exquisite sensibility and unshaken firmness. He acknowledged to me, that leaving his friends in France would cause him intense pain; but that nothing could prevent his return to America. He had hoped to complete his travels through France in the month of November; and, regardless of the sufferings to which he might be exposed, he resolved immediately to depart for his Diocese. "Undoubtedly," he remarked to me, "in this matter, I am thinking of self. At my age, one should think of death, and although, in Bardstown, I must experience privations, I prefer being there. My Coadjutor, seeing me infirm, will be with me as much as possible; he will be my consolation; but business will often call him to a distance, and I shall be left in my solitude. Yet what matters it, to suffer for one or two years?"

.One day, I had the curiosity to ask him, if he did not dread a sea-voyage. He replied: "I never think of such things; no, my child, I say to myself, what matter is it whether I die at sea, or in my chamber? I am certain, wherever I may die, I shall do the will of God."

This reply of the holy old man came from his heart. I have been told that, in one of his voyages across the ocean, while the vessel was driven about by a violent storm, he was buried in a profound sleep, tranquil as that of infancy. His traveling companion, who had not before crossed the ocean, was unable to sleep. Fear alone would have prevented him from closing his eyes. The storm increasing every moment, he went to awake the Bishop, who, raising his head, said to him, with the utmost calmness: "You are a child; you are too easily frightened by the cries of the sailors. Moreover, if God wishes to find us tombs here, what difference does it make! Is it not as well to be devoured by fish, as to be gnawed by worms?"

It is needless, however, to make farther quotations. The entire life of Bishop Flaget is an undubitable proof of his heroic fortitude. There was in his character a beautiful mingling of sweetness, condescension, and noble firmness. His extreme sensibility might have degenerated into weakness; but his generous faith sanctified and elevated it. To his fellow creatures, he was gentleness itself; in the service of God, he was firm and faithful. Thus it may be said of him, that he was beloved by God and man.

VII.

HIS CONFORMITY TO THE WILL OF GOD.

St. Francis of Sales, writing to St. Jane Frances de Chantal, besought her to lose her will in the divine will, as a drop of water is swallowed up in the ocean. It may be affirmed, that this counsel, which includes within itself all other counsels, had become the constant rule of the Bishop of Bardstown. He had so changed his will into the will of God, that those two wills seemed but one. Every thing with him was reducible to this problem:—to know what God required of him. Sometimes, the solution of it was difficult; then, he was undecided, irresolute; but as soon as all his doubts were removed, all hesitation ceased; not for a moment was he restrained by the apprehension of difficulties or obstacles. To do the will of God appeared to him always easy; nay, the thought of accomplishing that adorable will constituted his joy and happiness. This desire was his only passion.

These expressions might seem exaggerated; but all who have known Bishop Flaget intimately, can testify to their truth.

He was much indisposed at Rodez, and obliged to take remedies. The physicians had likewise recommended repose. Having expressed a desire to know on what day it was probable we should resume our journey, as I wished to make the necessary arrangements, I received the following answer: "I cannot yet inform you; all that I wish is, to do the will of God. What I ask of Him is, to make known to me His sacred will; either by causing me to become very sick, or by giving me such health, that, without imprudence, I may resume my journey."

On a similar occasion, the pious Bishop expressed the same thought and desire, but in terms still more impressive. He was then at Turin. "I have just," said he, "begged of God to make His holy will known to me; either by granting me health, if he wishes me to continue this visitation; or, if His glory will not thereby be promoted, to send me an attack of illness; but such illness as will leave me in no doubt as to what He requires of me. I have never prayed with so much fervor. All that I desire is, to know His holy will. I have never asked any thing else." Thus, he wished neither for health nor for sickness, neither for repose nor for action. All things were indifferent to him;—but to know the way which God had marked out for him.

Perceiving me at one time to be discouraged, he addressed me thus: "Whether our undertaking be successful or not, our consolation is, to know that we are doing the will of God. I also meet with things that annoy and discourage me, but what matter? If the carriage were to overset and crush me, and if I had time to utter a prayer, I would bless God, because in dying I was fulfilling His will."

Frequently I have heard him say, during our journey, that as the Pope had imposed on him the mission he was then fulfilling, he was sure that he was doing God's will, and that this assurance rendered him perfectly happy; whereas, in his own Diocese, two paths were sometimes before him, so that he was embarrassed, not knowing which to choose. Then he would add: "Yes, I should be most happy to die now, for I should be sure of dying in the accomplishment of God's will."

Such protestations were not, with the Bishop, vain forms of speech. Even had he desired to tell a falsehood, I do not believe he could have done it. As he thought, so he spoke. Besides, when divine Providence subjected him to trials, it was easy to see, that his expressions of submission to the decrees of heaven came from his heart.

The prelate, having asked for his Diocese a young ecclesiastic, who shortly after left for China, I inquired of him, whether the announcement of the departure of this gentleman had not saddened him? "Oh! not at all," he replied, "I have done all that I could to obtain his services for my Diocese, but God did not will it; who knows but that I would have deprived him of the grace of martyrdom?"

When he had received a letter bearing sad news, he consoled himself by repeating the prayer of the holy Pope, Pius VII.: "So be it; may He be praised;"—and he pronounced the following words with peculiar relish: "May the most amiable will of God be praised in all things."

Before setting out for Piedmont, the pious Bishop had consulted Gregory XVI., not wishing to proceed beyond France, without a special authorization. So soon as this authorization was received, he set out, without any solicitude; but the weather was extremely inclement when he left Chambery, to repair to Turin; the snow was falling heavily, and every thing prognosticated a most rigorous season. The good Bishop, reflecting that the snow would render the passage of Mt. Cenis exceedingly difficult, turning towards me, said, with a joyous manner: "We are now certain that we are doing the will of God; yes, it is He who wishes us to be in the midst of this snow. We must then be satisfied. Were I at present traveling to Turin, for my own satisfaction—for example, to solicit some valuable present—how anxious and tormented should I be! But, as it is, I do the will of God, and I am contented."

This determination of Bishop Flaget, to conform in all things to the will of God, caused him to watch carefully every emotion of his heart, and each impulse of his will. Thus, after having sent to the Sovereign Pontiff an humble letter, asking the commands of the Holy See as to his future movements, he said to me: "I confess, I am anxious to know what the Pope's answer will be;"—but correcting himself, he added: "No, no; I ought not to be anxious for any thing; what I desire is, to know the will of God." When he received this answer, it was easy to see how happy he felt to be thus assured of God's will. Frequently he was heard to exclaim: "Oh! how contented I feel! I ever feel satisfied when I know exactly what God wishes of me." He was no longer in doubt or hesitation; and he spoke frequently of his approaching return to America.

The merchant pursues not fortune, nor the soldier glory, with more ardor, than he sought to accomplish the will of God. He accepted beforehand all the sacrifices which his Sovereign Master should require of him, adding to the merit of his labors, that, still greater perhaps, of his intentions. No; he was not of the number of those indolent servants, who say much and do nothing; he did much, and would have desired to do still more. Thus, we may confidently hope, that He, who looks with complacency, not only upon the actions which we perform for His glory, but also upon the generous desires by which we anticipate, as it were, His will, has ordered his angels to prepare for the pious Bishop a crown of resplendent glory.

VIII.

HIS FILIAL OBEDIENCE TO THE SOVEREIGN PONTIFF.

It may be said, that the perfect conformity to the will of God, of which we have just spoken, explains the respectful and filial submission which Bishop Flaget ever rendered to the Sovereign Pontiff. His faith beheld in him the representative of Jesus Christ on earth; thus, to obey the Pope was to obey God. The will of the Pope, once expressed, was for him, so clear a manifestation of the will of God, that he hastened with a holy ardor to obey it. * * *

We have already seen that he was ready, at the mandate of His Holiness, to proceed to the most distant regions of the world. But it is well to examine what the good Bishop understood by an order of the Pope. One day, as he expressed a desire that the Sovereign Pontiff might decidedly pronounce, whether or not he should proceed on his travels, I took the liberty of asking him: "What would you do, my Lord, if the Pope were merely to manifest a desire for the prolongation of your visitation?" "Oh! I should set out," replied he, "immediately and without hesitation. The Pope, in such circumstances, will never give a positive order; but his wishes are commands. If the Pope were to show a desire that you should do something, and if you refused to do it, would you not, my dear child, have disobeyed him?" This language, from the lips of a Bishop, seventy-five years of age, is more instructive and impressive than a volume of controversy.

However, it conveys but an imperfect idea of the respectful tenderness, which he felt for the Sovereign Pontiff. He would often exclaim: "I assure you, if the Pope were to tell me to set out for Japan, I would immediately do so. It is my delight to do the will of Rome." He frequently received letters urging him to return to his Diocese;—the affectionate regret therein expressed that he remained still in Europe, deeply affected his heart; but his resolution was unshaken. His reply was: "I can do only as the Pope directs me to do."

At the time the Bishop was writing the letter to the Sovereign Pontiff, of which we have already spoken, he said to me, with a beaming countenance: "I am exposing to the Pope the reasons for and against the proposed measure. I then leave the decision to him. Now he will be obliged to express positively what his wishes are; whatever they may be, I am disposed to comply with them. Were he to tell me to go to China, I believe I would start instantly, if I found a vessel ready to sail." In fine, when the answer to this letter arrived from Rome, not only did the holy Bishop hasten to obey; but he submitted his own judgment, without comment and with evident joy, and availed himself of every opportunity to eulogize the decision of Gregory

XVI. In a moment of fatigue and suffering, he observed to me: "I see plainly that the Pope was right. I should not have been able to continue the journey; my health would not have permitted it." And, at another time, as he felt his strength gradually decreasing, he exclaimed: "Oh! blessed be God! How well the Church is governed! No; I do not believe I could have prosecuted this journey."

This respect and veneration—this more than filial tenderness for the Holy See,—was evidenced in the least, as well as in the greatest things. He took great delight in speaking of the Pope, in recounting the benefits he had received from him, and in exalting his goodness and wisdom. While at Rome, he obtained frequent audiences of Pope Gregory XVI. The Holy Pontiff had conceived a particular affection for him, and he treated him with unusual familarity. Once, in conversation with the Bishop, he familiarly opened his snuff-box, and presented it to the latter, who, taking a pinch, preserved it as something precious.

The Bishop and myself were, at one time, conversing on the subject of the congregation for the Propagation of Faith, and the zeal which the city of Lyons had always shown for that holy work. Among the causes to which he ascribed this piety, he failed not to mention the benediction which Pope Pius VII. had bestowed on this city, when he passed through it. "Oh! yes," said he; "I am sure that this Holy Father raised both his hands to heaven, and that an ocean of grace was poured upon this city."

IX.

HIS MORTIFICATION.

ALL those who have studied the secrets of the spiritual life, know that its maxims may be reduced to the two following: to die to ourselves, and to live of a new life; that is to say, to destroy in ourselves,—or at least, to subdue,—the fatal inclinations which have their origin in sin; in order that grace, acting with an entire liberty, may give us the habit of thinking and acting as Jesus Christ thought and acted. This virtue, which makes us thus die to ourselves, is called, in the language of the Church, the virtue of mortification. It controls the external senses, the divers faculties of the soul, the entire being;—for the whole man is bound by the chains of sin. The instincts of this body of clay draw us always towards the earth; and our soul, which ought to command and govern these earthly instincts, suffers itself to be subjected by them. Christian mortification, therefore, is constantly striving to restore to the soul its liberty, by recalling to it the remembrance of its primitive greatness. This mortification is not, then, an isolated virtue; it is the basis and the measure of all other virtues. Hence, wherever we behold great and heroic virtues, we may be assured that mortification is combined with them. But it manifests itself under different forms. In some persons, it is shown in the practice of voluntary penance; in others, it finds its exercise in the patient endurance of the trials and sorrows that beset the path of life; but, in all, its triumph consists in dying to one's self, and living of the life of the spirit.

In Bishop Flaget, its influence was visible in various ways. His body, accustomed to hardships, required but little ; and he was never seen to seek his own ease, nor the gratification of his own taste. His imagination, kept in a holy bondage, reposed in God ; his mind was occupied with God, and his heart loved only God ; for, having wisely disciplined his extreme sensibility, he loved those who were dear to him in God and for God. "My will," said he, "has been so subdued in the missions, that now it can submit to any thing. When I was at Baltimore, I loved study ; but I was frequently assigned duties which rendered it impossible for me to apply to it. At first, my will rebelled ; when I became conscious of it, 'oh !' I said to myself, 'this will must be trampled under foot.' It was well for me that I was obliged thus to conquer it; for now I am contented every where." The good Bishop spoke truly. He was never heard to complain of the fatigues of traveling, of bad lodgings, nor of a hard bed. He pleasantly remarked, "that at home he slept on an indifferent bed ; and that thus he was always sure of finding a better one, when he traveled, than that to which he was accustomed."

Nor was the holy prelate more fastidious with regard to his clothing. "You see," he would say to me, "I am not accustomed to all these little attentions. Sometimes, in my missions, I had good clothing ; sometimes I had not. Hence, such inconveniences do not annoy me."

The splendid repasts which were given, in his honor, were irksome to him ; yet he did not complain ; but he remarked : "We hear persons speak of good wines, and delicately prepared dishes, as if such things merited attention. This is always disagreeable to me. I acknowledge, that the magnificent entertainments to which I am invited cause me to think of God. Oh! God of Love!"

In one of the Departments of France, a commissary of police, accompanied by another officer, came to the presbytery, to inquire who the strange Bishop was, and whether he was provided with suitable papers! It was evident, they executed the commission with reluctance; but the curate of the parish was deeply mortified by this proceeding. When the prelate was informed of the object of their visit, he said with much gayety, "that he would consider it a happiness to be put in prison, and to glorify, by his chains, our Lord Jesus Christ."

The thought of honoring this divine Model, by imitating His severe and mortified life, was ever present to the holy Bishop. Had he, for this object, recourse to the instruments of penance, of which so many saints had made use? I cannot say;—the modesty of the prelate forbade my interrogating him on such matters. But a rapid view of the labors and trials, with which his whole life has been marked, suffices to show that he practiced heroic mortification. Towards the conclusion of his journey, I was conversing with him on his approaching return to America, and alluded to the joy he would experience on seeing again his two Coadjutors: "Ah!" he exclaimed, "that will be too much consolation for me; and, perhaps, too much natural satisfaction will accompany it." Thus we see, that this holy Bishop mistrusted the best emotions of the heart, and could say, with St. Francis of Sales: "If I were conscious of the least love which was not for God, I should instantly banish it from my heart."

Is not this condition of the soul a beginning of the celestial beatitude? It may be so called; but it is replete with pain and toil; for, however eagerly we may seek God, it must always be with fear and solicitude. Each instant we are in danger of losing Him; and we shall infallibly lose Him, if we place not a vigilant sentinel at the door of our heart. These continual struggles prevent our happiness from being perfect here below. But the day shall come when we will be permitted to lay down our arms; because, our enemies having been vanquished, it will be no longer necessary to combat. Our joy will then be augmented by the remembrance of past trials and labors; and we shall understand, with the Apostle, that there is no proportion between our sacrifices and the reward prepared for them.

X.

HIS PATIENCE IN THE TIME OF SICKNESS.

BISHOP FLAGET had naturally a robust constitution. Yet, from his correspondence, we ascertain that he was often attacked by severe illness. He was very near dying at Havana, and he was obliged to desist from his labors in the United States several times, in consequence of his bad health; but the laborious and agitated life which he led, may well account for these frequent indispositions.

The cholera which attacked him in 1833, a severe illness which afterwards detained him several months at Angers, and the infirmities of age, had greatly diminished the strength of the venerable prelate, when I had the honor of forming his acquaintance. Often, while we were traveling together, he was obliged to rest several days at a time, and to receive medical attention. He submitted to his physicians and nurses with the docility of a child, and bore the inconveniences and sufferings of his condition, as coming immediately from the hands of divine Providence.

At Rodez, it was deemed necessary that he should consult a physician. I was struck by the first interview between himself and the doctor. The prelate spoke on different subjects, but said not a word of his indisposition. I observed: "But, my Lord, you say nothing of your illness!" The physician, who understood his patient, rejoined, with a smile: "Oh! that is a matter of secondary consideration with the Bishop." Two or three days after this visit, I inquired of him what medicine the doctor had prescribed? "Ah!" said he, "I do not know; I have not inquired what it was. God has given me the grace always to practice great docility towards my physicians. I know it is the Almighty who imparts to medicines their efficacy. Physicians prescribe such or such remedies, but it is God who renders them efficacious. Hence I say to Him: I submit to whatever Thou shalt order; if it is a poison that is given me, I shall do Thy will in taking it."

He received, with effusions of gratitude, the cares

and attentions bestowed on him during sickness, and had always a kind and gracious word for each one that approached him. It was truly edifying, to see the readiness with which he took the prescribed remedies. He never manifested the slightest repugnance, nor made any objection to whatever might be proposed for his benefit; so that it was really a pleasure to nurse him.

Yet this venerable man, so mild, so patient, so resigned, was not satisfied with himself. "It is singular," said he to me, "that whenever I am indisposed, my head is affected; I am unable to fix my attention, to meditate and pray.—Oh! the saints were not so. Hence, I never fail to implore God to enable me to prepare for death before my last illness attacks me." God undoubtedly heard his prayer, as may be seen from perusing an account of the last years of his beautiful and holy life. What then must be the purity of heaven, since the pure gold of his eminent virtues was subjected to the crucible, in order to be purified from the stains of earth! How holy the society of the celestial Court, if those whose lives we have so justly admired in this world, are not found worthy to enter there, until they have effaced, by the tears of repentance, those slight stains, imperceptible to us! Such thoughts overwhelm the mind, but the heart draws from them hope and comfort; for He who requires of us such exalted virtues, has prepared for them an infinite recompense.

XI.
HIS LOVE FOR HIS DIOCESE.

A Bishop, on the day of his consecration, contracts a strict alliance with that portion of the Church which is then confided to his care. A ring is placed on his finger, as a sign and memorial of this sacred union, which he always wears,—thus indicating the indissolubility of his alliance. Hence, to love his Diocese becomes one of his first and sweetest duties.

Bishop Flaget spoke invariably of his diocesans with a truly fraternal affection. During his stay at the bishopric of Cahors, some friends were felicitating him, on the success of his journey, and the favors which heaven had bestowed on him at each step. He responded to these courteous expressions, by saying "that he was disposed to traverse the whole of France, if the Pope so ordered or desired; though, without doubt, he should prefer being in his Diocese;" then he added, with his wonted grace of manner: "Lately, I have received another letter, expressing the ardent desire of the people of Kentucky to see me. It is not astonishing; their father is absent, and they are beginning to think him indifferent towards them. Assuredly, thanks be to God, I am not guilty of this sin."

When he received good news from his beloved Kentucky,—as the announcement of a conversion, or the detail of some edifying event,—he was in an ecstasy of joy, and he spoke of it to all who approached him. One day, after the perusal of a letter, bearing such news, he said with deep emotion: "God is too good to me. I fear I shall never be sufficiently grateful."

Just before he left France, the good Bishop visited a city, where he had formerly sojourned for some time. The superior of the seminary, presuming that the prospect of his approaching departure was painful to him, addressed to him some words of encouragement. The Bishop listened to him politely; but at the close of his remarks, laughed heartily, saying: "Would you know, sir, the pain I experience, on the eve of returning to my Diocese? It is that which a father feels, on seeing again his children, from whom he has been long separated." At another time, he remarked to one of his friends: "I should wish to have wings, that I might fly to my own children."

After Bishop Flaget had decided upon his return to Kentucky, and while he was preparing for his immediate departure, he was informed that some of his friends had commenced negotiations with Rome, in order to keep him in France. They had hoped to persuade the Sovereign Pontiff, that the prelate, by remaining in Europe, could render himself useful, not only to one Diocese, but to all the missions. These tidings caused him great perplexity. He did not wish to disoblige the Pope by a refusal; but he was most anxious to return to his children. He wrote to this effect to the Cardinal Prefect of Propaganda, protesting, at the same time, his filial submission to the Sovereign Pontiff. The good Bishop was in suspense, and at a loss how to act. But he deferred, for a while, his departure. No answer coming from Rome, he wrote to me from Billom, on the 10th of June, 1839, stating that he had fixed his departure for the 8th of July following.

Almost immediately after receiving his letter, I understood that the Pope had rejected the proposition which was so repugnant to Bishop Flaget's feelings; I hastened to inform him of this. He wrote me thus in reply: "I thank God, my dear child, for the news you have communicated to me; for, in fixing the period of my departure three weeks earlier than I had at first intended, I was influenced by the desire to travel in company with the Rt. Rev. Bishop of Cincinnati; but my chief motive was, that I might be on the way before the arrival of the Sovereign Pontiff's letter. Thus I hoped to be able at least once more to see my spiritual children, and to prove to them that absence had not diminished my tender affection for them. My wooden palace in Bardstown is to me more charming than those magnificent mansions in which I have dwelt for the last three years. If after having resided five or six months with my beloved children, you should arrive with an order from the Pope for me to return to France, it would assuredly afflict me deeply; but a hundred times more poignant would have been my sorrow, had your letter announced to me that I must now remain in France."

☞POSTCRIPT.☜

A few errors were discovered while the preceding pages were passing through the press; too late, however, to have them corrected in the text. As our chief aim has been to be as accurate as possible, we will here point out two such mistakes, which are deem-of some importance, and will then add a few other remarks.

Page 40, line 18, for "civil court," read *parish*. Page 342, line 6, for "two years," read *one year*.

In reference to the account, (on page 21,) of the Bishop's mother having appeared to him when he was a child, it may be proper to state, that, while recounting the incident in his old age, the prelate appeared to be fully convinced of its reality.

The date assigned on page 24, as that at which he became a member of the Sulpician congregation, is more properly that of his first entrance into the Sulpician seminary at Clermont. He probably became a Sulpician only one or two years later; and very shortly afterwards was sent to the solitude of Issy. It is certain, as stated in the text, that he continued his theological studies for about two years, in the Sulpician seminary at Clermont, during which time he was ordained sub-deacon by Bishop De Bonald.—See his own letter on the subject, p. 23—*note*.

We will add, that the translation in the Appendix is occasionally somewhat free, both in order to give it the English turn of expression, and to condense the facts or reflections of the original, so that they might not occupy to much space. In a few instances, also, where shorter passages are not translated, the *asterisks* have been unintentionally omitted.